WHY
Smile?

WHY
Smile?

The science behind facial expressions

MARIANNE LaFRANCE

W. W. Norton & Company

New York · London

Excerpt from "Red Roses for Bronze" By H.D. (Hilda Doolittle), from *Collected Poems, 1912–1944*, copyright 1982 by the Estate of Hilda Doolittle. Reprinted by permission of New Directions Publishing Corp. Excerpt from "People Take Pictures of Each Other" by The Kinks. Used by permission of Alfred Music Publishing Co., Inc.

Photograph credits—p. 6: Megan Mangum; p. 8: Megan Mangum; p. 9: Megan Mangum; p. 15: Megan Mangum, adapted from an illustration by Peter Ratner, author of *3-D Human Modeling and Animation*; p. 16: Megan Mangum; p. 17: McNamee/Corbis; p. 29: copyright 2009, Oxford University Press; p. 35: Peter Turnley / Corbis; p. 39: from D. Messinger, "Positive and Negative: Infant Facial Expressions and Emotions," *Current Directions in Psychological Science* 11 (2002): 1–6, reprinted by permission of SAGE Publications; p. 40: Michel Bussy / PhotoAlto / Corbis; p. 66: AP Photo / Carlo Allegri; p. 74: Megan Mangum; p. 78: Ramin Talaie / Corbis; p. 81: AP Photo / Nick UT; p. 105: Getty Images; p. 129: David Turnley / Corbis; p. 134: Larry Downing / Sygma / Corbis; p. 139: from Parr, Waller, and Fugate, "Emotional Communication in Primates: Implications for Neurobiology," *Current Opinion in Neurobiology* 15 (2005): 716–20; p. 141: Bettmann/Corbis; p. 152: Stefanie Grewel / Corbis; p. 157: Holmes/Corbis; p. 169: courtesy Archives of Michigan; p. 174: Creasource/Corbis; p. 183: AP Photo / Annie Higbee; p. 197: Robert Eric / Corbis Sygma; p. 204: AP Photo / Carl de Souza; p. 220: Megan Mangum; p. 227: Peter Turnley / Corbis; p. 232: Kate Mitchell / Corbis;.p. 243: used by permission of Renso Dionigi, Mikey Siegel, MIT Media Lab.

For information about permission to reproduce selections from this book, write to Permissions, W. W. Norton & Company, Inc., 500 Fifth Avenue, New York, NY 10110

For information about special discounts for bulk purchases, please contact W. W. Norton Special Sales at specialsales@wwnorton.com or 800-233-4830

Manufacturing by Courier Westford
Book design by Chris Welch Design
Production manager: Julia Druskin

Library of Congress Cataloging-in-Publication Data

LaFrance, Marianne, 1947–
    [Lip service]
Why smile? : the science behind facial expressions / Marianne LaFrance.
        p. cm.
"Originally published under the title Lip Service: Smiles in Life, Death, Trust, Lies, Work, Memory, Sex, and Politics."
Includes bibliographical references and index.
ISBN 978-0-393-34422-6 (pbk.)
1. Smiling. 2. Nonverbal communication. 3. Body language. I. Title.
BF637.N66L34 2013
153.6'9—dc23

                                                    2012037667

W. W. Norton & Company, Inc.
500 Fifth Avenue, New York, N.Y. 10110
www.wwnorton.com

W. W. Norton & Company Ltd.
Castle House, 75/76 Wells Street, London W1T 3QT

1 2 3 4 5 6 7 8 9 0

To Megan, of course

contents

introduction

Brides do it; teasers do it; even educated geezers do it. You and I do it; we all share smiles. Salespeople, infants, politicians, and flirts, sadists and celebrities and children hoping for adoptive homes, they grin and smirk and put on a happy face. The anxious, the eager, the embarrassed . . . There is no one who has not smiled at least once, although some adhere to W. C. Fields's advice to start every day with a smile and get it over with.

Smiles are universally recognized and understood for what they show and convey, yet not necessarily for what they *do*. Smiles are much more than cheerful expressions. They are social acts with consequences. A special someone raises the corners of his mouth in a certain way, and your heart flutters wildly. A competitor or foe shoots you a grin and you find yourself smiling back against your will. In some instances, a smile can save lives: Early in the Iraq War, before the fall of Bagdad, the U.S. Army's 3rd Infantry entered the town of Najaf. As the soldiers marched toward the mosque, agitated residents began to congregate. The astute U.S. commander responded to the mounting tension by ordering his troops to point their guns to the ground and smile. In that moment, smiles—alongside other gestures of conciliation—prevented a possible clash.

While a well-timed lift of the lips might defuse a potentially antagonistic situation, sometimes failing to flash your pearly whites just might land you in a brawl. Indeed, a relationship has been found between the scarcity of an individual's smiles and the likelihood that he will be aggressive. In an experiment conducted at a college in Ohio, male undergraduates were assigned to compete in a game against someone they did not know. They were told they could administer an electric shock to their opponent, and set the shock level at whatever intensity they chose. When the game was over, results showed that those who smiled less often at their opponents set higher shock levels.

Part of what makes smiles so powerful, and powerfully consequential, are the multiple ways in which they affect those around us. As social psychologists Craig Smith and Heather Scott cleverly put it, "the face has the only skeletal muscles of the body that are used, not to move ourselves, but to move others."

When someone smiles, the consequences are often positive for the person who receives it: a glum mood lifts; an apology is accepted; a person's shaky self-confidence gets a boost; a deal is struck; the attraction is confirmed as mutual; a contribution is acknowledged; and everyone can now relax.

But change the circumstances or the cast of a smile, and the consequences shift: a rival grins to get under your skin; a bully's smirk unsettles his mark. Manipulators adopt faces to suit their ulterior motives; hypocrites smile at one and all.

When I say that a smile is a social act with consequences, I do not mean that smiling is necessarily intentional, nor do I mean that smilers and their recipients are necessarily conscious of, or have calibrated for, the gesture's impact. Just because an infant's gummy grin elicits gushing from an adult does not mean that was what the baby intended. But smiling *does* affect how we relate to each other, something a baby may not know or know how to control, but which is part of how our bodies and brains have evolved to help ensure our survival.

Scientists have observed babies practicing their smiles in the womb, showing recognizable smiles a month or two *before* birth. They smile involuntarily because they need to have these muscles operational so that they can entice supportive adults. Infants can do nothing for themselves—they cannot even hold their heads up, let alone feed and fend for themselves. Unless young ones can get others to sustain them, they will die, if not physically then emotionally. They smile for their supper and for other comforts as well. As they develop, they learn to smile deliberately; at the outset, their smiles are involuntary but no less consequential. It's likely their first social manipulation, and yet the act of smiling, in this first form, is unconscious. And unconscious smiling does not end at infancy.

Once, following a talk I gave on facial expressions, a woman from the audience told me about a stretch of time when she was unaware that she was smiling. She worked at a restaurant and smiled as she served customers. On her way home at night she would stop at a twenty-four-hour supermarket, and as she did her shopping, other shoppers would suddenly start talking to her. It took her a while to figure out that she had not stopped smiling since leaving work. Some shoppers took her positive facial expression as a conversational opener.

A smile produces an emotional current in people who see it, whether or not the smiler is aware of having done anything, and whether or not the recipient can identify the reason for his or her reaction. Nonetheless, there has been an act with consequences. Smiles not only have consequences for those who see them but also for those who do the smiling. A recent study showed that if you are generally disposed to smile, you may live longer. Researchers analyzed photographs of over two hundred professional baseball players in old issues of the *Baseball Register*. Rookies who smiled genuinely were found to have lived longer than those whose photograph showed either no smile or a "checked" smile.

This book shines a spotlight on the practice of smiling and explains why such a small muscle movement can have such substantial consequences. Might adopting a smile make a person feel better? Why do popular kids show more fake smiles than unpopular kids? What happens to close relationships when people cannot or will not smile? Is it a good sign or bad sign when a bereaved person smiles? Is service with a smile worth it?

A smile is a good deal more than a simple, pleasant facial display. Celebrated for their luminescence, smiles are often underestimated for their role in bringing people together and keeping them from each other's throats. Smiles do all of this because there is not one type of smile but many and not one consequence but quite a few.

It's easy to believe that spontaneous smiles are the genuine article because they happen naturally, and often we sense that. There is no doubt that deliberate smiles can be transparently phony, but they can also be genuine. A good friend, recently diagnosed with a life-threatening illness, has been eager to adopt an optimistic attitude, and asked his life partner not to look worried or sad when they were together. Fulfilling the ill partner's wish has entailed some deliberate, albeit heartfelt smiling.

Consider a more mundane example. A guest gives you a tacky gift. If you are like most people, you probably smile and say something like, "Thanks, you really shouldn't have." Psychologists and philosophers generally agree that such untruths are minor, since their motivation springs from wanting to spare another from small-scale hurt or embarrassment. Not all gift recipients, however, smile in this situation—some because they refuse to follow any social convention that requires a smile, others because they are physically unable to muster feigned appreciation, however strong their wish to do so.

Neuroscientists have found that voluntary and nonvoluntary smiles are under the control of separate neural pathways. In normal functioning individuals, both pathways work without notice. People smile when they feel happy and when they want to show that they feel happy, even if they don't. But on occasion, individuals have incurred injury to the neural pathway that makes it impossible for them to smile at will, although they can still break into a spontaneous grin. Damage to the other neural pathway has the opposite effect—now the ability to smile spontaneously is paralyzed while the ability to smile intentionally is unaffected.

Those of us on the receiving end of a smile will not always be sure whether another's smile is voluntary or involuntary. This makes deciphering any particular smile a bit of a challenge. Was it a spontaneous smile, reflecting authentic and unstoppable feelings of warmth? Or was it volitional, indicating more about the smiler's thoughts and intentions? It is possible to tell the difference if you know where to look.

For reasons that are not entirely clear, we possess two pathways to get smiles to our faces. Scientists speculate that the smile evolved in our ancient ancestors first as a true indicator of positive emotion. Later, a second system developed in which individuals began to smile voluntarily, in the midst of any emotional state, including grief and fury. This second system evolved, some argue, because it was not always in our best interest to be emotionally transparent, leaving ourselves vulnerable to those who would take advantage or manipulate our feelings. This system enabled us to control the broadcast of positive feeling—even when we weren't feeling positive—allowing us to cover disappointment or anger, to manufacture an often inauthentic but useful show of positive feelings in the absence of feeling anything. As we will see later, some people are better at producing authentic-looking smiles than others and some perceivers are better at detecting the difference.

This book is about the science of smiles, about the latest research in psychology, medicine, anthropology, biology, brain science, and computer science, about what motivates us to smile and what happens when we do. I have been researching smiles and scowls, grins and grimaces, frowns and facial expression adjustments for many years, from my perch as an experimental social psychologist, often in the light of real-world interactions but more frequently under cover of darkness in my lab at Yale (better to view minute facial changes in video records and from behind oneway mirrors).

Among the questions we have tackled are why men interpret a woman's smile as flirtatious while women seldom make the equivalent assumption about a man's grin; how it is that a smile can get you off the hook if you've made a mistake or broken a rule; why people with little power or status smile more; and what provokes those who are embarrassed or anxious to break into smiles. The results of these studies and many others are included in these pages to move you beyond the obvious meaning of a smile toward a richer understanding of why our occasionally random, sometimes accidental, and frequently deliberate choice to turn our mouths upward matters so much to us and those around us.

These facts about human smiles—that they are intentional acts as well as spontaneous outbursts; that they occasionally pop into awareness but more often work their magic without anyone being the wiser; and that they appear when people are happy but also when they are hurting—give us a base from which to probe why this universal expression is so effective at getting under everyone's skin.

LIFE

smile science

For nearly fifty years, American television has broadcast some version of a boy-girl dating contest. Originally it was *The Dating Game*, followed by *The Love Connection*, *The Bachelorette*, and *The New Dating Game*. In an early format, three young men vied for a date with a young woman. She asks each prospective date a few questions, they retort with amusing replies; she mulls and then picks one. The audience generally agrees with her choice and the new couple is awarded a night on the town or a vacation in a romantic locale. The TV dating game has had remarkable longevity and international appeal. In the United Kingdom, the show was called *Blind Date* and in Australia it went by the name of *Perfect Match*.

The idea of several suitors competing for a single lady did not originate in mid-twentieth-century television. In the nineteenth-century English novel, a courtship involving several suitors typically took several hundred pages rather than a twenty-one-minute time slot. Thomas Hardy published *Far from the Madding Crowd* in 1874; it is a story about the beautiful and spirited Bathsheba Everdene and the three men who loved her. One suitor was the dashing Sergeant Troy; a second was the wealthy farmer

Boldwood; and the third was steadfast Gabriel Oak. The last of
these had a noteworthy smile:

> When Farmer Oak smiled, the corners of his mouth spread
> till they were within an unimportant distance of his ears,
> his eyes were reduced to mere chinks, and diverging wrin-
> kles appeared round them, extending upon his countenance
> like the rays in a rudimentary sketch of the rising sun.

Alas, Gabriel's wonderful smile was not enough to attract Bathsheba. He lost to both Sergeant Troy and Farmer Boldwood. At
the end, and too late, Bathsheba realizes that Gabriel was *the one*.
Had she been more astute, she would have seen in Gabriel's smile
something beyond cachet or capital; she would have glimpsed
the genuineness missing from her other suitors. Had she been
scientifically inclined, she might have read Charles Darwin to
learn what to look for in a suitor's facial expressions. Darwin's
The Expression of the Emotions in Man and Animals was published
in 1872, just before Hardy's *Far from the Madding Crowd*.

From the late 1800s until now, researchers have examined how
and when people smile. They have determined that some smiles
are closely connected with feelings of joy, affection, and trust;
others are bound up with malice and manipulation. To understand all that smiles do, we first need to identify the variations
among them, and then we can examine the consequences they
have on our relationships and ourselves.

Back to the nineteenth century. Darwin and his contemporary
the French physiologist G.-B.-A. Duchenne de Boulogne noted
that there was one smile type in a category all by itself. That smile

arrives spontaneously and reflects pure delight. This is how Darwin described it:

> By the drawing backwards and upwards of the corners of the mouth, through the contraction of the great zygomatic muscles, and by the raising of the upper lip, the cheeks are drawn upwards . . . the upper lip is drawn up and the lower orbiculars contract, the wrinkles in the lower eyelids and those beneath the eyes are much strengthened or increased . . . the eyebrows are slightly lowered, which shows that the upper as well as the lower orbiculars contract at least to some degree. . . . In broadly smiling the cheeks and upper lip are much raised, the nose appears to be shortened. The upper front teeth are commonly exposed. A well-marked nasolabial fold is formed, which runs from the wing of each nostril to the corner of the mouth. . . .

Darwin's description is not how most would describe a "great smile." Yet that level of detail allowed scientists then and now to proceed with a common language. If it turned out that there was more than one kind of smile—and it seemed likely that there was—the differences would need to be precisely described and catalogued, using common terms and standards.

Meanwhile, across the English Channel, Duchenne was using electric current to induce smiles of various configurations. He attached electrodes to a man's face and sent galvanic current through them to activate muscles one at a time (presumably painless because the subject had lost all feeling in his face).

Activation of one muscle, the *zygomaticus major*, the same muscle described by Darwin, elicited a smile. It attaches at the corners of the mouth and pulls the mouth corners back and up at

French physiologist G.-B.-A. Duchenne applying electric current to
facial muscles

an oblique angle, producing the familiar upward curve. By altering the intensity of the current, Duchenne contracted the *zygomaticus major* muscle to various degrees—at low levels, the mouth corners hardly stirred into a barely detectable smile, while at higher levels, an expansive grin sprang to life.

When Duchenne applied electric current to other facial muscles, another expression looked like a smile, yet something wasn't quite right. It, too, involved contraction of the *zygomaticus major* muscle, resulting in "the same curved line separating the lips, the same sinuousity of the nasolabial fold, the same projection of the cheeks. . . ." But something was missing.

What was absent turned out to be contraction of the muscles that encircle the eyes—the way a ring goes around a finger. When these muscles contract, the cheeks lift, the skin under the lower eyelids bunches, the eyes brighten, and the skin at the outer eye corners produces familiar crow's-feet wrinkles. Duchenne called this muscle the "muscle of kindness." Its anatomical name is the *orbicularis oculi*. What most people think of as a great smile actually entails the action of two facial muscles: the *zygomaticus major* and the *orbicularis oculi*.

Duchenne also manipulated his own face to produce various expressions. Instead of electricity, he attempted to move one facial muscle at a time. Many of us have done something similar as we practice facial expressions in front of the mirror before a big date, an important audition, or the overdue apology. In his novel *Alice Adams*, Booth Tarkington wrote: "She saw herself dancing with him, saw the half-troubled smile she would give him; and she accurately smiled that smile as she rinsed the knives and forks."

Anybody who has ever smiled in response to "Say cheese" knows how easy it is to activate the *zygomaticus major* muscle that pulls the lip corners up. It can be done ever so slightly, as in the *Mona Lisa*, or with all the stops pulled out, resulting in a full toothy grin.

Deliberately contracting the *obicularis occuli* muscle, the one circling the eyes, however, is another story. Duchenne reported that try as he might he couldn't do it intentionally. In fact, most people cannot deliberately contract only this muscle. In a very big smile, the *obicularis occuli* muscle is sometimes inadvertently pulled along with contraction of the zygomaticus muscle.

I've now described two smile types—the simple smile produced by retracting the lip corners only and the combination of the lip

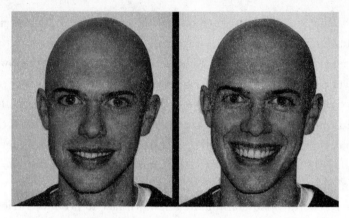

Left, non-Duchenne or social smile; right, Duchenne
or genuine smile

corner raise and the cheek raise. Of these two, Duchenne wrote:
"The first obeys the will but the second is only put into play by the
sweet emotions of the soul." When did scientists cease writing
like this? The spontaneous smile, now referred to in many quar-
ters as the *Duchenne* smile in honor of the man who first identified
its unique characteristics, is known for the combined activation
of changes around the mouth and the eyes. The *non-Duchenne* or
social smile involves retraction of the mouth corners only.

Many people, especially those in the public eye, aim for credible smiles, though the execution is sometimes less than successful. The writer Jonathan Franzen once referred to this as "the
hydraulics of insincere smiles." Look closely at the chrome-bright
smiles in photographs. Sometimes the *zygomaticus major* muscle
seems the only muscle alive and kicking. Or look at a photograph
of a smiling celebrity or candidate. First, cover the top half of
the person's face and look at the mouth. Then cover the mouth
and look at the eyes. At first glance, the number of visible teeth
may suggest that you are looking at a happy person. But when that

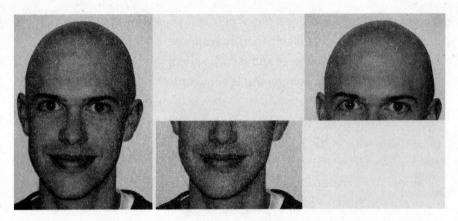

A smile deconstructed into non-smiling eyes and a smiling mouth

mouth is covered and only the eyes are visible, the happiness is often no longer apparent. Many a smile seems perfection if one looks only at the mouth. But if there is no visible skin bunching under the eyes or no creases discernible at the eye corners, the smile is most likely fabricated.

Consider again Hardy's description of Gabriel Oak's smile. It depicts a perfectly executed *obicularis occuli* contraction along with a *zygomaticus major* contraction. Gabriel's "eyes were reduced to mere chinks, and diverging wrinkles appeared round them, extending upon his countenance like the rays in a rudimentary sketch of the rising sun." His smile was the genuine article. For some emotion researchers, genuine smiles are real displays of positive emotion.

Many psychologists describe emotion as a fusion of several components: subjective experience, bodily changes, approach or avoidant behavior, and expressive display. You see a dog growling and running toward you. You feel fear (subjective experience), your breathing gets faster (bodily response), you freeze or flee (behavior), and your eyes and mouth spring wide open (expressive display). Each component is thought to be part of a single emotion system.

Consider a happier emotion scenario. Someone e-mails you with an offer of the job of your dreams, or the person you have long loved from afar calls to ask you out. You feel elated, your heart skips, you jump up and down, and you can't help grinning from ear to ear. If you're happy, you're going to show it. In other words, spontaneous facial expression is a core element of real emotion.

The fact that there are at least two different smile types has led psychologists to examine whether each one has its own associated subjective experiences and behaviors. In other words, the Duchenne smile should be associated with different feelings and behaviors than the non-Duchenne smile.

Consider people thought to be happy. If Duchenne smiles reflect happy feelings, then happily married couples should display more Duchenne smiles than unhappily married couples. Psychologists Robert Levenson and John Gottman looked to the faces of happily and unhappily married couples to see if this was true. In their studies, couples were brought to the lab and asked to converse as they normally do at home. Possible topics included good things in their relationship, while others centered on areas of disagreement. The conversations were videotaped, allowing the researchers to subsequently measure subtle facial changes. They found that happily married couples showed significantly more Duchenne smiles than the unhappily married couples. It's written all over their faces.

Infants also show both Duchenne and non-Duchenne smiles, although it is more of a challenge to see the difference since the fat on their cheeks covers the hallmark crow's-feet wrinkles of a genuine smile. Nonetheless, developmental psychologists hypothesized that baby-sized Duchenne smiles should occur when babies are happy. To test this, ten-month-olds were placed in infant seats on a table. Then, either the baby's mother or an unfamiliar person was asked to approach the baby. Lo and behold, as babies watched their mothers approach, they beamed Duchenne smiles significantly more often than when a stranger approached them.

Duchenne smiles also appear when a person is pleased, even if he or she makes protestations to the contrary. Julie Woodzicka and I asked a group of undergraduate women to listen to jokes, some of which were chosen to be deliberately sexist. Apologies for providing this example: "What do you do when the dishwasher stops working? You slap her and tell her to get back into the kitchen." As is the case with much smile research, we unobtrusively videotaped participants' faces while they listened to the prerecorded jokes.

Taking a line from Queen Victoria, most of the women participants "were not amused." When we asked them to rate the funniness of the sexist jokes, as well as jokes about lawyers (apologies now to attorneys), the sexist examples scraped the bottom of the amusement scale and reached the heights of the offensiveness measure. Some participants however showed unmistakable Duchenne smiles. These jokes evidently tickled their funny bones despite the fact that they said they did not.

Who were the women who said one thing but displayed something else with their faces? Where does the truth lie—in their words or in their smiles? Prior to the experiment, we had measured each participant's attitudes about the roles of women in modern society. At the conservative end of the scale were those who were more traditional and believed in profound differences between women and men, while those at the other end of the scale held more liberal and egalitarian beliefs. Conservative women genuinely smiled in reaction to the sexist jokes. It seems the more traditional women really enjoyed the sexist jokes, but when asked about them said the politically correct thing, namely, that the jokes were not amusing. In contrast, the faces of those with more egalitarian gender attitudes heard nothing there to make them smile.

Genuine smiles also have different consequences. Under the guise of a study of consumer behavior, researchers asked participants to evaluate a variety of T-shirts that came in several colors. A female model exhibited one of three facial expressions as she wore the shirts: a neutral expression; a social smile; or a genuine Duchenne smile. Participants were not told that the model's facial expressions varied, and when asked, none reported noticing any differences in how the model looked. Nonetheless, the type of smile she showed affected subjects' evaluations of the T-shirts—a Duchenne smile elicited more positive reactions than either the social smile or a neutral facial expression.

The Many Faces of Human Smiles

There are few more pervasive symbols than "the smiley face." It is the perfect icon: positive, simple, self-evident, and did I mention, vacuous. It's amazing that the smile, the most scientifically researched facial expression, could be summarized in a flat, yellow, round disc with two vertical ovals crowning a curved line. The Associated Press reported that in one year in the early 1970s, more than 50 million smiley face buttons were sold in the United States. Not to be outdone, the U.S. Postal Service issued a smiley face stamp in 1999. All this is innocuous, that is, if you don't count Texas judge Charles J. Hearn, who in 1993 signed his name and drew a smiley face on the bottom of an execution order, or Colorado senator Patricia Schroeder's wish to be taken seriously as a presidential prospect when she regularly drew a smiley face next to her signature.

There are definitely more smile types than the simple smiley face or the distinction between the Duchenne and non-Duchenne smiles. Graham Greene says of a character in *The Power and the Glory* that "He was appalled again by her maturity, as she whipped up a smile from a large and varied stock."

A minuscule facial movement can change a simple smile into something else altogether—attach wide eyes to a smile and you have the exhilaration of someone riding a roller coaster. Indeed, facial composites—sad smiles, contemptuous smiles, bored smiles, and angry smiles—are common occurrences. *Composite expressions* happen when two or more feelings occur simultaneously. We can be sad and happy and anxious at the same time—a combination of feelings often expressed by graduating college seniors. At other times, a facial composite may result when a person deliberately smiles to mask being angry or disappointed but the underlying feelings slip out from under the smile. And last but not least, a composite smile is sometimes the point. In Dan Brown's novel *Angels and Demons*, the secondary adversary Hassassin is appropriately described as having an evil smile. Villains let us see their true evil when they smile and ridicule at the same time.

Psychologists have found it helpful to describe different types of smiles along three yardsticks: *configuration*; *intensity*; and *timing*. *Configuration* describes the visual appearance of the smile, such as changes to the mouth corners, the eyes, or the cheeks.

Intensity refers to the size of the smile. And *timing* refers to how long a smile lasts as well as how quickly or slowly it appears and leaves the face.

Smile Configuration

The basic smile, as I have said, involves a simple oblique upward movement of the lip corners. Add to it contraction of the *obicularis occuli* muscle around the eyes and you have a winning smile. For a few lucky people, the *zygomaticus major* muscle has two heads where it joins the mouth, causing dimples to form.

Under the face runs a sort of Parisian subway map of overlapping and intersecting muscles that when in motion produce distinctive facial expressions. There are actually forty-three muscles at the ready to make up thousands of possible configurations: mouths close or open, brows lift or dip, cheeks puff or deflate, foreheads wrinkle, nostrils flair, chins pucker, lips purse.

Most facial muscles are actually twins—they are found on both sides of the face and can operate independently to produce lop-sided grins and cynical smirks. In fact, a manufactured smile often has an asymmetrical appearance due to the *zygomaticus major* muscle contracting with more intensity on one side of the mouth than the other. So, whether the smile is symmetrical or uneven can provide clues as to whether a smile is deliberate or felt. Picture Elvis Presley, Mae West, George W. Bush, and Voltaire.

Humans rarely experience unitary feelings and, as I have noted, the face reflects these combinations of feelings. Robert Louis Stevenson included such a mixed smile in *Treasure Island*. Our hero Jim Hawkins notices how the pirate Israel Hands looks

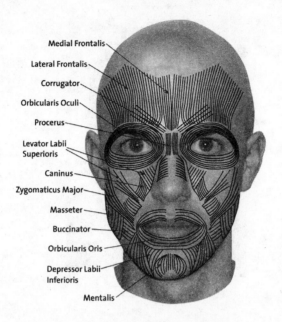

Medial Frontalis
Lateral Frontalis
Corrugator
Orbicularis Oculi
Procerus
Levator Labii
Superioris
Caninus
Zygomaticus Major
Masseter
Buccinator
Orbicularis Oris
Depressor Labii
Inferioris
Mentalis

Primary facial muscles

at him: "It was a smile that had in it something both of pain and weakness . . . but there was, besides that, a grain of derision, a shadow of treachery, in his expression as he craftily watched, and watched, and watched me at my work." A good thing he sees this, as later Hands will try to kill him. Although many facial composites are possible, some smile composites occur regularly. These include angry smiles, sad smiles, surprised smiles, relieved smiles, and condescending smiles.

Let's see what is involved in a smile composite from inside and outside the face. Consider an angry smile.

In this expression, the *zygomaticus major* muscle retracts the corners of the mouth, while contraction of the corrugator muscle,

Angry smile

beginning near the top of the nose and attaching above the center
of each eyebrow, introduces an angry element. When activated,
the corrugator muscle pulls the eyebrows in and down, typically
producing horizontal lines at the bridge of the nose or vertical
wrinkles between the brows. Activation of the corrugator muscle
is often associated with feelings of irritation or anger and occasionally with concentration. Sometimes, the presence of an angry
smile suggests someone is working hard to stay mad—a parent trying to convey that their child has done something wrong but the
child's behavior is hilarious. But an angry/happy blend might just
as easily mean that a person is relishing the thought of revenge.

Another smile composite is the sad smile. In this expression,
three facial muscles are activated—the medial *frontalis* muscle,
which pulls the middle forehead up; the corrugator muscle, which

President Ronald Reagan's concerned brows and suppressed smile

pulls the inner brows down and in; and the *zygomaticus major* muscle, which retracts the mouth corners. Psychologist Paul Ekman has labeled this expression a *miserable* smile. Depending on the circumstances, some see in it "concern furrows."

American president Ronald Reagan's frequent combination of a suppressed smile along with concern furrows conveyed that he was a down-to-earth guy, speaking his mind. But not everyone took it seriously. In *The Man Who Mistook His Wife for a Hat*, Oliver Sacks described a group of aphasic patients watching Reagan give a speech on television. Aphasia is a condition that damages the ability to understand verbal content but leaves its victims highly attentive to facial expressions. The patients were much amused by Reagan's expressions. They thought he was a clown (sad and earnest and putting a good face on things).

Smile Intensity

The *intensity* of a smile describes how big it is, from not detectable to the human eye to a grin that stretches the mouth corners until they are "within an unimportant distance of [the] ears." In most low-intensity smiles, the mouth corners raise a little, and the mouth is closed. With greater intensities, the mouth corners are pulled out and up enough so that the upper teeth become visible— that is except for the actor Dustin Hoffman, who is often photographed with a large, closed-mouth smile. At maximum intensity, the mouth is wide open so that both top and bottom teeth are visible. In *A Christmas Carol*, Dickens described an intense smile by an affable hostess this way: "In came Mrs. Fezziwig, one vast substantial smile."

At the low end of the intensity scale are invisible-to-the-naked-eye facial movements that can only be detected using *electromyography (EMG)*. In facial EMG, the tiny electrical discharges given off by moving muscles are amplified, providing proof of muscle activity just below the surface of the skin. Although fine wires can be directly inserted into muscle tissue, more often recording is done using surface electrodes. Despite the fact that facial EMG can be a pain (literally and figuratively), the device allows researchers to know what a person is feeling even when they are able to keep their expressions in check. Facial EMG also registers expressions too fleeting or too understated to be detected by astute observers.

In one experiment, research subjects watched humorous videos. Some participants were asked to adopt a poker face so that anyone observing them would not be able to guess what they were watching. Participants complied as best they could. Nonetheless, some faces "leaked" amusement. Despite the subjects' efforts to inhibit facial movements, the EMG recordings showed significant activation around the eyes, indicating involuntary smiling. It's difficult to keep a good smile down.

Of course, there are people who have trademark high-intensity smiles—Beverly Sills, Ray Charles, Julia Roberts, Miss America runners-up every year, fashion models alternate years, salespeople all the time, and Protestant ministers most of the time. The most legendary broad grin probably belongs to the Cheshire Cat from *Alice in Wonderland*. "Well! I've often seen a cat without a grin," thought Alice, "but a grin without a cat! It's the most curious thing I ever saw in all my life."

Now, the obvious question: Does the size of a smile reflect the amount of happy feelings? Not exactly. It is true that when people feel great joy, their smiles tend to be bigger than when they are pleased just a little bit. But oversized smiles often suggest a facial expression aimed at generating positive consequences. For example, psychophysiologist Gary Schwartz and his colleagues found that voluntary smiles are on average ten times bigger than spontaneous smiles. So, although a smile may be a mile wide, it may only be a millimeter deep.

Voluntary or deliberate smiles tend to be bigger because their point is to be seen. If you want someone's approval, a smile is often a good place to start, and just in case, it ought to be big enough to be noticed. But getting the size of the smile right can be a delicate calculation. Too much flattery, too much apple-polishing, too much smiling, and your motives become suspect. Psychologists call this predicament the *ingratiator's dilemma*: how do I create a positive impression without, at the same time, eliciting the unwanted impression that I am trying to create a good impression?

Because voluntary smiles tend to be more intense does not

mean that people who display them are necessarily aware of what they are doing. Indeed, smiling may be the most overlearned and out-of-awareness human behavior there is. As children, we learn that smiles are magnetic, that they often elicit positive consequences. But, as with any neuromuscular activity, the more one smiles, the more likely it is that one's central nervous system and muscular network become trained to produce smiles efficiently and unconsciously whenever relevant circumstances are present. So we may have started by consciously and deliberately telling ourselves to smile in social company, but the act becomes increasingly automatic with each repetition.

Smile Timing

A smile can flick on and off like a light switch. Or a smile can stretch across time like the Texan's smile in *Catch-22*—"[his] indestructible smile . . . cracked forever across the front of his face like the brim of a black ten-gallon hat." Smile timing involves how quickly a smile appears, how long it stays at its peak intensity, and how long it takes to disappear.

Researchers have reason to believe that the faster a smile comes on the face and the faster it leaves, the more likely it is that it was deliberately put there. For example, quick-on quick-off smiles are found more often when smiling is a job prerequisite. I observed this once watching a social director on a cruise ship. She beamed constantly in the company of passengers, enthusiastically and amicably attending to their questions and requests. But in the rare moments when she was alone and not smiling, the sight of a passenger looking her way caused a smile to materialize in a split second. It also went off just as quickly as her social work was done.

In smiling, as in many things, timing is everything. In snap-shots, people often look as though they are having the time of their lives. But if we had been able to see how the smile came onto and left the face and how long it lasted after the picture was taken, we would be better able to tell whether it was genuine. Deliberate smiles move in time to a different drummer. They appear abruptly, stay at their peak a disproportionately long time, and exit as quickly as they arrived. They also tend to be either very brief (less than two thirds of a second) or to hold on for longer stretches (more than four seconds).

In Doris Lessing's novel *The Summer Before the Dark*, the main character is a forty-five-year-old woman who is no longer needed by her husband or her grown children. As wife and social hostess, she has learned how to hide behind a smile, to be literally present yet emotionally absent. On one occasion as she pours coffee for her husband and his colleague, Lessing writes of her: "Having handed them coffee and chocolate wafers she set an attentive smile on her face, like a sentinel, behind which she could cultivate her own thoughts."

Do most normal people pay attention to something as minuscule as how long it takes a smile to come onto a person's face? Apparently they do. In one study, participants viewed a series of brief video segments that showed a person just starting to smile. The smile "starts" appeared at different speeds, with some arriving languidly and others appearing in a great rush. Participants much preferred those people whose smiles were slow to arrive. They were judged as more attractive and trustworthy than when a person's smile was fast to appear. They were also seen as more flirtatious.

In contrast to the quick-on, quick-off delivery of intentional smiles, spontaneous smiles are relatively brief but repetitive.

Genuine delight is reflected more often as a sequence of short smile bursts rather than arriving and setting up shop. To quote Flannery O'Connor in *Good Country People*, "His smiles came in succession like waves breaking on the surface of a little lake."

Deconstructing a Smile

We know that there are many smile types because scientists have had the doggedness to map out how the human face moves muscle by muscle. Darwin started us down this path by paying close attention to facial expressions of many kinds. He observed his own children. He studied people who were insane, blind, from other cultures, and he was incessantly eliciting descriptions from colleagues around the world.

A century later, Paul Ekman and Wallace Friesen at the University of California at San Francisco proposed a method for coding all visible movement on the face. They called their method the *Facial Action Coding System*, or FACS for short. First published in the 1970s, FACS has been updated several times since. In FACS, a facial expression is not described in terms of a verbal label like "sad," which could mean different things to different people. Rather, FACS codes movements on the surface of the face in terms of objective changes. Every visible change is called an *action unit* and there are action units for all visible facial movements. For example, movement of the smile muscle (*zygomaticus major*) is action unit twelve (AU12). Movement of the frown muscle (corrugator, which lowers and narrows the inner brow) is action unit four (AU4). Movement of the *frontalis* muscles (forehead furrows) involves two action units— AU1 describes movement in the middle of the forehead and AU2 describes movement on the sides of the forehead. With FACS facial expressions are typically coded from video recordings.

The FACS system bypasses the ambiguities of verbal labels in favor of objectivity and consistency. Early on, FACS included forty-six action units; it now contains more than sixty separate actions of the face, head, and eyes. If asked to describe a friend's facial expression, you might say that she looked sad. Users of the FACS system observing the same face would probably see AU1 and AU4 and possibly some AU15. The crunching of all these numbers—action units, intensities, durations, onsets, and offsets—produces distinctive facial profiles.

I spent a year in Paul Ekman's San Francisco lab with other face scientists and we all instinctively applied the FACS system to anyone who happened by. A member of the lab might come in on a Monday morning and be greeted with something like, "What's your AU6 and AU12 and AU25 all about?" Ordinary mortals would simply see a big smile. No one who ever used FACS would subscribe to the nonsensical idea that "it takes more muscles to frown than it does to smile." The precision afforded by FACS and similar systems allows scientists to know what particular facial expression is present, under what conditions, and with what consequences.

FACS is labor-intensive—I know from experience—but the output is equally concentrated, not just in revealing emotional depths that would otherwise remain hidden but in confirming the wondrous capacity humans have for communicating without words. The face is an ongoing parade of expressions.

In one of the first studies using FACS, student nurses watched a pleasant nature film and an unmistakably unpleasant film showing amputations and severe burns. Afterward, they were instructed to describe their feelings about the nature film honestly, but to lie about the ghastly film, telling the interviewer that it had been like a walk in the park. Participants' faces were surreptitiously videotaped during the interview and subsequently coded with FACS.

The nurses smiled both while telling the truth and while lying. They used their smiles while lying about the grisly film to hide their negative feelings. Nonetheless, other facial actions seeped through and were picked up, using FACS. Some faces revealed hints of disgust (raised upper lip—AU10) or sadness (lowered lip corners—AU15) or suffering (AU20), in spite of their efforts to keep negative expressions under the wraps of a smile. Again let me refer to a description by Doris Lessing: "You have to deduce a person's real feelings about a thing by a smile she does not know is on her face, by the way bitterness tightens muscles at a mouth's corner." That would be AU14.

Efforts are now under way to develop computerized systems to automate FACS coding, a worthy development if there ever was one. In one trial run, a team of Dutch and American scientists applied their expression recognition software to Leonardo da Vinci's painting, the *Mona Lisa*. Their analysis: Mona Lisa is 83 percent happy, 9 percent disgusted, 6 percent fearful, and 2 percent angry! Their system measures the degree of displacement of facial features, such as eyebrows, eyelids, cheeks, and mouth corners, from their neutral positions, and then compares the degree of the displacements to algorithms associated with each emotion.

Smiles are special. They assume multiple forms. They partner with other expressions. They can come and go in a nanosecond or stay interminably. They can be truly genuine or entirely false. They may surface with full awareness or appear as though by accident. Smiles do many things for human relationships; hence it is no wonder that a one-size-fits-all smile could never suffice. There is no such thing as a simple smile.

Now that we have the means to tell smiles apart—by virtue of their configuration, intensity, and timing—the way is clear to delve into their causes and consequences. In subsequent chapters, you will learn that your smiles can make other people happy and on occasion even make you happier. Some smiles establish social bonds, while others ward off angry actions and assuage hurt feelings. They can point to trustworthiness, sustain cooperation, and elicit support. In case all these desirable effects sound too good to be true, there are also negative actions associated with smiling, including ones that are malevolent, manipulative, and mendacious. This takes classic form in Shakespeare's *Third Part of Henry the Sixth* when Richard realizes he will never legitimately achieve the throne and must resort to other measures: "While I can smile and murder while I smile."

There is no getting away from the effects of smiling faces. But, in fact, when people do *not* smile because they cannot or choose not to do so, there are significant social and psychological consequences as well.

A short story by Jamaica Kincaid entitled "Girl" acknowledges some of this range:

> . . . this is how you sweep a yard; this is how you smile to someone you don't like too much; this is how you smile to someone you don't like at all; this is how you smile to someone you like completely; this is how you set a table for tea. . . .

out of the mouths of babes

A baby's first true social smile is often seen as the first among firsts—first tooth, first step, and first real word—all memorable and delightful. But the first social smile is something else again. It is noted in baby books, announced in e-mails, committed to memory, and, if in luck, captured on camera. Surveys report that seeing the baby's first "real" smile tops most moms' lists of the joys of being a new mother. For a young couple in England, it was heartbreak when thieves stole a video recorder holding the priceless videotape labeled "Molly's First Smile." All was not lost. Two weeks after the theft, the videotape in question was thrown over a back fence into the owners' yard. There may not be honor among thieves but there does appear to be sentimentality.

A baby's smile makes parents giddy and grandparents gaga. A smiling baby can take your breath away. It can elicit gushing from complete strangers. Sure, a baby's gurgles are endearing, their raspberries adorable, but there is nothing quite like watching a smile blossom on a baby's face. People will do all sorts of embarrassing things to get it to reappear. If they are successful, there is no achievement that's sweeter. Among the Navajo Indians, the person who first makes an infant smile hosts a celebration called the "First Laugh Ceremony." The Navajo believe when the baby gazes at someone and breaks into that outward-looking, open-mouth smile for the first time, the infant signals that he or she is ready to learn to speak.

Babies' smiles are as crucial to their survival as are their parents' "back-at-you smiles." Reciprocal smiling between child and parent is pivotal in a child's physical and psychological development. A baby's first "social" smile has been described as nature's way of duping parents into being attentive. And it is not just parents who are arrested by the first social smile. Writers over the ages have seen in that smile signs that the infant is now truly human; has intelligence, can reason, appreciates pleasure, and knows what love is. Psychologists for their part tend to steer clear of immoderate inferences like these; nonetheless, their studies lead them to conclude that smiling between infants and caregivers is a crucial dynamic in the development of a socially adept mature person.

Besides entrapping caregivers with their smiles, infants are also drawn to others' smiles and are especially miserable when active trade is not forthcoming. When the typical back-and-forth smile script between baby and caregiver is interrupted—by illness, depression, neglect, or abuse—prospects for that baby growing into a happy and emotionally healthy adult are considerably dimmed.

Babies' smiles seem the pinnacle of innocence—natural and spontaneous, without pretense or agenda. There is, however, much more than sweetness packed in those rosebud lips and raised chubby cheeks. Although infants come with the indubitable capacity to move their facial muscles into something that looks like a smile, these first expressions evolve into a socially calibrated and extensive roster of smiles for use in all kinds of situations. One of the most important things that babies come to understand is that their own smiles are actions with consequences. At the beginning, they smile instinctively. A short time later, they understand that their smiles make things happen.

It may come as a surprise to learn how early in life babies use smiles to entice and convince, mask and mislead. In fact, by three months, they can initiate face-to-face interaction with their mothers using simple acts of smiling and gazing at her face. To be sure, some baby smiles are genuine signs of delight, but in little time, little ones know how to perform their smiles to good effect. By the time they are toddlers, smiling is as much voluntary display as it spontaneous output of happy feelings. William Blake captured that artful capacity in his "Cradle Song": "Sweet babe, in thy face/Soft desires I can trace/Secret joys and secret smiles/Little pretty infant wiles."

Babies' Not-So-Simple Smiles

How are we to interpret the smiles of newborns? Do they signal relief that the outside world is manageable? Do they show that babies are in on the cosmic joke? Developmental psychologists, ever the objective scientists, prefer to characterize initial smiles as *endogenous*, that is, smiling without obvious cause. For example, both blind and sighted infants show endogenous smiles, as do infants who are born without higher brain structures even though their brain stems are intact. This evidence indicates that smiling is wired into the more primitive parts of the human brain.

Endogenous smiles occur too when newborns are asleep, which on average they are doing eighteen hours a day. Infant smiles mostly occur during REM (or rapid eye movement) sleep

| Neutral | Distress | Ambiguous | Joy |

A facially expressive infant

and take the two forms that we know as non-Duchenne smiles (mouth only) and Duchenne smiles (mouth–plus–cheek raise causing eye wrinkles). This is remarkable since babies in their first month rarely show a Duchenne smile when they are awake. To be sure, most sleeping infant smiles are modest in size and the mouth is usually closed.

Despite parents' injunction to their babies to have sweet dreams, we actually do not know of what babies' REM sleep is made. Most psychologists think that infants' "dream sleep" probably reflects ongoing development of the central nervous system.

This is not to say that an external stimulus cannot trigger a smile from a wide-awake infant. Give a newborn something sweet to taste, for example, and they reflexively smile. But scientists argue whether the smile stems from pleasure or is simply an instinctive bodily reaction. To study which is the case, researchers placed various drops of sweet, sour, and bitter substances on babies' tongues and assessed their facial reactions. The researchers found that a sweet taste evoked smiling and sucking. A sour taste elicited lip pursing, nose wrinkling, and eye blinking, and a bitter substance evoked turning away or spitting up. All responses appear to be instinctively useful in keeping a baby alive—steering it away from potentially dangerous material and toward substances not likely to cause intestinal trouble.

Researchers have also determined, contrary to popular belief, that infant smiles are *not* due to gas. Developmental scientists reasoned that if gas were responsible for the smilelike display, then that facial action should emerge around feeding times more than at other times. Robert Emde and his colleagues observed thirty newborns before, during, and after a feeding. They found no relationship between when the babies showed the smilelike expression and when they burped, spit up, or passed gas. Another study specifically looked at the types of facial expressions that actually occurred at the same time as gas in newborns and found not a smile amongst them. Instead, there was writhing and facial reddening and a grimace without the characteristic smile indicators.

First smiles are like warm-up exercises. But they have in them great potential. In fact, the French philosopher Merleau-Ponty labeled early smiles *motor smiles*. They provide babies with a running start on securing cooperative social relationships. But why can't a baby's smile simply mean that she or he is happy?

Infant Feelings

Although it may be hard to believe, there are scientists who do not think that an infant's smile has much to do with happy feelings. On the face of it, this probably seems absurd since it's obvious that a baby's smile means she is happy and her frowning indicates that she is not. How could one argue that facial expressions are anything other than straightforward indicators of an infant's emotional state? One might grant that the pleasure underlying a newborn's smile differs from that of an adult's pleasure, but it is nonetheless pleasure, and pleasure makes smiles happen.

But some scientists don't buy this. They argue that facial displays of newborns have little to do with internal emotional states and more to do with reflexive behaviors, and, once babies can focus visually, with imitation and then elicitation. A baby's first instinctive behavior, according to this view, is to snag nurturing caregivers, and it does this by smiling. Smiling is functional—it is nature's way of securing an infant's survival. Somewhat later, a baby's smile connects to feeling happy, but the association between smiling and being happy may not be there at the outset.

Other scientists think that the smile/happy connection is present from the beginning. I will refer to this group as EID (*emotions induce displays*) and the contrasting camp as DAF (*displays are functional*). According to EID, human infants begin life with a set of neurologically based emotions such as happiness, sadness, and anger. Each emotion is wired to a unique constellation of subjective, physiological, behavioral, and expressive conditions. Accordingly, a person who has just been insulted feels angry, experiences an increase in body temperature, bangs down the phone, and glowers.

Likewise, it is said, the brain of a normally developing baby already has in place similar circuitry for each emotion. EID advocates believe that the connections between feelings and facial expressions do not have to be learned; they arrive as a unit at birth. As soon as any emotion is elicited, a corresponding facial expression is instantaneously and involuntarily activated just like other physiological responses like burping.

In fact, EID proponents note that since the biological connection between emotion and expression is so tight, a facial expression itself can activate the associated feeling as well as the related physiological and behavioral responses. It is only later that the connection between an emotion like joy and a facial expression like a smile becomes less tied together as children start to manage what is revealed—or not—on their faces.

Scientists who believe that displays are functional, on the other hand, see no necessary connection between smiles and happiness. They see no inborn relationship between felt emotion and visible expression for infants or for adults. They point to evidence showing that feelings do not inevitably result in a facial expression—as with the proverbial poker face. They also note that individuals can easily adopt facial expressions without any real feeling—as with happy-talk newscasters. DAF advocates acknowledge that babies' smiles induce joy in those who see them, but they seriously question whether babies' smiles reflect positive emotion in the babies themselves. Some even question whether tiny babies have emotions at all—agitation and animation, yes, but not emotion as we normally understand it.

For the "functional" DAF group, facial display and emotion eventually come together so that some smiles become authentic indicators of positive emotion. But for this to happen, the brain needs more time to settle in, and there needs to be substantial social interaction with caregivers so that infants can come to understand when and how they are being emotional. "Look at that smile. What a happy baby you are!"

Research psychologists are still at it, trying to understand the nature of the relationship between facial expression and emotion. Nearly all agree that the connection between them is not always tight—certainly not among adults. But since newborns presumably cannot mask what they feel, some believe we should be able to see in them a clear link between feelings and facial displays if indeed they are neurologically bound together.

So, let's bring babies to the lab and see what the data show. In several studies, infants' facial expressions were observed in situations where there was good reason to expect that they were happy. In happy situations, the *emotions induce displays* contingent would predict smiling babies. The *displays are functional* camp, on the other hand, would be surprised if there was a consistent connection between a happy baby and a happy face.

One study observed infants mixing it up with some pretty cool toys, but alas there were no more smiles than when the same babies were not playing with the toys. It did not matter whether the infants were six months old or sixty months old. If playing with toys made the babies happy, it did not show on their faces. Following a similar strategy, other investigators tantalized three- and six-month-old infants with an assortment of interesting things to watch, listen to, and set in motion. They, too, found little smiling in the babies.

Not every study lines up behind these two, however. When babies were given a mallet and the opportunity to pound different-shaped pegs into a board with different-shaped holes, many beamed as they did so. Perhaps literally having clout is a better elicitor of positive emotion than simple play.

How about when babies see their moms coming toward them? Do they smile then? Yes, they do, and they smile significantly more than when they see a stranger approaching. But do they smile because they are delighted or might the mother's own facial expression be responsible for the smiles seen on the infants' faces? Newborns are in fact born mimics. Researchers have found that they are able to imitate unfamiliar facial movements on a stranger's face a mere few weeks after they are born.

Since the researchers in this study had not instructed the mothers and strangers about how to approach the infants, most of the mothers radiated positive greetings as they approached their babies while the stranger did not smile nearly as much. It seems possible then that the babies imitated the facial expressions they saw coming toward them. If so, it cannot be concluded that their smiles sprung from inner happy feelings.

Although the matter remains undecided, the data do suggest that we need to be cautious in assuming that smiling among the very young necessarily reflects positive emotion. In short, the link between feeling happy and smiling in infants is not as inevitable and invariant as it might at first seem. This issue is not trivial. Behavioral scientists want to understand why we feel what we do, why our bodies seem sometimes to have a mind of their own, and why our faces periodically give us away. Jerome Kagan, a respected developmental psychologist, proposed one resolution to this conundrum. According to Kagan, newborns (0–2 months) have sensations and stirrings of a kind, but it would be premature to call them emotions. They are not emotions because newborns do not yet have the ability to cognitively appraise internal sensory impressions, let alone evaluate external events and people. Most psychologists believe that "emotion would not be emotion without some evaluation at its heart." And while infants experience variations in internal tone, they do not make attributions about a possible external cause (Mommy was cranky just now) or internal cause (I think that milk may have passed its sell-by date).

What infants do have at the outset is considerable facial and

Inexpressive Russian orphans

vocal expressive capacity. A baby's cooing and crying, smiling and frowning, are actions with social and psychological conse-quences. "You are happy to see your Daddy, aren't you?" "What's making you so sad? Do you need a hug?" Babies let parents know that something needs to be done. Parents respond and by doing so let babies in on something really important, namely, that displays have meaning and consequences. Caregivers provide babies with a primer on emotion. Smiling means you're happy and this is what I do when you're happy.

By the age of three, toddlers have learned a lot about what emotion is and how each feeling is displayed on the face. When three-year-olds are given the names of several emotions, they can accurately enact the facial expression that goes with each one. However, when children do *not* receive feedback about emotions from caregivers, their emotional lives and expressive range suffer. Traumatized and institutionalized infants show little affect because they have had few opportunities to have tête-à-têtes with responsive adults who provide feedback and mirror back to them what emotions look like. Similarly, as they grow older, the facial expressions of babies who are blind from birth do not adjust and adapt as much as they do in sighted babies. Thus as adults, the facial expressions of congenitally blind persons tend either to be damped down or especially effusive. The singers Ray Charles and Stevie Wonder, who were both blind since childhood, are renowned for their ear-to-ear smiles, to say nothing of their oscillating bodies and lively feet.

Babies' Smiles Are People-Catchers

Five hundred years ago, Erasmus asked rhetorically: "What is there about babies which makes us hug and kiss and fondle them, so that even an enemy would give them help at that age?" Primatologist Sarah Blaffer Hrdy contends that infant smiles make mothers and others want to be close. Initially, babies may not smile so much because of what they feel but because of the way they make others feel. Using magnetic resonance imaging, researchers scanned mothers' brains while they were looking at photos of their babies smiling and found that the reward centers of their brains showed substantial activation. In fact, these are the same areas in the brain that other studies have shown to be associated with drug addiction.

Infants are more likely to smile if someone is watching them. The same is true of adults. For example, researchers observed that bowlers did not smile when they had their backs to their friends even if they had bowled a strike; they only smiled *when* they turned to face their friends. Moreover, solitary bowlers usually did not smile, irrespective of how well they were bowling. Two Spanish social psychologists, J. M. Fernandez-Dols and M. A. Ruiz-Belda, also observed winning Olympic athletes and noted that they smiled significantly more when acknowledging the cheers of the crowd than when they were alone.

Even the *imagined* presence of another person leads to more smiling among adults. In a series of studies, research subjects were asked to imagine something really splendid happening to them (e.g., getting great news) and to imagine it happening either when they were alone or when they were with other people. When participants *imagined* being with someone, they smiled more than when they imagined being alone, even though they reported the same amount of positive emotion in both situations. Smiling is meant for others, whether they are in front of us or in our heads.

Developmental psychologist Susan Jones has shown that the same thing happens with babies and toddlers. At eight months, babies are more likely to smile if others are present. By ten months, they clearly realize that a smile has first-rate consequences—hugs, tummy smooches, applesauce. By twelve months, babies understand that smiling makes others happy which prompts reciprocity that in turn gives them an emotional reason to smile.

Babies' smiles are there from day one because evolution has made that behavior adaptive. With growth, smiles become voluntary. This is an important aspect of human development, namely, that the factors responsible for initiating a behavior are not necessarily those that sustain it. Biology provides babies with the ability and inclination to flex their smile muscles but maturity and social context affect whether, when, and how they will materialize.

Growing Smiles

Smiles mature as babies grow. All smiles involve contraction of the *zygomaticus major* muscle that pulls the lip-corners upward and outward. When cheek rising, produced by the *obicularis oculi, pars lateralis* muscle, co-occurs with lip-corner pull, the result, as we have seen, is a Duchenne or genuine smile. During a heady game of peek-a-boo, infants display both Duchenne and non-Duchenne smiles. But now two additional smile variations are added to the repertoire: the *play* smile and the *duplay* smile. In the *play* smile, the baby's jaw drops a little, causing her mouth to open along with retraction of the lip corners. In the duplay smile, mouth opening accompanies a genuine Duchenne smile.

In peek-a-boo, the *play* smile tends to appear just before the adult's face magically reappears—a kind of looking-forward smile. The *duplay* smile appears more typically at the game's climax (Boo!). Developmental psychologists catalogue these distinctions because there is good reason to believe that such variations reflect different kinds of positive emotion or generate different social consequences.

As I mentioned early on in this chapter, the arrival of the social smile at about five or six weeks makes parents go positively weak in the knees. Psychologists call it the *social* smile because the infant locks eyes with the parent and smiles. Although parents *have* the baby, the baby, it is said, now *has* them.

With social smiles, babies go public. They set their sights on others and aim gummy grins in their direction. By the end of the second month, the social smile appears frequently, often

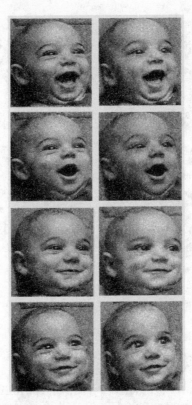

Smiles with and without cheek raising. The left photo in each pair shows a genuine Duchenne smile (with cheek raise); the right shows the non-Duchenne smile (without cheek raise)

accompanied by much arm waving and leg wiggling. Just why it takes several weeks for infants to show the social smile is not yet clear. One speculation—and it is just speculation—is that social smiling is delayed to spare parents from too much attachment in the first few weeks of life when mortality is relatively higher. Since parents' attachment jumps several notches once they see their infant's social smile, a delayed arrival might postpone

Signs of a low-intensity voluntary smile

serious emotional investment until the infant's survival is more likely. In the same speculative realm, one psychiatrist proposed that the arrival of the social smile in weeks 5 or 6 is "payment for services rendered."

By the ripe old age of ten months, an infant's social smile shows telltale signs of being voluntary. You might ask, how could one tell? Susan Jones and her research group observed ten-month-old infants playing with toys across a room from where their mothers were seated. The researchers were on particular lookout for what happens to an infant's smile when he or she turns to look at Mom and does not find her looking back. If the baby turns to look at his mother and continues to smile if she returns his expression but stops smiling if she does not look back at him, then the smile is characterized as voluntary. That smile is looking for a reply and varies depending on the answer it gets.

Coy smiles are also socially directed. In a coy smile, the infant starts to smile, then lowers its eyes or head, followed by a slight raising of one arm as though to cover its face. The baby looks adorable but is in shy or bashful mode. Fellow Yale psychologist Karen Wynn and I wondered about the possible function and consequences of coy smiles. We have been examining the conditions under which coy smiles are more likely to appear. Since they seem to be a mixed message, conveying both approach and withdrawal, we hypothesized that the coy smile would show itself more in the presence of a stranger than someone familiar to them. In one study, the babies are comfortably situated in an infant seat on a table. We then ask one of three adults (the baby's mother, a female graduate student, or a male graduate student) to enter, sit facing the baby, and try to get the baby to smile. They can make funny sounds or funny faces, but no tickling is allowed. We videotaped the interactions and coded whether the baby smiled and if so, in what type.

We found coy smiles are all but absent when the babies are alone or with their mothers but happen with some frequency with both strangers, especially male strangers. With their mothers, most babies have little to fear. Strangers, however, are another story, as their intentions are unknown. A coy smile may be one way to handle this ambiguity. The initial smile signals sociability, but the turning away suggests a readiness to hide just in case things go bad. Although infants do not yet have words, they can draw on several smile types to deal with their social environment. For the moment, Dr. Wynn and I are calling the coy smile the "Please don't eat me smile."

Smile Bonds

A baby's smile is unrivaled in helping to secure its survival. Psychologist Peter Wolff wrote a half century ago that mothers increase the attention they give their babies after the baby has flashed its social smile at them. Rene Spitz added the caveat that this smile innocently perpetuates a fraud by inducing parents to believe that their baby's smile is one of personal recognition. But almost any face at five or six weeks is enough to trigger the social smile. Well, not any face exactly—it just has to have the rudiments of a face: forehead, eyes, and a nose. It doesn't have to be animate, for instance, since a mask that moves up and down can elicit a social smile in the second to third month of a baby's life. Thus infants come equipped to smile and particularly to something that resembles a human face. As they get older, babies' smiles become more selective, aiming more frequently at familiar care-givers. These are the people that count.

The exchange in smiles between parent and child lays the groundwork for much else in a child's life. Just as adults are seduced by an infant's smile, infants are themselves drawn to the smiles of others, recognizing smiling faces before they can reliably perceive any other facial expression. And although they can discern a smile on the face of a stranger, they learn the difference between the smiling and frowning expressions of their mothers. In time, they learn to see these differences on the face of others.

Since mothers are suckers for their baby's smile they feel profound disappointment if their baby does not smile at them. Premature infants smile less than full-term infants. If a premature baby is also medically compromised, the mother sometimes feels her baby is never going to give her its stamp of approval. There are some babies who smile rarely because they are temperamentally inhibited. Alas, mothers tend to distance themselves from a non-smiling baby. They smile and talk less to them and hold them farther from their bodies.

Unfortunately, non-smiling is reciprocated in the same way smiling is. Premature babies and ill newborns are more likely to be neglected and abused than healthy, full-term infants. This is not to say that a non-smiling infant precipitates neglect or abuse, only that an expressionless baby exacts a heavy emotional toll on caregivers.

An unresponsive adult can also exact an emotional toll on infants. If the primary caregiver is unreliable or indifferent, babies are chilled to their emotional core. There is a substantial body of evidence showing that babies born to depressed or unresponsive mothers become depressed themselves. Their smiling recedes, as does their appetite and their ability to sleep soundly.

Smile reciprocity between infant and caregiver also plays a critical role in providing the template for how to have a conversation. Detailed observations of typical parent-infant interactions show that an infant's smile recurs if it is met with a smile, just as its vocalizations increase upon hearing similar sounds from a caregiver. Sensitive adults know intuitively to respond in like kind to whatever the baby communicates to them. Parents do not merely respond to their infants' smiles and vocalizations; they imitate them. The baby gurgles; the parent coos; the baby blows a raspberry; the parent smacks her lips; the baby smiles and the mother anticipates a lifetime of heart-to-heart conversations. The linguist and anthropologist Mary Catherine Bateson termed these early facial and vocal exchanges *proto-conversations*.

Proto-conversations have all the trademarks of adult verbal interactions. The mother's part in these conversations provides the "scaffolding" in which she offers support and adjustments to the child's responses. She looks for and facilitates more advanced behavior from the baby. John S. Watson proposed that these proto-conversations do something more than imitate adult conversations. They are a game in which the mother becomes important to the baby because she plays the game. When caregivers interact with babies in tit-for-tat exchanges, babies get it that the adult is responding to their actions. When that realization hits, there is much smiling and vocalizing on both sides.

In addition to producing delight and bonding in the moment, proto-conversations provide a foundation for a child's subsequent verbal competence. The more mothers reciprocate their infants' smiles and babbles, the more verbally competent the children are as two-year-olds, and the more socially competent they are with peers when they are three and half years old.

Smile Recommendations

A caregiver's smile conveys something else of importance to an infant, namely, information from a trustworthy source. Around their first birthday, infants begin to search for information about people and things that come into their immediate environment. An unfamiliar adult enters the room or an unknown furry object is noticed on the chair. How is a baby to react? Check in with Mom. Look at her face. If she smiles, it's good to go; if she frowns, "don't even think about going there." Developmental psychologists call this process *social referencing*. Social referencing is like reading a review before deciding whether a book or movie is worth tracking down.

The classic studies of social referencing involve observing how infants react to being beckoned to cross a "visual cliff." The visual cliff is a realistic-looking drop-off created by using adjacent checkerboard floor patterns. The "shallow" side is flush with the floor; the "deep" side is substantially lower but with a clear piece of sturdy Plexiglas making it flush with the shallow side. To a crawling infant, the deep side looks like a chasm. In the initial studies, one-year-old babies were placed on the shallow side with an attractive toy on the other side of the cliff. The baby's mother stood next to the deep side and gestured for her baby to come get the toy. Babies crawled until they got to the drop-off, at which point most looked to their mother as if to say, "Now what?"

Meanwhile, the mothers on the other side of the cliff showed their babies one of five different facial displays: joy, interest, fear, anger, or sadness. If the mothers smiled or showed interest, most babies put their crawl into high gear and went straight over the abyss. "I'll follow you anywhere." But if she frowned or showed fear, then most babies stayed put on the shallow side. An expression of sadness tended to confuse the babies, with some choosing to cross while others played it safe and stayed put. When there was no visual cliff, most babies didn't look to their mothers for advice and hence her facial expression had no effect either way.

Babies also look to other adults for cues as to what to do when a choice presents itself. University of Washington psychologist Betty Repacholi showed fourteen- and eighteen-month-olds two closed boxes. Upon opening one of the boxes she smiled and said, "Wow," but on opening the other box, she made a disgusted face and uttered, "Eww." When infants were then given the chance to explore the boxes, they were much more likely to look at and reach into the box that had precipitated the smile rather than the disgust reaction.

From many studies on social referencing, researchers have concluded that infants barely a year old who have the need to know but not the words to ask use others' facial expressions to find answers. Infants come to the table prepared to observe and copy, or, if uncertain, to observe and take note.

Toddlers watch adults' faces to gauge their feelings about all manner of things. They are quick to pick up caregivers' feelings irrespective of whether they are intentionally sent. For example, despite verbal assurances that everything is okay, adults' feelings of distress are still conveyed by facial expressions. This discrepancy between the verbal and nonverbal is often evident in children's books where illustrations say one thing and the text says another. So, in Maurice Sendak's *Where the Wild Things Are*, children tend to see the "wild things" as friendly since the illustrations show them smiling. Adults focus on the written text, which is frightening.

Tots rely too on their mothers' faces to help them distinguish between real and pretend—another developmental milestone. When a mother smiles as she talks into a banana as if it were a telephone, her child knows that bananas are not really an alternative form of communication. Indeed, the need to know what people *really* mean despite what they are saying never goes away.

The facial expressions of caregivers provide infants and toddlers with an illustrated manual for how to negotiate the physical and social world. Sometimes, parents offer up smiles that say, "Go for it," and frowns that say, "No." Children are heavily reliant on these voluntary facial displays.

Learning When Not to Smile

Working at Macy's as an elf at Christmas, the humorist David Sedaris describes seeing "a woman slap and shake her sobbing daughter," who was about to be photographed with the store Santa. The mother yelled: "Goddamn it, Rachel, get on that man's lap

and *smile* or I'll give you something to cry about." Most parental
instruction about when children should smile is not so graphic,
although it is often explicit. "Smile at the nice lady."

Children learn to smile to get through uncomfortable situations and they learn not to smile when to do so would be embarrassing or hurtful. Emotion researchers use the term *display
rules* to describe what most of us know as putting on a "front."
However one labels it, a crucial part of socialization is imparting
to children the idea that there are situations where one is not to
show what one truly feels. Display rules acknowledge that facial
expressions, voluntary and involuntary, are awash with consequences. In other words, one manages what is on one's face in
many social situations so as to choose the results one wants.

Developmental psychologist Carolyn Saarni developed a way to
study how and when children acquire the conventions for managing their faces. In the *mistaken gift paradigm*, researchers give
children a number of tasks to complete. After finishing the first
task, they receive a highly desirable gift and are led to believe
that other gifts will be forthcoming as they complete additional
tasks. After completing the second task, the children receive an
unattractive gift. Most are disappointed and upset. Do they show
this on their faces or do they cover their negative feelings? Many
did hide their disappointment by smiling, but only if others were
present. If no one was there to see it, their displeasure was clearly
visible.

Interestingly, although most preschoolers smile over their disappointment if others are present, for the life of them, they cannot explain why they smiled. Their action precedes the knowledge
of its rationale. Actually, psychologists now believe that adults
often act this way as well, making decisions moral and otherwise,
and only afterward searching for a good rationale for what they

have done. It takes several years before children, if pressed, can articulate why they adopt false faces. These justifications tend to fall into two broad categories: self-protective reasons and pro-social reasons.

Self-protection is generally good grounds for masking what one really feels. Perhaps the school bully can be deflected by a show of cool rather than signs of panic. Perhaps one can go for a comedy routine after having tripped to demonstrate it was intended all along.

On other occasions, one might express an emotion one does not feel to protect someone else, referred to by psychologists as *pro-social motivation*—responding to a lousy gift with a smile or smiling after a teammate has made a bad play, both put on so that others won't feel bad. A poignant example of this occurred recently from the five-year-old daughter of a friend. The daughter has a chronic medical condition that sometimes causes her to feel quite down. My friend noticed an uptick in her daughter's mood and said to her, "You seem to be feeling better." Her five-year-old replied, "Not really, Mommy, but I don't want you to feel bad too."

These emotion display rules highlight something important about social life: that emotion is sometimes spontaneous and unconscious while at other times it is intentional and conscious. Paul Harris and his colleagues at Harvard have been exploring when children grasp the difference between having a real emotion and putting on an apparent emotion. To get at this, they give children several stories to read. Some describe a child protagonist who feels bad physically (tummyache) but must hide it so as to be able to play outside. In other stories, the protagonist feels good because he or she has just won a game but has to hide it otherwise their playmate won't want to play anymore.

Children are asked two questions about the story they just

read: (1) What was the protagonist's real emotion? and (2) What was his apparent emotion? The second question is obviously tougher because it requires the child to understand that the protagonist does not want the other story character to know her real feelings. This means having to imagine what the other story character would see. Four-year-olds have trouble grasping that there is a difference between real and apparent emotion. People smile when they are happy, don't they? By six years, however, most children know that there is a difference and that apparent emotion is for others.

Children's emotional and expressive development is, of course, partly affected by primary caregivers. For instance, in one study, researchers observed how mothers responded to their toddlers' demands for something that had been put away. Some mothers simply gave in to their child's demand and returned the toy. Others questioned their child about why they wanted the toy and why they had to have it now. A few explained to the child why they could not have it now. And a final group of mothers tried to distract the child's attention away from the toy.

Two and a half years later, the now five-year-olds were exposed to the mistaken gift paradigm. Would the mothers' previous ways of dealing with her toddlers' demands translate into how their child now behaved when they didn't get something they wanted? If, in the first study, the mothers had used *distraction* or *explanation* to deal with their child's demand, their five-year-olds were more likely to smile even when they were given the disappointing gift. In other words, these kids had learned the social convention that calls for one to smile even if given a disappointing gift. If, on the other hand, the mothers had previously *caved in* to the child's demand or *questioned* his or her feelings about needing to have the toy, their five-year-olds were significantly less likely to cover their frustration with a smile. In short, mothers who used emotionally intelligent methods with their young children, such as distraction or explanation, were more likely to have emotionally intelligent children.

With a few more years under their belts, children begin to use facial expressions as an impression management system, that is, they manage their faces to get others to think of them as a particular kind of person—nice or funny or nobody's fool. It is not clear yet when children work at creating a good impression, but psychologists speculate that this probably does not happen until they are about eight years old.

Children know there are times when they should deliberately mask or manufacture facial expressions even before they know exactly why they are doing it. They partially understand that facial expressions have consequences, even if it is not always clear what they will be. They know that it has something to do with avoiding punishment or preventing hurt feelings. Such facial expressions acquired first as conscious social conventions later become second nature. As children grow, their smiles become both more voluntary and, paradoxically, more automatic. In his short story "Gesturing," John Updike put it this way:

> His smile was a gesture without an audience. He, who had originated his act among parents and grandparents, siblings and pets, and who had developed it for a public of schoolmates and teachers, and who had carried it to new refinements before an initially rapt audience of his own children, could not in solitude stop performing.

Although most children acquire some ability to manufacture facial expressions they don't feel, not everyone does this equally well or believes it to be a good thing. Some children, for example, do *not* suppress anger with a smile. These children tend to be the ones who more generally have behavior problems. Investigators have found that unpopular children are more likely to frown and grimace when they lose at a game and less likely to squelch their smiling when they win at a game than popular children. They will probably vent their "real" feelings and are less likely to suppress these for the sake of others' feelings. Lording a win over someone with an expansive grin is not likely to endear you to that person. All in all, kids who smile voluntarily have better social relationships. Socially competent children recognize that there are times when hiding or disguising emotions is what friends do.

Within a few days of birth, newborns show smiles of a kind, but usually while they are asleep. By six weeks, babies beam while looking directly into their parents' faces. By six months, they smile if others are watching. By six years, children can put on a smile they don't feel. Strategic control of facial displays might seem hypocritical and/or manipulative. After all, in doing so children suppress their own feelings to accommodate others. The sociologist Erving Goffman suggested that the refusal to put on a happy face is not a sign of authenticity but an overactive ego. Psychologists for their part see a rather amazing developmental trajectory as babies and children mature from a stage of purely involuntary and reflexive smiling to a place where their smiles can be voluntary and conscious and socially connected.

the indispensable smile

James Gatz, a poor white Midwestern kid, had ambition in spades and an equally outsized capacity for self-invention. By the time he is thirty, he appears to have it made, though by what means is not clear. Having renamed himself Jay Gatsby, he lives in a fabulous mansion on Long Island and throws lavish parties every weekend, but few if any guests seem to have actually met him. There are rumors, of course—that he doesn't live in the house but on a boat plying Long Island Sound; that he had been a German spy during the war; that he came from old money and graduated from Oxford; and that he may have once killed a man in cold blood. Jay Gatsby, the titular character in F. Scott Fitzgerald's novel *The Great Gatsby*, takes his time to appear. When Nick Carraway does meet him in person, although initially disapproving, he is won over by Gatsby's smile.

He smiled, understandingly—much more than understandingly. It was one of those rare smiles with a quality of eternal reassurance in it, that you may come across four or five times in life. It faced—or seemed to face—the whole external world for an instant, and then concentrated on *you* with an irresistible prejudice in your favor. It understood you just so far as you wanted to be understood, believed in you as you would like to believe in yourself, and assured you that it had precisely the impression of you that, at your best, you hoped to convey.

Not every smile is as magical as Jay Gatsby's, but even low-wattage smiles have power and consequences for human relationships. No wonder Gatsby had experienced success. In his smile, Nick saw not Gatsby but a reflection of himself, a self that was the best he could be.

Human smiles are designed to captivate. We see smiles, distinguish those that are genuine from those that are not, and move toward the former and away from the latter. All this happens in a split second and typically out of conscious awareness. This, then, is a key fact about smiles. They are consequential—they affect what others feel and do. Far from being merely a nice gesture or a great asset, a credible smile is a force to be reckoned with. Smiles are not merely consequential; they are indispensable to physical health, psychological well-being, and social viability.

How do smiles accomplish these amazing feats? In the first place, they contain everything in one neat little package. A smile is a very efficient signal. It is the most instantly recognizable of all facial expressions. It can be correctly identified from a greater distance and with a briefer exposure than any other facial expression.

More to the point, the human smile is a multifunctional tool. If a smile is present at first contact, it will get things off to a good start by sparking positive impressions. And beyond first impressions, a smile is a kind of golden compass. It is a social magnet, a trustworthiness meter, a device for diffusing anger, a patch for repairing frayed interpersonal bonds, and a lubricant for keeping social ties in good working order.

Snap Feelings

There are few compliments more flattering than being told that one has a great smile. In truth, smiles are unique in their ability to impart a positive impression. In one study, when research participants were asked to evaluate identical faces, some of which were smiling and some not, the smiling ones were judged to be more attractive, intelligent, and sincere, not to mention sociable, kindly, and competent. Attractive faces are believed to smile more than unattractive ones and smiling faces are judged to be more attractive than non-smiling ones. Moreover, the brain gets a charge from both smiling and attractiveness. Viewing either one instigates activation in the area in the brain known to process stimuli that people find rewarding.

The cluster of positive qualities associated with a person who smiles has been dubbed the *halo effect* by researchers—an effect that extends to babies as if they didn't already have enough going for them. Smiling infants are perceived to be cuter than non-smiling ones and teachers think that smiling children are smarter than those who do not smile. So, if you want others to think well of you, you could do no better than to smile. But there is more here than what first meets the eye—even the most fleeting of smiles has the capacity to burrow deep into the unconscious of whoever sees it and to set off positive charges from within.

We constantly take in huge amounts of visual information from our immediate environment and absorb most of it without being conscious of having taken note of much of anything in particular. In fact, most of what we perceive—space, people, and bustle—is taken in without conscious awareness. Our brains would implode if everything captured our conscious attention. One of the critical things we notice, if seldom consciously, are signs emanating from people's faces indicating what they are feeling or intending. The slightest smile or tiniest scowl transmits emotion or intent.

A smiling face shown for an exceedingly brief duration is enough to cause a viewer to instantly feel more positive without being aware of where that feeling came from. A smile of a mere four milliseconds' duration (four one thousands of a second) is sufficient to produce a mini emotional high. This brief exposure is faster than the minimum needed for perceivers to believe that they had seen a face, which is about ten milliseconds. Researchers call the method of presenting visual stimuli below the level of conscious awareness *subliminal priming*.

A subliminally primed smile causes people to see things around them in a more positive light. Boring material becomes a bit more interesting or a nondescript picture now seems to have more flair. Indeed, researchers have found that some things even taste better if they have been preceded by happy subliminal prime. In one study, participants who had been exposed to a smile prime later found the flavor of a so-so drink to be tastier than those who had not seen the smile.

Students of all ages know too that even the most ephemeral smile from a teacher (Sister Mary Jane in my case) is heady. In one study of this effect, graduate students evaluated their own ideas more positively if they were exposed to a photo of their smiling supervisor for an instant.

This positive spillover from a subliminal smile is no mere flash in the pan. It has staying power. Recently, a group of neuroscientists found, as have others, that a neutral face comes across more positively if a subliminally presented smile comes first.

They also found that when participants saw a fleeting smile just before they saw neutral faces, the neutral faces had stayed in their memory longer than neutral faces primed with other emotional expressions.

Subliminal smiles are also quite literally contagious. A team of Swedish psychologists discovered that when people were exposed to subliminal primes of happy and angry faces, their own faces mirrored the faces they "saw," even though they could not remember having seen them. And the halo may spread out even further. A recent article in the *British Medical Journal* reported that in social networks, happiness extends up to two people beyond the first. When you smile and feel in good spirits, a friend of a friend is slightly more likely to feel in good spirits as well. Three degrees of happiness.

Since these studies were carried out in the pristine conditions of research labs, one might reasonably wonder what would occur in the booming, buzzing confusion of the real world. The broadcast of a popular science program on BBC television in England provided the opportunity to look at this. Viewers of the program were asked to phone in their opinion as to whether a woman whose photograph was broadcast on their TVs was happy or sad. Her facial expression was designed to be neutral. In one part of the country, the broadcast of the program presented a subliminal smile just before showing the woman's neutral expression. In other parts of the country, viewers saw only the woman's neutral facial expression.

The researchers felt sure that a subliminal smile would affect what the viewers would see next. They expected the viewers would see the woman with the neutral expression as happier than those who did not first view the subliminal smile. Alas, the data did not oblige. More TV viewers voted that the woman was sad when a fleeting smile preceded her neutral face. What is one to make of these apparently contradictory results? The subliminal smile had an effect, but it was the opposite of what had been expected. Does this mean that the effect of subliminal smiles flies out the window as soon as researchers leave the lab?

But consider this—the BBC audience came to this experience with preconceived ideas about who tends to smile and who does not. For example, a picture of a dour Beverly Sills would strike most U.S. viewers as unusual, as would a photograph of a grim Julia Roberts. In fact, women do tend on average to smile more than men. A photograph of a non-smiling woman might have struck TV viewers as unusual. So, instead of getting a lift from the subliminal smile, the woman's neutral face may have looked sad in contrast to what came before it. Henry James wonderfully captured this distinction between a common appearance and a noteworthy event in his novel *The Wings of the Dove*: "When Milly smiled it was a public event—when she didn't it was a chapter of history."

My guess is that had the smile prime preceded a picture of a man with a neutral expression, the typical priming effect would have occurred. Since men on average smile less than women, viewers would likely have seen him as happy than sad compared to a condition where his neutral face had not been coupled with the subliminal smile. But until the BBC or some other network reruns the experiment, we won't know for sure.

Oscar Wilde said, "It is only shallow people who do not judge by appearances." In this, Wilde was wrong: both shallow and serious people judge on the basis of appearances. Moreover, everyone responds to appearances not so much with snap judgments but with *snap feelings*. Even before a smile is consciously identified as such, it has already imparted a positive vibe. It is only later (a few hundred milliseconds is forever to researchers) that a smile is recognized as being the familiar positive facial expression.

We possess especially sensitive antennae for detecting facial expressions in others. Even when we are distracted, a transient expression on the face of a companion registers on our emotion meters. Whether they are happy or sad, angry or scared, their nonverbal gestures sneak past our gated selves. Moreover, even when facial expressions are extraordinarily brief, their effects are anything but small. Unconsciously absorbed smiles cause us to see things as though through rose-colored glasses and can be enough to trigger the same smile muscles on our own faces. We may not be aware that we have seen a smile, but our feelings and our faces tell another story.

Smile Magnets

It doesn't take rocket science to know that smiles are contagious. You smile at me and I can hardly help but smile back at you, which is likely to elicit another from you. With all of this smiling, the probability goes up that we will come to be in each other's hearts and less that we will be at each other's throats. What science can tell us is why this happens and when it does not.

Smiles are like interpersonal *Velcro*. There are platitudes aplenty that attest to the social clout of a smile. Smile, and the world smiles with you; cry or weep, and you will do it alone. Smile, and you have a key that fits the lock of someone's heart. Smile, and you create a curve that sets everything straight. If you see a friend without a smile, give him one of yours. A smile is the universal welcome. Okay, okay, I'll stop, but not before reiterating the point that smiles make positive connections with others more likely. Indeed, when the social psychologist Lynden Miles used virtual reality to simulate the approach of a virtual human, he found that women allowed it to come closer when it showed a genuine smile than if it showed a social smile or no smile at all.

We are drawn to smiles because we need to connect with people. Indeed, most social psychologists theorize that humans' need to belong is hardwired into us and comes along with having big brains. Some people may fight the need to belong, resist it, deny it, but belongingness is a fact of human life. People reach for social connections—be they shallow or deep, a one-night stand or for the long haul—throughout their lives.

Smiling plays no small part in planting, developing, confirming, maintaining, and resuscitating social connections. Social interactions, including the vastly underappreciated superficial ones, are absolutely essential to our psychological well-being. We need to belong, and when we do not or fear that we may not, the consequences are not pretty. Social rejection hurts. In fact, social ostracism is literally painful. A recent study using functional magnetic resonance imaging (fMRI) showed that social exclusion activates the same brain regions as does physical pain. Social exclusion also takes a toll on our ability to think clearly and creates heightened anxiety.

Although it may seem paradoxical, the hurt produced by being rejected is actually a reminder *not* to get too far away from other people. Intuitively, it might seem to work in the opposite direction; that is, the pain of rejection would make people more skittish about establishing relationships lest there be even more rejection and pain. But actually the solution to the problem is within the problem—only other people can soothe the pain that comes from being ostracized. It is no wonder then that the threat of being cast aside by others leads one to actively search for signs of social acceptance. And the most reliable of these signs is a smiling face.

In an experiment probing the consequences of social rejection, researchers led some participants to believe that their personalities were such that there was a strong likelihood of their spending much of their lives alone, while other participants were led to believe that they would have fulfilling social lives. To produce these effects, the researchers gave all the participants a psychological test that purportedly measured future social success. They found that participants who had been misinformed about the likelihood of their being friendless in the future were faster at picking out pictures of smiling faces from a large array of various facial expressions than those anticipating a socially fulfilled future.

Not only are victims of social rejection quicker to identify smiling faces; they can read a whole range of emotional expressions more accurately. To get at this, some research participants were asked to recall an occasion when they had been rejected, while others were asked to recall an episode that had nothing to do with rejection. After they had thought about the incident for several minutes, all were tested on their ability to identify the feelings expressed in photographs of people's faces. Sure enough, those who had just ruminated over a prior rejection were more accurate at reading the whole range of facial expressions than were those who recalled an innocuous event. They saw that a sad face was sad; a disgusted face was disgusted; a scared face was scared. They saw this even when the expressions were quite subtle. The lesson from having been dropped: pay attention.

Since social rejection smarts, most people work at avoiding it. We do this by being promiscuously nice. Relationship expert John Gottman has argued that strong connections between people do not start with a bang but with a few simple, positive, and recip-rocated bids for connection. In *The Book of Laugher and Forgetting*, Milan Kundera describes one such moment. "She looked at him and was unable to hold back a smile. It was a nearly tender smile, filled with fondness and understanding, a shy smile. . . . He had great difficulty restraining himself from returning that smile." Smiles tentatively offered and reciprocated often begin as volleys that lead to deeper and more important liaisons.

This need we have to belong is rooted in our long-distant evolutionary past. Social psychologists Geoff MacDonald and Mark Leary maintain that humans are hardwired to avoid being separated from others because separation would have made the survival of our human ancestors unlikely. Survival was more probable when people combined forces. Combining forces required not only being cooperative but knowing how to sig-nal to others' cooperative tendencies. In contrast, those who were antisocial, uncooperative, and uncommunicative would have had a tougher time staying out of harm's way because they would have been cast out of the group. Going it alone in the wild would simply not have worked. Those individuals able to have and hold onto harmonious relationships would have had the evolutionary advantage. So humans acquired the smile as a way to signal friendliness.

The poet H.D. wrote in "Red Roses for Bronze":

The half-caught smile,
The subtle little sort of differentiating
Between the thing that's said
and that's said not;
the "have I seen you somewhere else?
forgot? Impossible."

Studies support what H.D. knew: that people think they already know someone if that person smiles at them, even if it is an absolute stranger. When research participants were presented with photos of famous and not so famous people, half of each depicting smiling faces, they were more likely to believe that they had seen the smiling faces before, whether it was someone famous or not. A smile is like already having one foot in the door.

From studies done over nearly a century, psychologists have concluded that people feel more comfortable with almost anything with which they are familiar—food, ideas, brand of beer, ways of loading the dishwasher. Indeed, when we are reminded of something familiar, we react in a positive way. Susan Anderson and her colleagues found that people smiled more at a stranger who they believed was similar to someone they already knew and liked.

So, a smile can get the social ball rolling, and subsequent smiles keep it moving along. Seeing someone smile induces a sense of agreeable familiarity and a shared history, even if there isn't one yet. And smiles can tip off the possibility that a current social connection has staying power and something to look forward to. As Ring Lardner put in one of his short stories: "They gave each other a smile with a future in it."

In Smiles We Trust

When he goes to work in his job as a taxi driver, Hyder fears for his life. Edwina, Hyder's wife, worries too about the dangers of his job, although Hyder hasn't told her half of it. "Someone flags you down and you don't know if they're going to pay you or kill you." In their book *Streetwise: How Taxi Drivers Establish Their Customers' Trustworthiness*, sociologists Gambetta and Hamill describe how taxi drivers in New York and Belfast sized up potential passengers.

They found that when drivers are suspicious, they rapidly calculate a number of factors, preferring older over younger, women over men, a city's safe zones over its "danger zones"; they also look for signs of trustworthiness in the person's face, but also understand that a would-be robber can fake a nice smile.

Trust assessment is something we all do. It would be great if there were reliable signs we could draw on, especially in regard to strangers with whom we have no history. Is this someone I can confide in or count on? Are there cues to a person's trustworthiness? In my lab, we examined whether a smile indicates that a person can be trusted.

In one study, we had undergraduates imagine they were members of a college disciplinary panel with the task of determining whether a student had cheated on an exam. The written materials suggested that the accused student had broken this cardinal academic rule. Clipped to the outside of the folder containing the materials was a small photo of the female student. In some photos, she was smiling, while in others she showed a neutral expression. Participants were asked to review the materials and decide whether the student was guilty of cheating, and if so, what disciplinary action should be taken. Nearly all the participants thought the student was guilty, but those who had seen the photograph of the accused smiling thought she should be given more benefit of the doubt.

Why would a smiling defendant be given more benefit of the doubt? We considered a number of possibilities. Possibly panelists simply liked a smiling defendant more or saw her as more attractive. Maybe the smile implied that the accused was embarrassed and therefore contrite. In actuality, the panelists took the accused student's smile to mean that she was a basically trustworthy person.

Trust is frequently an issue in everyday social interactions. Let's say you are thinking about going into a business with a partner or sharing something of importance with a colleague. If you are like most people, you weigh the pros and cons but then go with your gut feelings. Economist Robert Frank contends that without necessarily knowing it, it is often the facial expressions we see that drive our gut feelings toward others. Does that mean one should simply check off whether the person smiles or not? Would that it were so simple.

Nonetheless, some people can be trusted, and this shows itself in *how* they smile. In short, unselfish people show more genuine involuntary smiles. A Canadian psychologist, Michael Brown, measured altruism by asking people about their altruistic behaviors, such as how frequently they donated blood, put in hours for a charity, paid more to shop at a store deserving of support, and so on. Then, on videotape, participants briefly described themselves, after which their facial expressions were coded to differentiate spontaneous or Duchenne smiles from social or fake smiles. The altruists produced significantly more Duchenne smiles than the non-altruists. Their smiles were also shorter and more symmetrical—brevity and symmetry being two additional characteristics of authentic smiles.

Can ordinary mortals pick out genuine smiles to help them decide whether a person can be trusted or not? To determine whether they can, a group of European psychologists set up two-person games of trust which involved the exchange of money. Participants chose a partner, with the only significant difference being whether the counterpart's smile was genuine or fake. Moreover, the only difference between the genuine smile and the fake one was in the timing of the counterpart's smile. You may recall that authentic smiles have relatively long onset and offset times—they arrive and leave the face at a leisurely pace and spend a relatively brief time at their maximum intensity. In contrast, fake smiles arrive and depart relatively quickly and stay at their maximum intensity for a longer time. Whether conscious of it or not, the participants took note of these subtle differences and were more likely to choose to play the trust game with those who displayed authentic smiles.

Resilient Smiles

Emma Woodhouse is a clever young woman whose mischievous and misguided attempts at matchmaking very nearly ruin her own chance at romance. *Emma*, like all of Jane Austen's novels, is full of microscopic details of character. At one point, Austen describes two men who could stand some makeover of how they smile:

> Some change of countenance was necessary for each gentle-man as they walked into Mrs. Weston's drawing-room—Mr. Elton must compose his joyous looks, and Mr. John Knight-ley disperse his ill-humour. Mr. Elton must smile less, and Mr. John Knightley more, to fit them for the place. Emma only might be as nature prompted, and show herself just as happy as she was.

If Mr. Knightley borrowed a little of Mr. Elton's happy face, both might be better off.

There is evidence a person's habitual facial expressions leave behind a facial trail. Psychologist Carol Malatesta Magai examined individuals' faces to determine whether it was possible to see if some emotions were favored over others throughout their lives.

The face of actor Edie Falco shows traces of a lifetime of smiling

One person, for example, often felt angry (at the boss, at traffic congestion, at people who didn't return her messages, etc.),
and as a result there were traces of anger on her face even when
she adopted what she thought was a neutral expression. Another
individual described herself as being sad much of the time (missing friends, listening to Bette Midler sing "Wind Beneath My
Wings," watching *Terms of Endearment* . . . again). Her face, too,
had traces of past emotions—even when she was asked not to show
any expression.

One adage has it that before the age of forty we have the face
we are born with, but by fifty we have the face we deserve. Psychologists would say instead we have the face we use. The current
psychological focus on facial expression differs from the previous
and popular idea that personality is revealed in a person's static
facial features—nose shape, forehead size, cheekbone height, and
the like. In the nineteenth century, society was especially keen
on the idea that personality could be read from bumps and clefts

on people's heads. In fact, the Swiss theologian Johann Kaspar Lavater provided a guide to this "science" in the form of several lavishly illustrated volumes.

On a similar note, Franz Joseph Gall contended that phrenology, the study of an individual's skull, revealed a person's character and mental capacity. How can one argue with the idea that character is revealed in chins and noses? That something feels true, however, does not make it so. But researchers have found that facial expressions, rather than facial structure, really do reveal something true about a person's life path.

In a longitudinal study that followed a group of women over the course of their lives, social psychologist Dacher Keltner looked to see if characteristic facial expressions said something about how a person's life would turn out. First, the women's facial expressions were coded from their yearbook photos at Mills College, in Oakland, California, circa the late 1950s. Over the next several decades, their life experiences were documented at interviews with the women at twenty-seven, forty-three, and fifty-two years old.

Keltner's findings, which show there are links between early facial expressions and later life outcomes, are remarkable. The women who displayed more intense smiles in their college yearbook photographs were more content with their lives many years later. They had fewer psychological and physical problems and were more satisfied in their marriages. If that were not enough, years later the ones who smiled in their college yearbook photos were those who scored higher on tests of mental focus and showed more motivation to achieve.

Smiles have other impressive effects. They keep people nearby when they are most needed. Researchers have observed individuals who have recently lost a spouse or child and noted that even in mourning, some people show bright smiles. The grief is real and the smiles are genuine. But what is even more interesting is that these same individuals are doing much better months and years later than those who did not smile in the immediate aftermath of a loved one's death.

How can this be? We know that seeing a person smile induces the wish to approach. If, on the other hand, someone close to you is grieving, it's tough to be around them despite one's desire to be supportive. But if the bereaved person occasionally smiles, it can have the effect of causing the sorrow to lift for a bit. Seeing a smile, friends and family feel less helpless and more positive, and they are more inclined to stay close. That is all to the good for everyone involved. Research has even shown that when people feel social support, they experience less pain.

One Chinese proverb holds that a smile adds ten years to your life. A Japanese adage avows that the one who smiles rather than rages is always stronger. Ben Franklin advised that "a cheerful face is nearly as good for an invalid as healthy weather." If there is truth here, as the Mills College study suggests, the question becomes *Why*? Why would smiling as a young adult predict later life satisfaction? Is it simply that happy young people are happy older people? Or might smiling as a young adult have consequences for one's social life both at the time and over time?

People who smile draw others to them. The predisposition to be positive leads to more and stronger social bonds, which in turn provides lifelong support. Indeed, some have found a relationship between being positive and living a long life. In one study, researchers coded autobiographies written by a group of nuns when they were novices many years earlier. Then the researchers went about finding who among them was still alive. Those whose early diaries had many positive themes were more likely to be alive sixty years later than those who had been less optimistic as young adults.

These results are provocative and require more research to uncover the details of how optimism affects longevity. Nonetheless, the data support the idea of a reinforcing process wherein smiles beget smiles and good feelings, which, when repeated, generate trust and inclusion.

In the past, psychotherapists held that a positive disposition probably reflected deep denial and that the hallmark of psychological health was a hard-boiled, clear-eyed, realistic acceptance of a dark and threatening world. As Freud saw it, therapy was deemed successful when neurotic misery had been converted into ordinary unhappiness.

But positive psychology is currently in ascendance. Today, psychologists endorse the idea that one should let-a-smile-be-your-umbrella. Positive emotion broadens and builds a person's psyche, argues the social psychologist Barbara Fredrickson. It can also undo the damage that negative emotion may have wrought. In fact, evidence indicates that the experience of positive emotion reduces accelerated cardiovascular reactivity and heightened anxiety caused by negative emotions.

Whereas negative emotions like anger speed a person up, prompting quick thought and quick action—"I have to get out of here, now!"—positive emotion slows a person down, prompting expanded ways of thinking and prying people loose from "I'll have the usual."

Smile Patches

Just as a positive stance toward the world incurs benefits, a negative one incurs costs. Health psychologists have shown how having a chip on one's shoulder negatively influences one's health. For cynics, this news is not great (but then again the news is never great for cynics). People who are often angry appear to be at greater risk for an early death. This happens in part because angry and hostile outbursts tend to be hard on a person's cardiovascular system. And angry outbursts tend to cause others to respond in kind, which ratchets up the hostility even more. Is there a way to interrupt this spiral? A social smile may do the trick. A study by two Canadian psychologists, Kenneth Prkachin and Barbara Silverman, demonstrated how this works.

These psychologists measured male and female subjects' customary tendency to be either hostile or agreeable. Then each participant was deliberately aggravated in two ways. In the first, the interviewer challenged the participant on nearly everything they said. Respondent: "I believe in the golden rule." Interviewer: "That's such a simplistic basis for conduct." Respondent: "Psychologists will never know as much as poets." Interviewer: "What do you know?" In the second method, the interviewer came across as flat and uninterested in anything the participant had to say. To make matters worse, the subjects were told that their conversational skills were being analyzed.

What did hostile people do when aggravated? They did *not* glower or scowl or fume any more than the agreeable people. But they did show fewer *polite* smiles when they were aggravated. A polite smile, intentional and voluntary though it is, can deflect or deflate a tense situation. In *Othello*, Shakespeare has the Duke of Venice say: "The robb'd that smiles steals something from the thief." People who are inclined to be hostile refuse to turn a smiling cheek; agreeable people, on the other hand, smile more, which has the effect of short-circuiting angry exchanges. Even fabricated smiles generate positive consequences.

Analyze friends' conversations over cocktails, teens' cell phone banter on the move, or parishioner's chat after church, and you will observe people doing a lot of *small talk*. Small talk entails innocuous pleasantries coupled with social smiles. The verbal exchange is trivial and the smiles shallow, but neither are pointless. Among those who are barely acquainted, small talk is a superb "reconnaissance dance," during which individuals explore possibilities; among neighbors and associates, small talk checks and confirms that all is as expected; among longtime companions, small talk is the thing to smooth over rough patches. These smiles help keep the social fabric intact.

Superficial interactions, marked by pleasant smiles and token queries about one another's health, are exactly what the sociologist ordered. Mark Granovetter calls some of these skin-deep interactions *weak ties* and argues that they do important social work. They can tie people together who probably will never be fast friends but might one day be ready to stand in, lend a hand, mention a job opening, or suggest an inexpensive white burgundy.

In many superficial conversations, there is value in appearing interested. Agreeable listeners lend an ease to chance encounters. They issue small cues that indicate they are attending and are interested. Communication scholars call these cues *back-channel responses*. Smiles and head nods are the primary nonverbal back channels, while verbal injections such as "uh-huh," "really," and "wow" are the typical verbal ones. In fact, the absence of back-channel responses is a surefire way to communicate disinterest or disrespect.

To demonstrate what happens when back channels go missing, I sometimes ask my students to drop them from conversations for a day—no smiling or nodding when someone else is talking. They return with stories attesting to the fact that the absence of smiling and nodding was taken as rudeness, disinterest, or evasion; some students simply report that they cannot do it.

Smiles allow quotidian social encounters to pass without fuss. Slight smiles say "thank you" and "your welcome" when someone gives way or holds a door. Brief smiles acknowledge a fellow commuter at the train station or elevator but commit to nothing more. Micro smiles communicate transient alliances in long meetings and undercut potential annoyance at having to make a request or apology. "Do you mind if I . . . ?" or, "Oh, excuse me." Polite smiles can be a mini "time-out" for adults. A Miss Manners column described such an example. A hostess pauses after noticing that her couch has been ruined by spilled wine. She adopts a wooden smile and says, "Oh . . . that is . . . quite . . . all . . . right." A perfectly formed social smile does wonders too when one has nothing to say.

Since social smiles are deliberate, they are often judged to be phony. Vladimir Nabokov has a good example in *Laughter in the Dark*: "Margot was vexed that he did not recognize her. 'We had a talk a couple of years ago,' she said slyly. 'Quite right,' he replied with a polite smile. 'I remember you perfectly.' (He did not)." But perhaps the classic rejection of phony smiles comes from J. D. Salinger's *Catcher in the Rye*. Recall Holden's description of Mr. Haas, the headmaster at Holden's old prep school:

> I mean if a boy's mother was sort of fat or corny-looking or
> something, or if somebody's father was one of those guys
> that wear those suits with very big shoulders and corny

black-and-white shoes, then old Haas would just shake
hands with them and give them a phony smile and then
he'd go talk, for maybe a half an hour, with somebody else's
parents. I can't stand that stuff. It drives me crazy.

Politeness by definition is voluntary and deliberate but nonetheless crucial to social life. For sociolinguists, every conversation is rife with possibilities for insult and discord. (And you
thought you were just having a friendly chat.) Politeness, they
argue, is a system of actions aimed at smoothing over inevitable
moments of discord or disagreement so each is respected and
the social connection is maintained. From that vantage, then,
far from being hypocritical, a polite smile conveys that the other
person's feelings matter.

An embarrassed smile plays a similar function. Spill a drink,
forget a person's name, get caught in a fib—not major events to
be sure, but awkward, nonetheless. Dacher Keltner and his colleagues have shown that embarrassed smiles smooth uncomfortable incidents. In the throes of mortification, it is hard to imagine
how blushing, cringing, and grinning can be useful; but even
children and nonhuman primates understand that embarrassed
smiles allow people to excuse social faux pas.

An embarrassment smile actually has a particular signature.
In less than a second, the embarrassed person looks down, begins
to smile, and then attempts to quell the smile by pressing the lips.
Since initial attempts to exert control over the unwanted smile
usually fail, the embarrassed person lowers his or her head further and looks away in one direction and then the other, seeming
to want to hide the smile. An embarrassed smile says to observers
that the smiler acknowledges a mistake while pointing to it as
an exception. It also offers other benefits. Several studies have

Embarrassment smile

found that subjects like and forgive people more who show genuine embarrassment. And parents have been found to punish their children less if the latter show embarrassed smiles.

Smiles have much to commend them. At the top of the list is their talent for attracting and keeping other people close, a feature that serves us well and is especially valuable in times of trouble when we need the endorsement and support of others. Duchenne or felt smiles do something even more remarkable—they are a guarantee of sorts that the person smiling can be counted on.

Smiles can also deflect anger or at the very least buy some time when an altercation seems likely. While there is still much to learn about which circumstances make this likely, and why, the fact that it sometimes works is no small feat in times when revenge seems more likely than reconciliation.

And smiles produce dividends too for the smiler over and above the ability to draw people close. Felt smiles in particular can erase negative emotion. At the risk of sounding like a fortune cookie, the more Duchenne smiles are part of one's life, the more likely it is that that life will be longer and possibly even happier.

missing smiles, frozen smiles

A couple of years ago, a good friend of mine suddenly came down with Bell's palsy. One evening she was her usual animated self, playing with her six-year-old daughter, and the next morning half of her face was paralyzed. The right side was alert, but the left side had completely wilted. When she tried to smile, her mouth beckoned upward on the right, but the left side stayed stubbornly still, as did her left eye, which could not blink. She appeared to be sneering and she is the least likely of people to sneer. As is often the case with Bell's palsy, there are few other physical symptoms. But there are substantial interpersonal consequences.

For one thing, my friend's daughter needed to know what was going on, and so Mom did the thing professorial parents do: she explained; she clarified; and she asked if her daughter had any questions. She told her daughter that she had come down with something sort of like a cold, and that even though it might look like it, it didn't hurt, and besides she was going to be fine very soon. That seemed to do the trick. Or at least it did until the next morning, when her daughter said to her, "You are not my real mommy. Where is my *real* mommy?"

What happens when smiles go missing or seem stuck in place? Babies whose mothers are depressed and inexpressive have a tough time of it, as do parents of children born with Moebius syndrome, which prevents the children from smiling or making any facial expression. Kids diagnosed with autism or Asperger's syndrome, both included under Autism Spectrum Disorder, are unresponsive to other people's facial expressions even to the point of avoiding looking at them. People whose facial expressions have become masklike due to Parkinson's disease leave spouses despairing at no longer having access to the person they thought they knew. And when women who lunch use Botox or men who meet have cosmetic surgery to rid their faces of wrinkles, what they gain in smoother faces they may well lose in emotional self-awareness.

In short, when smiles are absent or attached in place—whether due to illness, injury, intention, or intervention—then the central artery by which people know their social world is shut off. Human beings are so dependent on facial expressions that a person with an unchanging face raises doubts about their essential humanity. Medical anthropologists report that the Comanche Indians of Oklahoma call Bell's palsy the "Ghost Sickness." Little wonder then that a six-year-old might think she had lost her real mother when half her face was frozen.

Children are not the only ones who are discombobulated when they run up against a person with an unresponsive face. Talking to someone whose face is inert feels like standing on quicksand. It's tough to get one's social footing. Facial movement, even of the most modest sort, is present in most conversations, and when it is not forthcoming, social partners are at a loss as to what to do. Transient smiles from others let us know that we matter and the absence of them calls that into question.

Ralph Nader shows facial remnants of having had Bell's palsy

Facial immobility doesn't just affect those on the receiving end. When a person's face is frozen, Dutch social psychologists found that their ability to empathize with others' feelings is substantially reduced. My friend with Bell's palsy became a stranger to her daughter, and for a time also a stranger to her friends, who had trouble seeing themselves in her expressionless face. Worse still, because matching other people's facial expressions is one point of access to another's emotional world, she may have had difficulty understanding us.

Pick a face, any face, out of a crowd. What do you see? Scientists for their part see both *stable* features that allow a person to be recognized and *transient* features that convey an individual's current state. Our brains come prepared to tell these two facial aspects apart. One neurological system is called into play when we recognize a person we know. Another part of the brain goes to work when we detect what someone is feeling from changes in their facial expression.

High cheekbones, a wide forehead, and a pug nose are examples of stable features, as are skin color and eye shape, permanent creases and scars. The arrangement of stable features makes one person's face unlike any other. In contrast, transient features, including blushing and perspiring, and eye movements like blinking, winking, and nodding, come and go. The dividing line between stable and transient features is blurred when a facial expression is adopted so frequently that it becomes more stable than transient. Hamlet says to Ophelia: "God hath given you one face, and you make yourself another." Art historians, noting a dour expression in Rembrandt's many self-portraits, have speculated that Rembrandt often depicted himself with a frown because he probably had one most of the time.

Stable facial features mark individuality. Transient facial expressions, on the other hand, provide connections with others. For the six-year-old whose mother's face was partially paralyzed, the loss of connection was nothing less than having lost her real mother. Her mother's face was structurally the same, but in its lack of expression, everything about her had changed. Transient facial expressions provide us with a status report of another person's ongoing emotional life and link to us.

Masks

When we see an impassive face, we take it personally. This non-smiling person has no interest in me or no understanding. Period. Unfortunately, Bell's palsy is not the only affliction that freezes a face and chills relationships.

Parkinson's disease has among its symptoms the *Parkinson's mask*. As this noncurable degenerative disease progresses, the facial muscles cease to function, robbing the Parkinson's sufferer of the ability to smile or frown or make most facial movements. The face is silenced. As one researcher put it, Parkinson's disease reduces "the body's capacity to embody emotion, thought, and the unique character and spirit of the individual."

Even people who are aware they are dealing with a person afflicted with the disease tend to react as though the Parkinson's mask is deliberate or can be controlled. Spouses are frequently frustrated by the facial impassivity they see in their significant other. Health professionals are also prone to characterize Parkinson's patients as difficult because of their nonresponsivity. It is not a surprise therefore that these individuals report that they often feel misunderstood. A frozen face is hard to ignore for it makes those of us who face it feel irrelevant or invisible.

A doctoral student of mine conducted a study with married couples where one spouse had Parkinson's disease. The goal was to see if Parkinson's sufferers had more trouble communicating some emotions than others, and whether spouses were able to see their way around the reduced expressivity. In the study, the spouses with Parkinson's were asked to communicate a simple verbal message to their partners in one of three ways: in a positive manner; in a negative manner; or neutrally. For example, the patient was to say to his spouse, "I can do it myself," in three different ways—with good humor, or cranky impatience, or no feeling one way or the other. The most conspicuous finding was that messages that the Parkinson's sufferers intended to be positive were not perceived as such—both spouses and strangers saw them as neutral or negative. Many sufferers reported that they had smiled. It may have felt that way from the inside but it did not

A girl with Moebius syndrome with the hallmark expressionless face

look that way from the outside. Their smiles went missing, and with it a lot to miss.

Unhappily, smiles can also go missing in children's faces. Moebius syndrome, for example, is recognized by a child's complete "inability to smile." Neurologist Jonathan Cole affectionately calls these children "Moebians," and notes that the small jaws and absence of facial expression that are often part of the syndrome give the affected child the appearance of a Modigliani painting. Unfortunately, an inexpressive infant presents a huge challenge to parents who will never see delight in their child's face. And parents, being parents, worry about the future and how their expressionless child will be received by playmates when they are young and by adults when they are older.

Surgeons are currently working on ways to inject Moebius

faces with life. In one procedure, a nerve graft is taken from the patient's leg, and, along with a muscle from the thigh, transplanted into the cheek area. The smile is activated by a tiny twitch in the jaw. The results thus far are not perfect, but for the patients and their families, being able to maneuver their face into something resembling a smile feels nothing short of a miracle.

Absent Smiles in Autism

One sign that all is not well with a child is that he or she smiles infrequently or mostly to himself. Autism Spectrum Disorder (ASD) is sometimes considered in such circumstances, since avoiding social and emotional engagement with others is one of its key symptoms. The child may smile as much as a normally developing peer of the same age. But while the normally developing child smiles most when he or she is engaged with other people, autistic children do not.

ASD usually cannot be diagnosed with certainty until a child is nearly three years old. Yet an inexpressive face (among other indicators) in babies as young as twelve months suggests an eventual diagnosis of autism. Researchers have noted that pictures and videos of very young autistic children show behaviors subsequently linked with ASD. The French psychologist Jean-Louis Adrien and his colleagues detected telltale signs of autism—little social smiling, few and atypical facial expressions, and near-complete avoidance of eye contact—when they analyzed home movies of children less than a year old.

In 1943, Leo Kanner was the first to use the term *autistic aloneness* to describe children who paid little attention to those around them. Studies highlight the tendency of autistic children to attend to the objective features of "things" and steer clear of the emotional features of human faces. When autistic children look at photos of facial expressions, brain scans indicate that they are seeing faces as they would any other object, no different from cars or buildings. Meanwhile, the areas of the brain that normally show activity when looking at people showed no activation. In one study, investigators asked autistic and normally developing children to look at photographs of people and to sort the photos in whatever way made the most sense to them. The normally developing children tended to sort the photos according to the facial expressions they saw in the pictures—some people were happy while others were sad. In contrast, children with ASD ignored facial expressions and sorted the photos on the basis of the hats the people wore.

Temple Grandin, an accomplished writer, researcher, and highly articulate autistic adult, describes having to learn to attend to people's facial expressions. Grandin reports: "I need to rely on pure logic, like an expert computer program, to guide my behavior . . . I can't read subtle emotional cues. I have had to learn by trial and error what certain gestures and facial expressions mean."

Bell's palsy, Parkinson's disease, Moebius syndrome, and Autism Spectrum Disorder represent sizable challenges for the people close to them, but they also say a lot about normal social interactions. Humans rely heavily on expressive faces to know what to do and how to feel. Other people's faces provide a manual for how to behave in social relationships. When they are unavailable, we feel disconnected and unintelligible even to ourselves. Even when we know that an impassive face has a physical cause, it is still hard not to take the lack of responsivity personally.

Smile Transplants

A few years ago, news flashed around the world about the first face transplant. A thirty-eight-year-old French woman had been severely bitten by her dog, and as a result had to endure amputation of her nose, lips, chin, and cheeks. In many news reports, the face transplant was widely discussed on medical as well as moral grounds. Was it ethical to replace one person's most recognizable and distinguishing feature with that of some other person? The enormity of the event was made all the more poignant by accounts suggesting that the transplant recipient did not at first recognize herself with her new face. Isabelle Dinoire saw a stranger when she first looked in a mirror. Four months after surgery, doctors reported that she was beginning to return to a normal life, the telltale sign of which was some facial activity. The change that received the most comment was that she could "literally smile again," although it took nearly eighteen months for her smile to begin to look normal. That is when the operation was deemed a success. Being able to smile is a mark of normality.

A face that never smiles is noteworthy, but a face that never seems to be without a smile is disconcerting in its own way. A person who constantly smiles might be preternaturally cheerful—in theory a good thing. But too much smiling for too long a time, and it's likely that the smiling has ceased to bear any relation to positive feelings, if indeed positive feelings were ever there to begin with. The English spy novelist Eric Ambler described one constant smile this way: "He had a smile, fixed like that of a ventriloquist's doll: a standing apology for the iniquity of his existence." Another English novelist, G. K. Chesterton, expressed similar reservations about someone who smiled too much: "He was a man still young, but already corpulent, with

sleek dark hair, heavy handsome clothes, and a full, fat, permanent smile, which looked at the first glance kindly, and at the
second cowardly."

Both missing smiles and fixed smiles have significant social
consequences, disrupting interactions that we usually take for
granted. These smiles raise important questions about the relationship between our faces and our feelings: Can adopting a smile
cure a bad mood? If one adopts a stiff upper lip (assuming one
knew how to do it), can fear or sorrow be reduced? Before answer-
ing these questions, let's look at other people who never or hardly
ever smile.

Expressionless Mothers and Woebegone Babies

Brand-new infants, once believed to be inattentive to anything
but a few physical sensations, are actually on the lookout for smiling faces. Babies as young as a few months are already happy-face
experts. They know that smiles differ from frowns and pouts.
They can even detect degrees of happy faces. Babies are able to
detect a smiling face before they can reliably identify any other
facial expression. This capacity to zero in on a smiling adult is
exactly what they need because sleuthing out an affectionate
caregiver is a baby's primary quest.

Smiles are the seeds from which attachment grows. Nowhere is
this more apparent than in the exchange of grins between babies
and parents. Babies beam and moms swear lasting allegiance;
mothers gleam and babies hold on for dear life. Alas, when one or
the other fails to smile, there may be very serious consequences
for both. Consider the fact that 10 to 20 percent of new mothers
experience serious postpartum depression. If that isn't enough,
public health researchers have found that women at home raising

small children, who were not depressed when the baby was born, are at risk for developing serious depression later on.

Depressed mothers put a different face on parenting than non-depressed mothers. They are less likely to smile and less likely to intentionally match their baby's cooing. Tiffany Field and her colleagues, who have seen a lot of depressed moms and babies in several decades of research, find that infants whose mothers are depressed are themselves fussier and drowsier, and show less contentment than infants whose mothers are not depressed. Unfortunately, the babies of depressed mothers take their lead. Their own smiling stops, they coo and babble less, and become less playful. An infant with damped-down affect and reduced activity is a sorry sight indeed.

When a mother becomes emotionally unavailable—one of the common symptoms of depression—her infant's expectations are upended. This is not the way it is supposed to work. Indeed, there are data suggesting that when a depressed mother leaves a baby's side, the baby's stress level drops—the opposite of how it usually works. Having a mother physically present but emotionally unavailable is very hard on a child. Even worse, a few minutes with a baby who has become depressed because his mother is depressed can even dampen the spirits of an otherwise genial stranger.

Unfortunately, if smiles are not a regular part of their experience, babies come to find them baffling when they do occur. When the key adult in a baby's life does not smile, she will be unable to take her eyes off an adult who does. One study showed that infants of depressed mothers tended to stare at photographs of smiling faces longer than typically developing infants, because the smiling faces are strange rather than familiar sights. Abraham Lincoln, no stranger himself to depression, said of babies, "In this sad world of ours, sorrow comes to all; and, to the young, it comes with bitterest agony, because it takes them unawares."

Infants develop what psychologists call a "working model" of what it means to be in a relationship from their first primary connection. If the baby cannot find a smiling adult and seduce her with her own smiles, she starts out in life harboring grave reservations about getting involved with another human being.

Besides upsetting a baby in the moment, a mother's passivity leaves a negative residue. Investigators have found, for example, that children of depressed parents show less capacity to regulate their own emotions as they get older. This is especially true of angry feelings in children who have had a depressed parent. The child's feelings are more likely to get out of control because he has not learned that emotions can be modulated. These children also tend to develop fewer social skills, which are essential to attracting and keeping playmates. Being cheerful didn't work before, why should it work now? If the mom's depression lasts beyond a baby's first year, the effects ripple outward to touch other developmental milestones, including less physical coordination and mental organization.

Absent Faces

Developmental psychologists have a nifty way to assess how facial inexpressiveness affects normally developing small children and by extension how a parent's emotional disengagement affects an infant. It is called the *still-face procedure*, and consists of three phases. First, a non-depressed mother sits across from her normally developing baby and interacts as she typically would for a few minutes. Then the mother is asked to shift into a *still-face* mode, where she adopts a still but neutral facial expression for about three minutes. During this phase, she is asked not to respond to signals from her baby. In the third and final phase, the *reunion*, the mother is told that she can now resume playful interaction with her baby.

How does the baby respond to its mother's "still-face"? Usually, he starts by smiling. When that smile doesn't interrupt his mother's impassive face, he is likely to look away. If the mother continues to be facially unresponsive, he begins to protest—he fusses, cries, and squirms. After a bit, seeing the futility of his efforts to get his mother to respond, the protests recede and the baby withdraws into a state of wariness. It is worth noting that this three-stage response to the still-face procedure has been observed in babies as young as two months. In a still-face period of a mere three minutes, normally developing babies of non-depressed mothers show the same sequence of behaviors as those babies whose mothers are actually depressed. First, they smile; when that doesn't work, they protest; and when that doesn't work, they retreat from the world. A baby's smile, usually so effective at drawing his mother in, now shows itself to be futile.

Since a smile is one of the few behaviors a baby has to attract a caregiver, it is easy to see why a baby gives up when it doesn't work. We know, for example, that institutionalized and neglected infants begin smiling at the same time as infants reared at home with loving parents, but unlike them, their smiling then drops away. Some neglected babies go in the opposite direction with their smiling: they smile constantly in the vain hope that it will eventually work. When they reach adulthood, they tend to smile in nearly every social situation, whether it is appropriate or not.

Psychologists call this unfortunate consequence *indiscriminate friendliness*.

Infants are able to accurately read several facial expressions as early as seven months, and at an even younger age if the face is familiar to them. Infants are able to see in their mothers' expression if she is overwhelmed or badly treated. But if infants are themselves abused, their ability to accurately read adults' expressions deteriorates. Instead, they are on the lookout for one particular facial display: an angry one. Abused preschoolers are extremely accurate in identifying angry faces, even "seeing" angry expressions when they are looking at a neutral expression.

Fathers' Faces

Fathers, too, can show postpartum depression after the birth of a child. And like some mothers, they may have been depressed well before a child's birth. Mothers get more attention, of course, because of their greater availability for research studies and because nearly everyone presumes their singular effect on children. But now that researchers have turned their attention to depressed fathers, it has been found that there is a higher incidence of mental health problems among their children, regardless of the mother's mental health.

Depressed fathers affect children in a striking way. Researchers call the effect of paternal depression on the family *positivity suppression*. When a father is depressed, everyone in the family keeps happy feelings to themselves—even to the point of responding negatively when a young child spontaneously expresses delight. In short, a depressed father keeps the whole family from showing happy feelings, even in interactions in which he is not directly involved.

Facing Depression

Young children are not the only ones affected by the face of another person's depression. Depressed adults leave an unhappy wake behind them. Psychologists have studied how this happens by pairing clinically depressed and non-depressed people in conversation. For example, a college student is asked to converse with a depressed person on the telephone on whatever topics they wish. It doesn't take long for the college-age subjects to feel down in the dumps themselves. It is no surprise then that they were also less willing to have more conversations with the depressed person. Face-to-face conversations have the same effect. After just a few minutes of talking with a depressed person, the smiling of non-depressed subjects declined considerably. They also became less animated and ended up joining the depressed person in generating negative things to talk about.

Just what is it that depressed people do that leads others to take a negative turn? At first pass it may seem obvious since it certainly doesn't take rocket science to know that spending time with a depressed person can be tough going. But are depressed people too negative or are they insufficiently positive? The distinction is important because psychologists now believe that positive and negative emotions are not at the opposite ends of a single scale but are actually relatively independent of each other. Consequently, it is possible to feel both at the same time, or neither, or one or the other to various degrees.

Imagine that you are at a social gathering and are telling one of your more entertaining stories to several people. Among those listening is someone with a vacant facial expression, while another looks downcast. Okay, so you won't tell that story again.

However, which listener upsets you more? Apparently, an expressionless face is just as unsettling to an adult as it is to a baby. The hallmark of depression is not profound sadness, but lack of feeling—what psychologists call *flat affect*. Depressed people tend not to be mournful or sad. The telltale sign of depression is the near-total lack of positive affect.

Most people have a default emotional setting for everyday social encounters that is a mildly positive. "Hi. Hi. How are you? Good, you? Good . . . the kids? Good, yours?" We expect most encounters to be pleasant. But depressed people tend not to rise to these expectations. They do not perform good-naturedly; they do not do what the social historian Christina Korchemidova calls "drive-by smiling."

Consider the following experiment. Depressed and non-depressed participants viewed pictures of happy or unhappy people while researchers measured small muscle movements on their faces. Two facial muscles were of particular interest—the smile muscle (*zygomaticus major*) and the frown muscle (corrugator). When participants viewed unhappy people, depressed and non-depressed participants responded similarly—they frowned. However, their facial responses differed when viewing pictures of happy people. Non-depressed participants smiled, but depressed participants showed no smile muscle activity. In fact, depressed people frowned when they looked at happy people. "You can't make me happy. I won't. You can't." Unfortunately, the absence of positive expressivity gives others little incentive to want to continue the conversation and every reason to withdraw.

Anthropologist Catherine Lutz argues that many people, although perhaps more in the United States than anywhere else, work at appearing happy when other people are around—having thoroughly adopted the belief that positive is "normal" and everyone should strive to be happy. Consequently, depressive people, Lutz argues, are avoided for their failure to actively pursue happiness. What would it cost them to smile once in a while?

Smile Back Talk

The commonsense view of the relationship between emotion and expression goes something like this: something happens (an insult, a compliment, a surprise); emotion is aroused (anger, delight, surprise); and signs of the feeling burst onto the face. In short, events trigger feelings that prompt overt expressions. A man is cut off in traffic, he is startled and feels angry, he shouts: "#@!$!%!" A woman receives a great job offer, she feels elated, and a grin erupts on her face. A sad memory intrudes and the individual begins to tear up and their lower lip trembles. Most people believe a person's facial expression is an outward manifestation of an internal feeling. The expressions may be subtle or quick, but they reflect what is going on inside.

What if the process actually works the other way round? What if facial expressions don't just reflect feelings but actually cause them? Bell's palsy, Parkinson's disease, depression, even a pervasive tendency to present a stoic face to the world all raise the possibility that limited facial expressivity may limit what people feel. If a person's face is stilled, might emotions be shut down as well?

The idea that one's face affects what one feels has been a staple of psychological thinking for over a century. Darwin speculated that exaggerating or inhibiting a facial expression of emotion could affect how much one felt. William James went so far as to propose that when we are happy, it is *because* we are smiling, and when we are sad, it is *because* we are crying. In other words, facial expressions and bodily changes *are* the emotions, not mere reflections of them. James did not advise everyone to put on a happy face, but he did come pretty close: "The sovereign voluntary path to cheerfulness, if our spontaneous cheerfulness be lost, is to sit up cheerfully, to look around cheerfully, and to act and speak as if cheerfulness were already there."

Many a guru has channeled this path into a significant life lesson. At one end of the philosophical spectrum is the Vietnamese peace activist Thich Nhat Hanh, who said, "Sometimes your joy is the source of your smile, but sometimes your smile can be the source of your joy." And then there was the American capitalist Malcolm Forbes, who advised, "To live long and achieve happiness, cultivate the art of radiating happiness." Regrettably, for everyone who advises that smiling will cure all that ails you, there are others who believe that the most smiling can do is to mask the misery that lies beneath.

Ever ready to bring coherence to contradictory positions—"Smiles turn a bad feeling around," "No, smiles only cover bad feelings"—psychologists have stepped in to name the issue, clarify the differing strands of the argument, and conduct experiments to see what's what. The theory that facial expressions affect feelings is known as the *facial feedback hypothesis (FFH)*.

The strongest version of the facial feedback hypothesis is that in order for there to be feeling, there needs to be facial expression. Lacking facial expression, there can be no emotion. "If I am successful in suppressing all facial expression, then I will feel nothing." There is however little support for this particular hypothesis. Case in point, a woman with complete facial paralysis showed that she nonetheless responded in other ways to emotionally evocative photographs.

An alternative way of thinking about how facial expressions might affect feelings proposes that expressions moderate or curb feelings rather than cause them outright. "If I already feel a little happy, might I be happier still if I smile more? If, on the other hand, I feel a little blue, might I feel better if I frown less?" So, facial expressions could act like the volume control on an MP3 player—turn up the expressions, turn up the feelings; turn down the expressions, turn down the feelings.

Experimental psychologists have devised some clever ways to get people to change their facial expression without them being aware of the purpose of the exercise. If I ask you to smile and then ask you what you feel, you might say, "Happy." But I could not take this as evidence that your smiling *caused* you to *feel* happy because in asking you to smile, in using the word "smile," you might think, "People smile when they are happy; ergo, if I smile, I should be happy." In so doing you would be giving me what you think is a reasonable answer, but it would not be an answer to whether facial changes affect feelings.

James Laird was one of the first researchers to get subjects to alter their facial expressions without using the words "smile" or "frown." He did this by instructing them to tense or relax the muscles at the location of fake electrodes he placed on their faces. The electrodes were positioned either on the cheeks above the zygomaticus smile muscle or between the subjects' brows where the corrugator frown muscle is located. He did not mention the words "smile" or "frown," nor did he show the subjects by his own expression what he wanted them to do.

The participants looked at pictures, and as they did so, they were asked to tense the facial muscle at the locale of the electrode. He found that people felt more intense feelings when they tensed the relevant facial muscles. When looking at pictures of the Ku

Klux Klan, subjects were angrier when simultaneously contracting their frown muscle than if they were not. Likewise, subjects who smiled while viewing pictures of playing children reported feeling happier than those who were not contracting the smile muscle while taking in the same image. The results clearly support the idea that facial expressions can moderate or intensify a feeling that is already present.

The German social psychologist Fritz Strack devised another ingenious way to get subjects to move their facial muscles while diverting them from the real purpose of the task. He told subjects (okay, so he lied to them) that he was interested in whether people could learn to use different body parts to accomplish a task, as might happen when people are physically handicapped. Participants were asked either to hold a pen in their teeth crossways without touching the pen with their lips (causing their mouths to smile) or to hold the pen in their lips pointing outward without touching it with their teeth, which prevented them from smiling.

While doing this, the subjects were asked to watch cartoons and rate how funny they were. Those who "smiled" due to holding the pen in their teeth thought the cartoons were funnier than those who held the pen in pursed lips.

Other investigators borrowed Strack's procedure to determine if a prejudice could be changed by altering someone's facial expression. Subjects either "smiled" or not while viewing photographs of unfamiliar black or white faces. Those who "smiled" while holding a pen in their teeth subsequently showed less racial bias against blacks than those who viewed the photos while holding the pen in their lips.

In yet another method of manipulating faces and feelings, two parallel golf tees are taped vertically about a quarter inch apart just above and between the brows. The subjects' task is to get the tips of the tees to touch. This could be done when they contracted their frown muscle. When successful, they perceived sad photographs as sadder than when they were instructed to keep the tees apart.

Three decades of research using techniques such as these have converged on the conclusion that facial expressions do in fact have consequences for those who exhibit them. But there are limits to how changing one's facial expression can affect what one feels. First, changing facial expressions does not affect all feelings. For example, increased smiling intensifies happy feelings, but exaggerating expressions of disgust does little to increase actual feelings of disgust—probably a good thing.

Second, adopting a facial expression that is the opposite of one's current feelings is difficult to pull off. A smile has some capacity to reduce sadness but it cannot completely turn it around. And finally, complete suppression of all facial expression is seldom successful in stamping out all feeling. People who aim for the prototypical poker face can quell most facial expression, yet even among practiced suppressors, strong feelings can leak out at the edges of the face.

Attempts at suppressing facial expression can also generate unexpected results. In one experiment, subjects were instructed to suppress any display of being amused as they watched a series of funny videos. While some were successful at adopting a blank face, others showed sad expressions. It appears that their efforts to not smile led them to feel something sad.

There are those who regard even the occasional smile as an unseemly show of emotion. The motivation is often self-protective—give nothing away and no one can get to you. It usually works, but can include keeping people away who would otherwise be supportive. Inexpressivity acts on others just as smiles do. The difference is that smiles solicit approach while inexpressivity promotes distance.

Reducing Those Pesky Smile Wrinkles

While not being averse to having feelings, there are increasing numbers of people who don't want the facial creases and wrinkles that come from being emotionally expressive. I am speaking here of *Botox* injections, which have become the number one nonsurgical procedure for reducing facial wrinkles in both men and women. Botox contains a neurotoxin that blocks release of the neurotransmitter acetylcholine, leaving the muscle in a state of flaccid paralysis. This causes the skin over it to relax and even out. Currently, Botox is injected most frequently in the *obicularis occuli* muscle that encircles the eyes and causes those awful crow's-feet wrinkles. One small problem with this solution is that this muscle is the core component of the genuine smile. Not to worry, though; Botox does not affect the fake smile.

Some people in the dramatic arts worry about the widespread use of Botox among actors. Film director Martin Scorsese has been heard to complain that he finds it difficult to find an actress over the age of thirty-five with the ability to look credibly angry because so many have made their frown muscles inert. But psychiatrists have found this same inactivity may have emotional benefits. An initial study of ten clinically depressed women showed that botulinum toxin reduced the extent to which they felt bad. However, subsequent studies suggest that the effect of facial muscle paralysis is a little more complicated than "eliminate the frown muscle and you can get rid of miserable feelings." So, hold on before canceling that appointment with your psychotherapist and substituting it with a visit to the dermatologist.

In a recently completed doctoral dissertation, Joshua Davis compared two methods for the temporary treatment of facial wrinkles, Botox and Restylane. While Botox paralyzes facial muscles, Restylane reduces wrinkles by filling the area under the skin with water. Based on prior studies, Davis predicted that Botox should reduce depression but that Restylane would not have this effect.

Seventy-two women between the ages of twenty-seven and sixty were injected with either Botox or Restylane. None had previously been judged to be depressed or had had facial treatments. Several psychological measures were given a week before the injections, and a second time, between two and three weeks after the injections. The key test was an established measure for depression. Surprisingly, and counter to predictions, the Botox group had *higher* depression scores in the second session than in the first. Those in the Restylane group showed neither more nor less depression across the two sessions.

The expectation was that the Botox group would show less depression after the treatment. They did not. Why not? The study was a model of scientific rigor, so the problem did not lie there. But there was one important difference between this study and the study mentioned earlier with depressed women. In the current study, the female participants were *not* clinically depressed at the outset. What the Botox treatment did was to inhibit *normal* facial expressions. It constrained action of the frown muscle but also unintentionally made their faces inert, which restricted normal everyday feelings. In the non-depressed women, that was not a positive experience. Participants' ordinary facial muscles conveying delight or curiosity or even irritation were rendered inert by the Botox. People need to feel their own facial muscles to be themselves.

Forever Smiling

Psychologists know that something is up, and it is not positive emotion, when people smile all the time. Novelists also know it. Henry James wrote in *Portrait of a Lady*: "She shook hands with Lord Warburton and stood looking up into his face with a fixed smile—a smile that Isabel knew, though his lordship probably never suspected it, to be near akin to a burst of tears."

Chronic social anxiety is associated with chronic smiling, which is often adopted to camouflage a pervasive unease in the world. We know that genuine smiles are animated and brief, often running into each other like puppies chasing a ball, while deliberate smiles tend to last beyond their expiration date. A smile with a long duration often appears when a conversation turns toward a potentially uncomfortable topic. Psychologist George Bonanno and his colleagues at Columbia University recently found this in interviews with women who had a documented history of having been sexually abused. These women were encouraged to talk about significant events in their lives. The women who had a history of having been abused but who chose not to disclose it in this context displayed longer social smiles during their interviews than the women who had been abused but were comfortable talking about it. The investigators interpreted these smiles as a cover for the continuing shame of what had happened to them.

Buster Keaton was reported never to have smiled, ever—"He had a mouth as stiff and flat as the brim of his porkpie hat." Keaton did smile, however, as a child; that is, he did until his not-very-funny vaudeville parents learned that audiences would howl with laughter if the five-year-old Buster was tossed into scenery or had chairs busted over him and showed no expression.

It is no laughing matter, however, for those who cannot smile because of a physical or psychological problem. Since people find it disconcerting to interact with a person whose face shows no feeling, they often look for an exit strategy. And so the inexpressive person is ostracized or disparaged. Or sometimes it is the person attempting to interact who responds by blaming themselves—am I really that tedious? Either outcome is challenging. When smiles are missing, we are reminded of their significance.

LIES

two-faced smiles

On December 22, 1984, Bernard Goetz, a white, self-employed electronics specialist of thirty-nine, boarded the Seventh Avenue express train in New York. Four noisy African-American youths boarded the same subway train, and one of them, Troy Canby, approached Goetz and said, "Mister, can I have five dollars?" When Goetz didn't comply, the youth moved closer, smiled, and said, "Give me five dollars." Goetz responded by pulling a gun from his coat pocket and firing five shots. One of the young men was permanently paralyzed. Canby's smile, Goetz later reported, was the last straw.

How could a smile transform a mild-looking electronics repairman into "the subway vigilante"? According to conventional wisdom, smiles spark feelings of well-being, not wellsprings of rage. Alas, smiles can be two-faced. Taken at face value, a smile typically casts a positive glow, but the person behind the smile may have something entirely different in mind. The result is a *disconnect* between outward expression and inner feelings. Some disconnects are the result of unconscious processes while others are deliberately produced.

An *unconscious disconnect* may result from having spent a

lifetime pushing negative feelings way out of awareness. For
example, a person may have heard repeatedly when young that
angry feelings are bad and should *never* be expressed. So even
the slightest inkling of anger or frustration is automatically
covered over with a smile. On the other hand, *deliberate disconnects* result when an outward show of positivity is intentionally
used to camouflage the fact that a person is lying through their
teeth.

Although scammers and dupers often smile to keep people in
the dark, there are still others with malevolent intent who actually
want the recipients to see their glee, albeit through a glass darkly.
Ironically, a smile is often the perfect way to convey contempt.
Several times in his trial for crimes against humanity, Saddam
Hussein scoffed at the proceedings by smiling at the presiding
justices. The so-called Unabomber, Ted Kaczynski, smiled after
his arraignment as the police paraded him in front of reporters and photographers. During one of the several recent school
shootings in the United States, students were horrified that the
shooter smiled as he fired his gun. And to the chagrin of many,
photographs of three men responsible for mass murder—Joseph
Stalin, Pol Pot, and Osama bin Laden—have shown all of them
smiling. We expect to find evil in the faces of tyrants, tormenters,
assassins, and murderers. Instead, their smiles mock our respect
for human life.

Evildoers, of course, are not the only ones to undercut a smile
with malice. Bullies on the playground, teasers at the office,
and trash talkers on the basketball court smile to exhibit their
eagerness to discombobulate the other. Taken at face value,
these smiles look like the real thing, but they are Janus-faced. As
a British journalist, Marshall Pugh, said of one example, "They

Osama bin Laden smiling

exchanged the quick, brilliant smile of women who dislike each other on sight."

But smile recipients are part of the exchange, too, and sometimes it is how a smile is read that turns it upside down. Smile recipients interpret the smiles they see, occasionally perceiving wickedness when none was intended. Anytime a person sees a smile, it will be seen through the lens of the perceiver's personal history, which will affect reactions to it. When U.S. house majority leader Tom DeLay was arrested on conspiracy and money-laundering charges, his mug shot showed him with a full toothy grin. What perceivers saw in that grin depended entirely on which side of the political aisle they stood. Republican members of the House were delighted to see their leader

Mug shot of former U.S. congressional leader Tom DeLay

smiling, while Democrats saw only reptilian gloating in DeLay's expression.

In short, some individuals see smiles through a grimy lens of distrust. The distrust may be the result of a prior bad experience. Or other aspects of the scene may suggest that not everything is to be trusted. A facial expression does not speak for itself. Consider two men at a party who watch their respective wives smile at another man. The facial expression is the same, but it could be interpreted via different filters. For a trusting husband, seeing his wife smile makes him happy because he interprets it as indicating that she is having a good time. For a jealous husband, seeing his wife smile makes him angry because it indicates that she is flirting. The same smile seen through different psychological filters will produce different consequences. And each will have been there for anyone to see.

Thus, a smile can appear alarming, not because the perceiver is paranoid, although he certainly could be, but because the immediate context nudges the interpretation in that direction. Consider the setting in which Bernard Goetz saw Troy Canby's smile. Goetz had previously been mugged—in fact, more than once—and had begun to carry a firearm. Around that same time, the news media were full of stories about how dangerous the streets and subways of New York City had become, casting shadows on any encounter with a stranger. Into this dicey history and context come four male strangers who ratchet an initial request for money into a demand sheathed in a smile.

In the dark subway, Canby's smile seemed to mock Goetz's vulnerability. It would have been one thing had a friend of Goetz smiled and asked for five dollars. But in the subway context, combined with Goetz's history, Canby's smile came across as a barefaced taunt. At another time, or in another place, or with a different person, that particular smile might have led Goetz to give the shirt off his back; in the subway, the smile triggered instead the desire to "wipe that smile off his face."

Setting the Stage for a Smile

Half a century ago, social psychologist Marvin Cline showed how context affects the perception of smiles. He placed pictures of two faces, each with a different expression, side by side. He asked research participants to look at the pictures and to describe what was happening. He found, as has been found before and since, that people are natural-born storytellers. Give a person a lead-in and a storyboard comes into being.

In Cline's study, when participants saw a smiling face next to a sad face, most participants saw the smiling face as gloating, the result of the smiling person being victorious over the glum one.

When, however, a smiling face was set next to an irritated face, the stories more often included themes of the person with the smiling face as poking fun at the one who looked irritated.

Using a variation of this design, a recent British study examined how a smile was interpreted when placed in two slightly different photographs. All of the participants looked at two photos placed next to each other. In both, a photo of a man showed him looking out at the camera. The difference was in the picture of a woman placed to the left of the man. In both photos she was smiling, but in one she was seen in profile so that it appeared she was looking at the man. The other group of subjects viewed the same woman to the left of the man, but here she was also looking at the camera. When asked how attractive they found the man, female subjects rated him as more attractive when the photo of the smiling woman faced in his direction rather than facing forward. If the adjacent photo showed a non-smiling woman, the female participants gave the man in the photograph a complete pass. Like babies looking to their moms for guidance, these women took another woman's facial expression and orientation as clues to what the man was like.

Lev Kuleshov, an early Soviet filmmaker, was one of the first to use minor changes in context to produce dramatic cinematic effects. He took a close-up of an actor's expressionless face and placed it in three different frames: looking at a plate of soup; at a dead woman in a coffin; or at a playing child. Audiences who viewed the three frames were convinced that the actor's facial expression changed from one to the next when, actually, only the contextual frames had changed. In fact, those who viewed the pictures were impressed with the actor's ability to communicate different emotional reactions via subtle changes in his facial expression, when none had actually occurred. So, some actors may be able to get away with conveying the "emotional gamut from A to B" if the surrounding frames vary enough.

Mixed-up Smiles

Smiles sometimes find themselves in mixed company, mixing it up with other communicative signals such as words.

Consider a familiar situation. You need to reprimand someone, but you also want to convey that you appreciate him. A mixed message is the likely outcome. Your words say, "You've messed up," but your smile says, "I value you." What comes across in the message? Or think about times when you have felt the need to disagree with someone's point of view but do not want to be seen as antagonistic. You phrase your disagreement clearly, but have you possibly undercut your position by smiling?

What is the take-home message for recipients of mixed messages? To study how people respond to them, psychologists have fabricated all kinds of mixed messages by combining communication channels (facial expression, vocal intonation, words) with positivity or negativity, and measuring reactions to them. For instance, positive words such as, "Your report is terrific," are paired with a negative facial expression or a negative statement like, "You're a klutz," communicated with a neutral voice. Subjects are exposed to many examples and their responses are noted.

A frequent finding in lab studies is that when presented with mixed messages, recipients rely on *how* something is said rather than *what* is said. Thus, a frown or positive intonation usually trumps whatever was said. In the real world, however, mixed messages are more likely to elicit confusion about what is being said or uneasiness about who said it. For example, mixed messages have been found to be more frequent in marriages where difficulties abound than in marriages where there is satisfaction, although it is not clear whether the mixed messages are the cause or symptom of the marital difficulties. Researchers have also found that patients have more doubts about physicians who communicate in mixed messages than about those who are straight talkers. Doctors often opt to package bad news with a positive face, while patients may simply come away confused.

Given that mixed messages are potentially confusing, you might wonder why people cannot simply be more consistent in what they say and how they say it. If only it were so simple. How would you respond if a close friend asks what you think of his new heartthrob or a colleague asks what you think of the lecture she just gave? What if you really think that she or it is/was dreadful? If you are consistent and candid, hurt feelings would likely result, even if your friend or colleague says they *really* want you to be honest with them. On the other hand, lying is seldom a great solution. So you equivocate. You dance with your words and distract with your smile. You change the subject, postpone your answer, or focus on some inoffensive yet irrelevant feature ("She's got a great laugh"). But balancing all these considerations has its own costs. Studies show that when you are working to show how pleased you are when you are not, your physiology goes into overdrive and your capacity to think sputters.

In modern-day life, the blatant expression of prejudice is frowned on but often leaks out nonetheless. An Emory University social psychologist, Eric Vanman, studied this among white racially prejudiced individuals when they were asked to evaluate an African-American co-worker. Prejudiced participants tended to say all the right things, like declaring their very high regard for their black co-workers. However, their faces told another story.

They showed more corrugator facial muscle, which indicates the presence of antagonism.

Does everyone catch the prejudicial feelings seeping in at the edges of the nice words? Those with lots of experience with mixed messages tend to be more alert to the possibility of a cover-up, that the words being expressed are not consistent with underlying feelings. For example, African-Americans are significantly better than whites at seeing through a Mr. Nice Guy act to the bigotry it is attempting to conceal. How do whites let slip their antiblack prejudice despite their efforts to conceal it? Sometimes they just smile too much. All that smiling suggests that they do "protest too much."

Jokes can also be understood as mixed messages, and with similar confusion. The aim is to amuse, but they often come packaged with a sharp edge. In her research, developmental psychologist Daphne Bugental defined a joking message as one that combined negative words with a positive nonverbal expression. For example, a speaker might say, "You're hopeless; you're really hopeless," with a smile. Although adults mostly found such messages amusing, school-aged children did not find them funny in the least. The smile failed to take the sharp edge off the critical words. However, neither adults nor children were amused by sarcastic messages that flip the combination to positive words and negative facial expression. A verbal statement like, "That's good . . . that's really great," said with a negative facial expression, did not come across as amusing to anyone, young or old.

Deceptive Smiles

If one is to believe the evidence, humans deceive each other all the time. Among adults, the sheer frequency of lying is astonishing.

Social psychologist Bella DePaulo asked all sorts of people to keep a diary for a week and to record any lie they told during encounters that lasted for more than ten minutes. Since this requires people to enumerate instances of questionable behavior, one might expect small numbers. Yet, on average, people reported saying something that was not true in more than a third of their conversations. Respondents also admitted to lying in at least 10 percent of the interactions they had with their spouse or romantic partner.

To be sure, some lies are told to protect another's feelings or are written off as no big deal because they make conversations more interesting. However it is rationalized, lying is something that humans do as easily (and more regularly) as brushing their teeth. And the ability to come up with a lie at a second's notice seems to be associated with having a bigger brain. Neuroscientists find that the occurrence of lying is correlated with the size of the neocortex, that part of the brain involved in conscious thought. Scientists have found that the likelihood of deception in primates (including apes) goes up as the size of the neocortex goes up. Although it is not clear which came first—a larger neocortex or lying—it is clear that lying is something humans do easily. And it starts early; children engage in some forms of lying by the time they are two and a half years old. One particularly heartrending kind of lie involves what researchers call "Doesn't hurt bravado." In these cases, toddlers deny feeling pain ("doesn't hurt") or fear ("don't care") when it is clear that it does and they do.

Ralph Waldo Emerson had mousetraps in mind when he suggested that, if one were to build a better one, people would beat a path to your door; but it could as easily apply to lie detectors. Law enforcement officials, oversight committees, job interviewers, immigration officers, poker players, parents of adolescents, and

suspicious spouses are among those on the lookout for deception. Conventional wisdom has it that deceivers will be caught
if one knows where to look. Freud, for one, held that "betrayal
oozes out of him at every pore"; Nietszche stated, "One can lie with
the mouth, but with the accompanying grimace one neverthe-
less tells the truth." And Pinocchio certainly knew that the nose
knows lying when it sees it.

Social psychologists have long been a part of the scientific
effort to determine if faces, gestures, voices, or some other body
part reveal that someone is lying. The results from many studies indicate that no one should be beating a path to the door that
offers a surefire deception detector. That has not stopped the traffic, of course. Psychologists have looked at data on scores of cues
across thousands of participants and concluded that clues that a
person is lying are few and uncertain. All the usual culprits that
many believe are dead giveaways to deception have been studied.
For example, gaze aversion, fidgeting, blinking, shrugging, nose
rubbing, as well as more esoteric ones like face-touching, lip-
pressing, pitch rise, and lip-corner pulling, have not proved to
be indicative of dishonesty. All told, the evidence is compelling.
Deception is *not* reliably revealed by any of these behaviors.

Since no reliable behavioral tip-off has been found (and
that includes the discredited but not disowned polygraph), it is
not surprising that liars typically get away with lying. Average
accuracy at detecting lies is only slightly greater than would be
expected by a flip of a coin, and often worse, because people tend
to rely on flawed theories about what we do when we are lying. The
fact that no reliable deception sensor has been identified, that
no meter rings or flashes, vibrates or whistles, when people lie
has not discouraged those who claim to *know* a liar when they see
one. And it has not stopped those who are able convince others

that they possess such a detection device. For example, the most frequently mentioned indicator of lying across the planet draws on the idea that liars cannot and will not look you in the eye. But since everyone, including liars, knows that others "know" this, liars are hardly going to avert their gaze. Yet the lack of reliable evidence linking lying to looking away has done little to dent this piece of tenaciously held folk wisdom.

Since humans lie so frequently, one would think that we as a species would have developed the means to detect when we are being had. But no, evolution has sided with the liars. Psychologists think the evolutionary edge has gone to the liars because the species would stand more chance of survival if the fittest were able to hide or divert important information from others. In our long-distant past, behaviors that allowed humans to feign and fake were adaptive, and behaviors that gave deception away would have dropped by the evolutionary wayside. If human beings regularly let slip what they were up to, they would not likely have survived to tell any tale, tall or otherwise. So, natural selection favored those who were able to keep their business to themselves.

Nonetheless, with the scientific news that some smiles are involuntary while others are intentional, researchers are now taking a closer look at whether particular smiles might disclose that something does not look altogether right while other smile types might successfully deflect targets away from an ongoing deception. While the *amount of smiling* provides no reliable gauge as to whether someone is lying, a *particular smile configuration* might hint that not everything is as it seems.

A recent study has confirmed earlier findings that liars do not smile *more* than truth tellers; however, they do show more deliberate smiles than truth tellers. And some on occasion exhibit more spontaneous embarrassed smiles. In one study, female subjects were asked to lie to another person, to tell her that the task they were about to undertake was fun when in fact it was tedious. Some liars had time to prepare their lie while others had to do it on the spot. For a comparison, some participants were told to tell the whole truth and nothing but the truth about the task.

Liars showed significantly more deliberate smiles than truth tellers. Apparently the strategy involved a smile offense as a way to divert their audience from the fact that they were being handed a bill of goods. But liars who had to make up a lie on the spur of the moment displayed more embarrassed smiles than those who told the truth, suggesting some discomfort with lying.

Clearly, not all liars feel shame. In fact, some deceivers positively relish the act of putting something over on someone, and that may slip out in a spontaneous smile, what Paul Ekman calls *Duper's delight*.

Finally, other smiles may cue that someone is not telling the whole truth. A genuine smile may be part of a mixed message. As you saw earlier, facial expressions are rarely unadulterated. Smiles, even spontaneous smiles, can co-exist with other emotion signs. Can people detect this appended facial indicator? In one test, adults and children viewed video clips of a man and a woman showing three types of smiles. One smile was the genuine article (raise of the lip corners along with crow's-feet wrinkles around the eyes). The second smile included genuineness indicators (raised mouth corners and crinkling eye corners), but there was also a trace of anger in the expression, revealed in a slight tightening of the lips. The third expression was also a genuine smile with even more lip tightening.

For each smile, participants were asked to indicate whether the person was really happy or only pretending to be. Some adults (not all) and some children (not all) were able to read the targets' lips. They didn't know what it was that alerted them to the possibility that the person was pretending to be happy rather than being truly happy; they simply felt that some smiles didn't ring true.

In Nathaniel Hawthorne's *The Scarlet Letter*, the spiteful Roger Chillingworth seeks to mask his fierce expression with a smile, "but the latter played him false, and flickered over his visage so derisively, that the spectator could see his blackness all the better for it." Smiles, even genuine ones, do not always mask other emotional eruptions.

More than forty years ago, two clinical psychologists focused their trained eyes on films of psychotherapy sessions shown in slow motion. Under those special viewing circumstances, they were able to see facial expressions that flashed by rapidly on otherwise passive faces. The term they assigned these now-you-see-them-now-you-don't displays was *micromomentary facial expressions*. In real time, most people miss them not only because they are extraordinarily brief but also because observers are usually not paying close attention.

The rock song "Reason to Believe" communicates the sad tale of a man dealing with his love's infidelity. He missed the telltale signs because he did not want to see what they meant. While she "lied straightfaced," he continued to look for "a reason to believe." Tears have a disconcerting way of blurring vision, but lovers as well as most of the rest of us are often motivated *not* to look closely. Psychologists call this not wanting to know the "truth bias."

Machiavellian Smiles

Niccolò Machiavelli, the Italian Renaissance philosopher and politician, wrote the first self-help book for politicians. The central idea of *The Prince* (1513) is that "Cunning and deceit will every time serve a man better than force." Although Machiavelli himself did not mention smiling as an excellent cover for cunning and deceit, the most prominent portrait of him by Santi di Tito shows a faint smile that is every bit as ambiguous as that of da Vinci's *Mona Lisa*.

Five hundred years after Machiavelli, two social psychologists, Richard Christie and Florence Geis, conjectured that princes and politicians were not alone in subscribing to Machiavellian principles. Drawing on *The Prince*, Christie and Geis developed a scale to measure the degree to which anyone endorses a Machiavellian worldview. This measure came to be known as the *Mach scale*, and its most definitive version as the *Mach IV*. The Mach IV scale consists of twenty statements and asks respondents the degree to which they agree with each one. Sample items are, "Never tell anyone the real reason you did something unless it is useful to do so," and, "Anyone who completely trusts anyone else is asking for trouble." With the scale in hand, psychologists went about studying *high Machs*, as high scorers are called.

Hundred of studies later, psychologists find that high Machs are a type unto themselves, although there appears to be a little Machiavellianism in all of us. The high Machs' modus operandi is calculating and manipulative. They are suspicious and cynical about interpersonal relationships and believe that if they don't exploit people first, others will do so to them. High Machs look at altruistic and generous people and presuppose that underneath all that goodness they are just as self-centered as everyone else, although they go considerable ways to disguise that fact.

High Machs also are more competent and more confident than those scoring lower on the Mach scale, and they are better negotiators and persuaders in general.

In fact, a study of U.S. presidents using extensive biographical material concluded that presidents who were more Machiavellian passed more legislation during their terms in office and had more legislative victories than their less Machiavellian counterparts.

From all this you might imagine that Machiavellians are cold and impersonal people. Nothing could be further from the truth. People who know them use terms like "charming" and "sociable," even "charismatic." In short, Machiavellians possess the classic two-faced smile. They seem appealing and amiable, but all of that is designed to mask their hidden agendas. Most of us can be had by charm; we are susceptible to a smile's warmth, and besides, we want to believe. According to Donald Barthelme, "The distinction between children and adults, while probably useful for some purposes, is at bottom a specious one. . . . There are only individual egos, crazy for love."

Con artists and psychopaths, too, take a page out of *The Prince*. Like Machiavellians, con artists use reassuring smiles and pleasant conversation to establish a trusting relationship with their victims, so effectively in fact that victims have a difficult time letting go of the "friendly" relationship even after the gig is up. They stroke, dispensing subtle positive reinforcements to elicit positive feelings. Cons are called confidence artists for good reason—tokens of appreciation, displays of respect, signs of affection are generously bestowed, all the better to defraud a person of whatever it is that they can ill afford to lose.

Psychopaths reliably are enthusiastic users of two-faced smiles. Clinical psychologists use the word "charming" to describe psychopaths, for they are clever and interpersonally engaging. Clinical psychologist Robert Hare noted for example that the psychopath's lack of true feeling for others is "hidden by an amazing smile, captivating body language, and smooth

talk, all of which enable him or her to gain the trust of others."
But beneath the charming smile, psychopaths are manipulative,
irresponsible, antisocial, cruel, and totally without conscience.
Like Machiavellians and con artists, psychopaths display two-
faced smiles in abundance. But unlike them, their Janus-faced
smiles are not a means but an end. They gain intense pleasure
from taking others on a destructive ride.

"Jeer Pressure"

It was said of Voltaire that he had the "most hideous" smile in
Europe. "It was a thin, skull-like smile that sneered at everything
sacred: religion, love, patriotism, censorship, and the harmony of
the spheres." Simply put, sneers and smirks are smiles gone bad.
Readers of Lemony Snicket's *A Series of Unfortunate Events* learn
that a smirk means "smiled in an unfriendly, phony way." Or as
the poet Shelley put it, "There is a snake in thy smile, my dear."
    Smirks and sneers twist symmetrical smiles out of shape.
Darwin noted that the *derisive and sardonic smile* had the familiar
retraction or oblique upward movement of the lip corner but only
one lip corner. When smiles morph into smirks in intimate relationships, the signs are not auspicious for survival of that union.
Fake smiles and stainless steel smirks coupled with scathing
comments like, "You couldn't balance the checkbook if you tried,"
suggest that divorce will not be far behind.
    The British psychologist Michael Billig contends that much
that goes by the name of humor in interpersonal relationships
is actually barely disguised ridicule. Though seemingly playful,
ridicule is often used to discipline, correct, or socialize someone
into the right way of doing things. "Jeer pressure" is effective at
eliciting conformity to that which a group thinks is right. Even

viewing someone else being ridiculed elicits conformity to group norms.

Teasing is ridicule-lite. Parents tease, siblings and lovers tease, friends and team members tease, supervisors and co-workers tease, fraternities and sororities tease, even babies and toddlers tease. Take Bart Simpson's comment: "I will not tease Fatty." Like other intentional two-faced smiles, a tease is a deliberate provocation in playful packaging. People are teased about their physical attributes and appearance, personality and habits, intelligence and skills, and social behavior and relationships. So we have in teasing a prototypical two-faced smile: a little aggression, a touch of amusement, and considerable room for interpretation.

The context for teasing has been found to affect how fraternity brothers rib one another and how they react to it. As you might guess, high-status frat brothers hold little back when they tease new pledges. In response, new pledges show more embarrassed smiles and fewer genuine smiles when teased.

The element most people use in deciding whether a comment is a tease or an insult is the presence of a "playful marker." Playful markers consist of behaviors like smiling, exaggerated intonation, or adding a wink and an elbow in the ribs. Like other mixed messages, these markers are designed to change a cut that metaphorically draws blood to one that merely ruffles feathers. Infants as young as seven months look for the playful marker of an adult's smile to help them decide whether they are being teased or not.

The playful marker says to the target and audience that the tease is to be taken in jest. People who are socially skilled are more likely to catch the playful markers, and as a result, don't react to the teasing as if it was fighting words. Those with underdeveloped social skills, however, are more likely to miss the markers and hear only ridicule.

Schadenfreude and Gloating

Schadenfreude, a German word describing the experience of great pleasure at another's low fortunes, also gives rise to two-faced smiles. That great curmudgeon Ambrose Bierce even defined basic happiness in schadenfreude terms: "Happiness is an agreeable sensation arising from contemplating the misery of another." Gloating is the behavioral manifestation of schadenfreude, openly expressing pleasure that someone else's misfortune has resulted in our gain. Schadenfreude is clearly not a noble sentiment, nor is gloating an admirable behavior, but psychologists are seeking to understand why it is that people feel strong positive emotion about other people's singularly bad outcomes. For example, most Americans cannot comprehend nor will they forget the joy seen in parts of the Arab world in response to the suffering inflicted on Americans in the September 11 attacks on the World Trade Center and Pentagon.

Insight into the nature of schadenfreude comes from examining the circumstances in which it occurs. In one study, participants saw one of two films depicting a person applying to medical school. In the first film, the student was an aspiring medical student who had a BMW, an attractive girlfriend, and a wealthy family, and who boasted of being able to get straight As by barely studying at all. The second film showed a young man of modest means, with no girlfriend or car, who studied himself ragged just to get Bs.

When participants learn that the privileged person has recently experienced adversity, they expressed more delight, even if the misfortune was undeserved, than when the adversity befalls the person who was barely getting by. It appears that schadenfreude occurs when bad things happen to someone who has everything going for them. In other words, we feel pleasure when bad things happen to people we envy because it seems to even the score somehow.

Meanwhile brain scientists have examined the neurological underpinnings of schadenfreude. A group of Israeli scientists found that patients with damage to the ventromedial prefrontal cortex of the brain were unable to identify gloating, even though they were able to recognize basic emotions like happiness and anger. This is noteworthy because that particular region of the brain is linked with the ability to empathize—being able to see things from the other person's perspective. The irony here, of course, is that one has to know how to empathize with someone in order to know they will feel pain when something bad happens to them. If one cannot empathize, then the suffering of an adversary would not be a joyous event.

We know that smiles are often contagious—one person's smile can cause another to smile. We do this because mirroring one another's smiles is one way we come to know and trust each other. When people share the same fate, they also smile when the other person is pleased. But there are times when having warm fuzzy feelings about another person is the last thing we want. In that contrarian place, we again find two-faced smiles. When two individuals compete, they do not mirror but countermirror with their faces. They adopt facial expressions that are the opposite of what the opponent is showing. They smile when the opponent is upset and frown when the opponent is pleased.

Schadenfreude does not, of course, manifest itself in everyone to the same degree. People with low self-esteem appear to be more susceptible to schadenfreude than those whose self-esteem is in better shape. And not everyone relishes feeling good when someone else is feeling bad. Instead, they feel guilty or sympathetic.

And so we find that smiling also has a dark side. Some two-faced smiles are deliberate fabrications, the outward pleasantness adopted to divert attention from actualizing ulterior motives. Other two-faced smiles are involuntary, the result of having learned to smile at the first sign of negative feelings to prevent them from being expressed. Still other two-faced smiles are baldly hostile—nasty through and through. The smile morphs into smirks, sneers, and gloating, letting everyone know that the recipient is beneath contempt.

In acknowledging two-faced smiles, we are faced with the fact that some smiles are treacherous. A smile, though often charming, cannot be taken at face value on every occasion. To do so risks being victimized. However, it is possible to see through them. There are clues if you know where to look; nonetheless, these clues are often missed because it is psychologically more comfortable to find a reason to believe.

smile politics

The scene is a political convention in the United States at which the party's nominee for president will be chosen. The choice is down to three men, but the dynamics are especially contentious between the two front-runners. One of these is a principled and sophisticated liberal with a couple of skeletons in his closet (infidelity, depression). The other is a ruthless and double-dealing conservative who may actually be in the closet. That is the framework for Gore Vidal's play, and subsequent movie, *The Best Man*. Vidal knew something about politics, having run for office himself as well as having a relative or two in the business. Besides, a good deal of politics is theater in any case.

In the first scene, as several reporters leave a hotel room, William Russell, the liberal candidate, says to his wife:

> From now on we project blandness. . . . And no matter what happens, I shall smile serenely, fatuously. A nuclear reactor melts down in Colorado, and I smile. The Supreme Court abolishes the Bill of Rights, and I smile. Armageddon. Boom. . . . And slightly irradiated . . . I smile.

There is no arena that takes its smiles more seriously than politics. Russell, the presidential hopeful, says out loud what many politicians take to be self-evident, namely that the path to political success involves lots of smiling. No matter the issue: smile.

There are few domains where the act of smiling is more volitional, less spontaneous, and more premeditated than political campaigns—except maybe in sales and megachurches. If a candidate smiles in the right way, pundits are inclined to apply the word "charismatic." If the wrong way—smiles arriving too late or snapped off too soon or staying on too long—then the words "slick," "crooked," "tough," or "maniacal" come to mind. The British press often mocked the former prime minister of England Gordon Brown for his excruciatingly painful public smiles, and a few went so far as to suggest that they had something to do with his being voted out of office in 2010.

Smiles are also political in ways that have nothing to do with conventional politics. They make their appearance anywhere power is an issue, and there are few social relationships where power is not an issue. When people control other people's outcomes—that's power. When people exert influence—that's power. As you will see, smiles are consequential in affecting and reflecting who is on top and who is not, who is aiming to move up and who doesn't want to offend anyone.

Political leaders keep their options open with smile diplomacy; candidate smiles help win over fence-sitters; and underling smiles confirm that everything is as it should be.

What's in a Presidential Smile?

Smiling by U.S. presidents is now standard practice, but it was not always so. Political scientist Richard Ellis contends that

presidents in the early days were never shown smiling in public. Their facial expressions were invariably stern because the
presidency was regarded as a duty that one accepted with grave
responsibility and certainly not with relish. Over the last century, a change has come over the land, with presidents smiling
whenever they are in the public eye.

Presidential smiling began in earnest with Franklin Delano
Roosevelt, who Ellis argues was the first president that Americans pictured grinning. In fact, Calvin Coolidge, two presidents
before FDR, had such a dour demeanor that his campaign committee brought in Al Jolson to sing and joke so Coolidge might
be caught on camera with an actual smile. It worked, but it was a
shock to the nation. *The New York Times* reported: "Coolidge nearly
laughs!"

Since FDR, presidents have taken great care to polish their
public smiles because advisers know that U.S. voters want their
commanders in chief to be likable. Some voters even imagine
being on such friendly terms with the president that they could
have a beer with him.

Each president in recent times has had a recognizable smile
that defined his character and imprint. Common man Harry
Truman's triumphant smile as he held up a newspaper prema-
turely and erroneously announcing: DEWEY DEFEATS TRUMAN is
firmly etched in American memory. Eisenhower's congenial
retired general, frequent golfer smile was the perfect accom-
paniment to the buttoned-down 1950s. Some said of John Kennedy's smile that its charm allowed him to get away with nearly
anything, while Richard Nixon's always late to arrive grin had
people wondering what he was up to. Indeed, the difference
between Kennedy's charming smile and Nixon's ill-fitting one
probably contributed to the fact that those who heard the 1960

presidential debate on the radio thought Nixon had won, but those who saw the debate on television were convinced that Kennedy had. Nixon did eventually become president, but apparently still worried how to get his smile right—he sent a memo to his chief of staff urging White House staffers to talk up what a warm human being he was.

Early in Lyndon Johnson's political career, he is described by one biographer: "Tall as a plow horse and slim as a lodgepole, he boasted a slick of black curly hair and a smile as wide as the Pedernales." His smile, part of a substantial persuasive arsenal, all but disappeared as the Vietnam War became intractable. Jimmy Carter's toothy, Southern farmer grin cemented in place as the Iranian hostage crisis took hold and blocked his bid for a second term.

Ronald Reagan's smile, in equal measure earnest and jaunty, got him through misdeeds and lapses of memory so effectively that many then and still regard him as the "Great Communicator." Bill Clinton's barely contained grins and George W. Bush's barely contained smirks were their respective trademarks. Barack Obama was the first to have been voted by dentists and citizens alike as having the most winning smile. A "winning smile" by definition is defined by its consequences.

Do presidents pay attention to other presidents' smiles? Three years before he became president, and even before he announced that he was running for president, Obama wrote tellingly about a portrait of Lincoln: "It would be a sorrowful picture except for the fact that Lincoln's mouth is turned ever so slightly into a smile. The smile does not negate the sorrow. But it alters tragedy into grace."

A few of these presidents have been called "charismatic," which has something to do with how they smile.

The Face of Charisma

When Nelson Mandela was a poor law student he was taken to meet Walter Sisula, then leader of South Africa's fledging African National Congress. On first seeing Mandela, Sisula is said to have declared, "A mass leader walked into my office." Mandela was tall and handsome, carried himself with a regal air, and he "had a smile that was like the sun coming out on a cloudy day."

"Charisma," once used to describe leaders with divine and superhuman powers, now applies to leaders with the ability to exercise diffuse and intense influence over the beliefs, values, and behavior of others through their own behavior, beliefs, and example. A colleague of mine at Yale, Joseph Roach, professor of theater and English, defines "charisma" as the ability to convey two apparently opposite qualities at the same time—strength and warmth, or grandeur and humility. According to Professor Roach, the contradiction works because we want to have "public intimacy" with our leaders—that is, assurance that he or she is not like anyone we've ever met but still is just like one of us after all.

Though a student and wearing a threadbare suit, Nelson Mandela had what people saw as the charismatic gene. Sisula noticed a regal presence coupled with a spectacular smile. Curious about what most people think is charismatic, political psychologists have looked to biographies, letters, and diaries for indicators. Three telltale traits recur over and over: high energy; social assertiveness; and an intense interest in power. In business contexts, charisma tends to take a more pragmatic form; charismatic executives perform well in front of large audiences, grasp situations easily, and recognize members' needs.

For the social psychologist Howard Friedman, one quality stands head and shoulders above the rest in differentiating what

Charismatic former South African president Nelson Mandela

charismatic leaders have that lackluster ones do not: emotional eloquence. Friedman and his colleagues at the University of California at Riverside devised a test to measure this trait, a measure they called the *Affective Communication Test*, or ACT. Instead of asking other people to point to charismatic leaders, ACT asks respondents to report on themselves. They are told to rate how expressive they are in thirteen situations, such as, "I can easily express emotion over the telephone."

Friedman found what many political scientists had noted, that charismatic people are extroverted, exhibitionistic, and relish power ("I am the decider"). They think well of themselves, and even when young have been involved in school politics, public speaking, and theater. A good smile is "job one" in all these activities. High ACT scorers know how to use their faces to touch others' emotional buttons.

Emotional eloquence causes other people to be emboldened. As a demonstration of this, Friedman put unacquainted individuals into three-person groups, one of which scored at the high end of the ACT while the other two had low scores. Whose emotions were most affected? Whatever the mood of the single expressive individual at the start, the moods of the other two came around to mirror it. The mood of the highly expressive person was clearly contagious.

Charismatic leaders are particularly adept at infecting others with positive feelings. For example, when a group of business students was asked to describe their vision for their respective companies, those who had been judged by their managers to be charismatic were brimming with upbeat possibilities. When these same fledgling but charismatic managers made a presentation to a large group, they smiled to beat the band. A case in point: journalists often use "brilliant smile" and "successful entrepreneur" in the same breath to describe Richard Branson (now Sir Richard), CEO of Virgin Airways.

Presentational Politics

Should we conclude that American presidents smile more now than in times past because twentieth- and twenty-first-century citizens vote for candidates who are extroverted and confident? Or is more smiling by presidents due to a change in how presidents and presidential aspirants are presented to voters, sometimes known as *presentational politics*. When presentation matters, as it does in our nonstop, vision-saturated world, smiling may have become the default look for leaders and leader wannabes. Political commentator Joe McGinniss put it rather starkly by noting that on television a candidate does not need ideas for "style becomes substance."

We certainly *see* presidents a good deal more now than in the past. Paid television advertising has escalated over the last half century. In fact, television is now the preeminent mode through which candidates present themselves to voters. This itself has become big business, a response to the need for an appealing videostyle.

Televised spots are not the only presentational conduit. We see political leaders incessantly in news photographs, in televised interviews, and on YouTube. At present, we know our presidents cinematically, and so "face time" with the president takes on a whole new meaning. It makes sense that smiling would become the go-to facial expression for American presidents because it is seen in the visual channel to which most voters have access.

In the 1960s, Marshall McLuhan predicted that politics would be replaced by imagery since the image would become more powerful than a politician could ever be. We are not too far from that now, when many citizens are better acquainted with visual images of politicians than they are with particulars of their policies. Pictures of politicians waving at unseen audiences, delivering speeches, shaking hands with world leaders, and modeling for photo ops occupy a lot of media time. Political scientists argue about whether the increasing importance of the visual is the cause of voters' current low interest in political ideas and less commitment to a particular party, or whether increased visibility shows the effects of these changes. Whatever the case, there is agreement that politics is now heavily saturated with the visual.

Television news with its ever present background visuals has also transformed the way we see political leaders. Roger Masters introduced the term *visual quotes* to describe the video clips or photographs that serve as background to television stories about political leaders. When viewers "watch" a TV newscast about a political leader, their attention is drawn more to the visual images than to what is being said. Many news watchers assume that brief video segments are merely background to the real story, but in truth they occupy the foreground in people's consciousness and memory. In earlier times, citizens learned their political news through partisan politics and exposure to pamphlets, broadsides, and newspapers. Information previously arrived by words; now it comes via pixels.

This emphasis on the visual has altered what we know or, more precisely, what we *think* we know about politicians. Policies and politics are usually complex and difficult to get a handle on, but a politician's personality—or more specifically the impression we have of the individual's personality—seems straightforward and conclusive. Words too often seem slippery and untrustworthy, compared to our personal impressions, which we believe are firmly grounded in what we see with our own eyes. We trust what is in front of our eyes and in close-ups—presidents look very much like the way people appear to us in real face-to-face interactions.

In the jurisdiction of political image bites, politicians' facial expressions take center stage and smiles get the spotlight. Political figures appear to us up close and personal. As McLuhan foresaw, the political visual image constitutes a lot of what we have. No wonder it is intensely managed. Bill Clinton once complained to his adviser Dick Morris that in campaigning, he felt he was auctioning off his body parts by giving a smile here and a handshake there.

The emphasis on presentation politics is not news to most people, who know gloss when they see it. But if it is gloss, it is persuasive gloss—smiles have real consequences. If a politician smiles while delivering a speech, those individuals who tend to listen carefully think about what is being said even more deeply than when there is little or no smiling. That would seem to be a good result. Yet we also need to consider the effect of smiling on people who are not particularly motivated to think deeply about what they hear. They are even less likely to attend to what is being said if what the politician says is said with a smile.

Politicians ought not to adopt perma-cheer smiles. Smiles must adapt to the context and be variable enough in display to be seen as sincere. Of course, some politicians need to start by learning the basics. When advisers told Thomas Dewey to smile during his run for president against Harry Truman, he replied, "But I thought I was smiling."

Even when politicians know how to smile, there are situations where it is best not to. Voters sense when a politician's facial expressions are phony or extravagant. On the one hand, voters are made nervous when a politician smiles in an awkward or stilted fashion; but effusive smiling also can be jarring in its own way. During Bill Clinton's 1992 run for president, he was advised to smile less. His all-systems-go smile came across as slick and insincere. He erred again as far as the public was concerned when he laughed briefly during the funeral of his friend and commerce secretary Ronald Brown. Studies have shown that effusive reactions by political leaders, even if positive, make the public nervous.

Not surprisingly, revolutionary leaders do not do a whole lot of smiling. Indeed, a smiling revolutionary seems an oxymoron. A real revolutionary is dissatisfied with the status quo—not cheerful in the face of it. Consider the iconic image of Ché Guevara, which survives today on posters, mugs, and T-shirts forty years after his death: Ché gazes off in the middle distance, and

President Bill Clinton showing a characteristic attempt to
suppress smiling

his facial expression is one of seriousness and resolve. In short,
political audiences have standards for appropriate emotional display by their leaders. Too much or too little sends out alarm bells
about their leaders' competency and their humanity.

Appearances to the contrary, presidents display facial expressions besides smiling. Anger expressed by lowered brows and
fixed gaze is sometimes useful. In his memoirs, French president Charles de Gaulle described being impressed with Winston
Churchill's persuasive use of anger during negotiations. In fact,
several studies show that participants often concede more to
negotiators who are angry than to those who are happy. When
confronted with an angry opponent, they tend to believe the other
is not going to budge, and so make relatively large concessions.
Conversely, smiling opponents indicate to the other side that

their proposals are flexible. In that case, one need not resort to large concessions.

While smiling is generally advised on the campaign trail, a neutral demeanor tends to arouse less resistance from the other side. In one study of this dynamic, video clips of presidential candidates in the 1984 U.S. elections were shown to viewers who differed in their preferred candidate. In general, smiling proved better than not smiling for voters, whether they were for or against someone. In fact, it was especially effective for those voters who had yet to make up their mind. Angry displays by candidates sent supporters and opponents in opposite directions. Supporters were delighted when their candidate showed anger, although citizens inclined toward the other party saw only bombast by the irate candidate.

Political opponents have also been known to manipulate another candidate's smile for nefarious purposes. During the 1968 presidential campaign between Richard Nixon and Hubert Humphrey, a television spot aired by the Republicans presented a broadly smiling Hubert Humphrey juxtaposed with a set of negative images. The images: Humphrey smiling followed by bloodshed in Vietnam; Humphrey smiling followed by backwoods poverty; Humphrey smiling followed by street rioting outside the Democratic Convention in Chicago.

Republicans used this disingenuous technique again in the 1988 presidential election between G. H. W. Bush and Michael Dukakis. In one TV spot, viewers saw images of criminals walking to freedom through penitentiary gates or disgusting pools of industrial pollution interspersed with shots of Dukakis smiling from the turret of an Army tank as it drove in circles around an open field.

In both contexts, Humphrey's and Dukakis's smiling faces

invited the inference that they either had something to do with the unsettling events or at the very least were unconcerned about them.

Political Profiling

It is said that a politician's personality opens or closes doors but actually how a candidate's personality is perceived holds more sway. There is, in fact, a startling consensus among voters across several countries as to what traits they want to see in their political leaders. The desired traits are *extroversion* and *trustworthiness*.

Across the ideological spectrum, these two traits trump all other, ostensibly relevant characteristics. When people think about family, friends, co-workers, and celebrities, extroversion and trustworthiness are not the first traits that come to mind, but they are at the top of voters' lists for what they want in a political leader.

How do constituents detect a candidate's level of extroversion and trustworthiness? Despite claims by some that they can look a person in the eye and know whether that person can be trusted, the eyes themselves are not a measure of character. The muscles around the eyes are where the cues lie.

We glean impressions of people from what the social psychologist Nalini Ambady calls "thin slices," glimpses of their faces and brief sounds of their voices. Indeed, psychologists have a wealth of data showing that impressions about what a person is like are made extraordinarily quickly and from amazingly little information. Often enough, these impressions are dead on. In one study, research subjects were shown pictures of unfamiliar candidates for less than a second and asked to hazard a guess about whether they would win elections in which they were running. Not everyone was up to the task, but a significant number were able to do so with striking accuracy.

These findings deserve a second look because of what they tell us about what the research participants were actually able to do. Subjects were *not* asked whom they personally would vote for after having a fleeting glance at a photograph. Rather, they were asked to consider what a *majority* of voters would do. The essence of their accuracy was in knowing other people's preferences in political candidates. Faces matter hugely in our assessment of people, and many of us are on the same page about what those assessments are.

Do faces also tell us something about voters? Amazingly, yes. Citizens who lean in a liberal direction smile more on average than citizens who bend in a conservative direction. Does this mean that liberals are happier than conservatives? No, actually conservatives are happier. According to a recent survey by the Pew Research Center, 47 percent of conservative Republicans in the United States described themselves as "very happy" as compared with only 28 percent of liberal Democrats.

So, why do liberals smile more than conservatives, if it is not because they're feeling jollier than conservatives? You will recall that while spontaneous smiles reflect positive emotion, people also smile voluntarily, and those smiles reflect not inner emotion but outer intentions. In short, liberals' smiles signal a more cooperative, nonaggressive orientation. This sounds a little like the poet Robert Frost's definition of a liberal as a man too broadminded to take his own side in a quarrel.

New findings also indicate that liberals are perceived differently from conservatives by those who do not know their political slant. If a person comes across as warm, it is more likely that he or she is a Democrat. If a person comes across as powerful, the data show that he or she is more likely to be a Republican.

Appeasing Smiles

It thus appears that political candidates are under a mandate to smile a lot, which means that many of their smiles are enacted deliberately and consciously. Miraculously, some of them still come across as convincing.

Once a person has achieved office, or is in any position of power for that matter, he may smile for other reasons. Many people find in power a positive, even exhilarating experience. But lack of power has also been linked with smiling in the company of those in charge. Consider the iconic image of the ever-smiling underling who grins to show how happy he is to be of service. These are submissive, appeasing smiles—smiles that say to anyone who is watching, "I know my place and I am not about to challenge yours."

These are the smiles that primatologists believe provided the foundation for our own. Nonhuman primates like orangutans and baboons show something that looks awfully like a human smile in particular circumstances, namely, when the alpha animal in the group dominates them into submission.

The *silent bared teeth (SBT) display* is the label given by ethologists to the facial expression shown by lower-status animals in response to a threat display by a more dominant animal. The more dominant animal sees the bared teeth display and concludes that the contest is over, if indeed it was ever a contest. The SBT display says, "You win," which allows the more dominant animal to back off since the battle is done. The potential hostilities have been

Silent bared teeth grin (left) and play face (right)

settled with nary a spot of blood. Threat displays followed by submissive displays are an efficient and painless way to settle who
is where in the pecking order without having to resort to actual
fighting.

The SBT display in many primates is not arbitrary; rather, it
is the outgrowth of the expression of fear—the same open mouth
and gritted teeth and wide eyes. And so it conveys a clear message: I give up.

Dominance-submissive displays are an indispensable pro-
tocol in many nonhuman primates and probably in human
primates as well. Nobel laureate Konrad Lorenz, best known
as the Pied Piper of ducklings, argued that human smiling is
remarkably similar in appearance to the silent bared teeth display shown by nonhuman primates when threatened by a more
dominant animal. More recently, psychologists have suggested
that the human appeasement smile differs from the SBT of
other primates. Deferential humans often briefly press their
lips together while smiling. You have likely displayed this very

thing when you stepped aside to let someone pass or arrived late for a meeting.

Submissive smiles in humans produce analogous consequences to our primate relatives—they ward off something potentially unpleasant. Like our primate relatives, the lower-status human strokes the more dominant person's ego so that both can turn their attention to other matters. Psychologist Carolyn Keating and her colleagues asked research participants to rate several people on how dominant they looked. Some smiled; others did not. Smiling people were rated as significantly less dominant than those who did not smile.

Some human smiles serve as excellent appeasement gestures because they look genuine while at the same time serving as affirmation of the person's lower station. Black porters in the United States in the days of the Pullman trains were required to show this smile nonstop. In his book *Miles of Smiles, Years of Struggle*, sociologist Jack Santino wrote that the mostly white train passengers expected to see smiling porters, so much so that the eager-to-please smiles were apparently included in the price of a train ride. Black porters knew the drill—smile each and every time they encountered a passenger. No matter whether they were shining shoes or hanging clothes or being called "George," black porters smiled to let the predominately white passengers know how pleased they were to be serving them. The historian Bernard Mergen likened porters' smiles to minstrels' smiles, since both were performances designed to dilute any impression that they might be insubordinate. The good thing in all this was that the porters knew it was an act and that they could maintain a sense of self behind the facade.

Appeasement in human terms means having to be ready to say you're sorry, all the time. Submissive smiles are public displays

Smiling was required of Pullman porters

that announce to all that no one here is about to challenge the social order. Appeasing smiles, however, like many other smiles, are acts with a conscious agenda. They are designed to send the message that one knows one's place and is happy with it.

Appeasement smiles are especially endearing when displayed by those with high status. England's Princess Diana was often photographed showing a smile with appeasing overtones. It consisted of a low-intensity smile issued behind a slightly lowered head. She was royalty and quite literally self-effacing, a perfect expression for the "people's princess."

A little bowing, a little scraping, a little smiling, and the social order is confirmed. But it is not immutable. Toward the end of *Jane Eyre*, Jane's employer, Edward Rochester, orders her to speak, but this time her smile does not concede anything. "Instead of speaking, I smiled; and not a very complacent or submissive smile either."

Alas, popular translations of scientific findings often present as simple fact the idea that the human smile at its core is basically nothing more than an appeasement gesture. Wrong. Well not wrong exactly, but way oversimplified. We smile not because the other person will attack if we do not but simply to communicate that nothing is amiss. We smile to nip possible dissension or tension in the bud. We smile to smooth troubled waters. We smile to signal our wish for a pleasant interaction. We smile to say we can work this out. While such volitional smiling sometimes emerges in the low-power person, more often it derives from the stance that getting along is a good thing.

Smile Politics in Nonhuman Primates

Communication is almost as essential to nonhuman primates as it is to human primates. They too have lots of things to communicate: the occasional challenge to a higher-ranking animal; periodic reaffirmation of the chimpanzee power structure; and good relationships with other baboons, including the periodic need to reconcile after an altercation. And these do not even begin to cover all the communication involved in mating, playing, and taking care of baby baboons.

Nonhuman species do not have a single communication system, even though many facial expressions are shared across species. The import of any expression thus depends not on an inherent meaning but on which species and subspecies is under consideration. Just as the dominance-submission rituals shown by humans are not identical to those shown by chimpanzees either in form or in consequence, the communication among bonobos, squirrel monkeys, orangutans, and chimpanzees is far from identical.

With evolution, as various species branched into subspecies and took up different ecological niches, the silent bared teeth grin too branched out to signal different messages in different groups. Like human cultures, some nonhuman primate species show strict hierarchical relationships where the powerful are clearly distinguishable from the powerless. For example, rhesus macaques live in rigid, essentially "despotic" dominance chains of command, marked by high rates of aggression and low rates of reconciliation after fighting. Other species, however, have more egalitarian arrangements. Stumptail macaques, for one, have a flatter pecking order where positions change rather frequently. They also show much lower rates of aggression and higher rates of reconciliation after fighting.

When the silent bared teeth display appears in hierarchical species, it is an appeasement gesture. When it appears in egalitarian species, it occurs more frequently in nonconfrontational encounters, such as greeting a non-threatening approach by another animal ("How are you?" "No, how are you?" "No, I asked first").

Smile Politics Among Human Primates

Power is also a fact of social life for humans. It operates in Oval Offices and home offices, via explicit orders of command or through tacit agreement, across borders and within cliques, in casual relationships and intimate ones. Social psychologists define "power" as the capacity for one party to control another's resources and outcomes.

The matter at hand may be of considerable consequence or as mundane as who gets to hold the remote control. Power is sometimes exercised coercively, as when a person or group gets its way by force or threat of force. More often, social power works without obvious intimidation or even awareness. It works so subtly and smoothly that it doesn't look like power has anything to do with what's going on.

Within most groups, members know who is on top and who is closer to the bottom; who is vying for the top spot or who has been toppled. The signs are clear, even though understated, because everyone needs to know who is where in the pecking order. When everyone knows what to expect, stress is minimized.

Among humans, nonverbal cues typically reflect one's position. Professor Joan Chiao of Northwestern University found that observers knew a dominant person when they saw one. Powerful people are likely to tilt their head ever so slightly upward and look the other person in the eye. Averted gaze and lowered heads indicate that the person is not the boss, at least not yet. How we address someone also signals status differences. A lower-status person is more likely to use a formal than familiar mode: "Hello, Professor LaFrance," versus, "Hey, Marianne, what's up?"

People higher up on the socioeconomic ladder get away with not having to convey interest in getting to know someone if they are not interested. They are less likely to look, laugh, and nod at the other person, and more likely to doodle and fidget, than those who have less wealth and less education.

Where does the smile stand in the worlds of power, politics, and money? Powerful people smile and nonpowerful people smile. But it is not the same smile, nor does it have the same consequences.

The hallmark of having power is being able to act at will, to do what one wants to do, when one wants to do it, how one wants to do it. People who have little power do not have this prerogative. Rather, they need to adjust their behavior to accommodate what other people want. Higher-status people tend to say whatever is on their minds, while lower-status people often have to hold their tongues. Those of higher status do not have to bide their time, while low-status people have to wait their turn.

It seemed likely that these sizable psychological differences would translate into different smile dynamics. It also seemed likely that if you have power, you have the licence to smile when you want to and not because it is expected. No display rules for me! Conversely, being in a position of lower power means following someone else's rules and not revealing one's inner feelings.

So, we designed an experiment to test these ideas. In our lab, we created power differences between people by giving participants high or low control over another person's outcome. For example, high-powered people allotted bonus points however they wanted. Bottom line: We found that high- and low-power participants smiled in similar amounts but for different reasons. Lower-status participants smiled because they felt they had to; people with higher power smiled because they felt like it. High power gives options; low power imposes obligations. To have power means having the freedom to be spontaneous; if you don't have power, then it behooves you to monitor when it is a good idea to smile and when you should keep it to yourself.

People play politics and power games, and smiling is part of the action. In national politics, smiles are as inescapable in political campaigns as bumper stickers and sound bites. Every political smile is polished and practiced to within an inch of its life. The wonder of it is that some of these smiles actually come across as credible, affirming that a smile does not have to be spontaneous to be sincere. But if a candidate's smile looks as if someone else is pulling the strings or as though it hurts to do it, then doubts take shape.

In personal relationships, too, smiles are political. They are part of attempts to wield influence by converting blatant pressure into a softball suggestion. From the opposite side, a smile might signal acquiescence, for the moment.

service with a smile

Early in my father's working life, he was a salesman for a company that made dairy equipment, including the thingamajigs that made ice cream. It was obvious to me that selling ice cream was easy as pie but selling the machines that made ice cream was probably hard. Dad did some adjusting to my dualistic conception: the product, he said, didn't matter because what he was really selling was himself.

By the early twentieth century, advertisers had learned there was cash value in presenting their products with a smiling face. A century later, an immense service economy has signed on, promising to conduct business with a smile. In fact, service with a smile is now believed to be the only way, symbolically and literally, to operate a successful service business. Not exactly cutting-edge business thinking, but in truth, service with a smile is not as simple a strategy or as innocuous an endeavor as it might first appear.

Some years after my father shared the essence of selling, I heard an interviewer ask Arthur Miller, author of *Death of a Salesman*, what it was exactly that his protagonist Willy Loman sold. Miller responded, as had my father, "Himself." In the second act,

Willy reminisces about how to make a sale: ". . . it's not what you do, Ben. It's who you know and the smile on your face! . . . and that's the wonder, the wonder of this country, that a man can end with diamonds here on the basis of being liked!"

A brilliant playwright, not a motivational speaker, wrote *Death of a Salesman*, which is probably why at the end of the play diamonds are nowhere to be found. Instead, Willy's dream has collapsed and he has committed suicide. His friend Charlie eulogizes him this way, "He's a man way out there in the blue, riding on a smile and a shoeshine. And when they start not smiling back—that's an earthquake. And then you get yourself a couple of spots on your hat, and you're finished."

Outside the theater, service with a smile is typically not tragic. It is simply the name of the game—smile consequences measured in sales figures. But for those for whom smiling is a job requirement, emotional fallout sometimes follows, since one can lose oneself behind a constantly smiling face. Smiling on demand saps social strength and emotional energy. It is true that service with a smile is associated with positive results—sales are made, customers sign on—but the consequences for the smiler are not always so rewarding.

The goal is to treat customers with good-natured attention. That is good as far as it goes, but what about the worker, the service provider who is required to smile as part of the job description. Might that be too much to ask? Recall that the relationship between positive emotion and positive display is not automatic. People smile when they are happy, but they also smile when they are not happy. The first of these requires no premeditation. The second one takes motivation and effort. If one has good reasons for putting in the effort, the outcome can be satisfying; if not, then there is a psychological price to be paid. There also may be a wide social toll when human smiles are turned into commodities to be traded for profit.

Strategic Smiles

Salespeople and service providers are not alone in using smiles as a means to an end. Welfare recipients are instructed to smile during job interviews to reduce prospective employers' reservations. Female ice skaters smile to charm judges. The Professional Golf Association instructed its players on tour to sign more autographs and show more smiles. Supervisors attach mirrors to the computers of telemarketers as a reminder to "smile down the phone" when they make their pitches to customers. Research has in fact shown that people hear more pleasantness in the voices of people who smile while they are talking on the telephone. Highway toll takers in Massachusetts received bonuses for coming to work with smile on their face. A railway company in Japan has gone so far as to install computerized smile monitors, allowing employees to get feedback on the quality of their smiles.

Adoption agency Web sites post pictures of smiling children since adoptive parents frequently say that they were drawn inexorably to their child by virtue of their endearing smile. Appeals for donations to starving children overseas are more effective if they feature smiling children than sad ones. Fashion models' smiles are seldom described as endearing, but they do use strategic friendliness with agents, bookers, clients, and photographers in order to get assignments. Publicists urge authors on book tours to smile even if their books deal with corruption, war, poverty, torture, or environmental degradation. Larry Heinemann, author of several books about the Vietnam War, often groused about having to smile for book jacket photographs.

The advice to supply service with a smile is found everywhere, in orientation manuals, employee handbooks, and training books, to name but a few. At the Ritz-Carlton hotels, employees are required to memorize credo cards that explicitly assert the basics of Ritz service. One of their cardinal tenets: "Smile—we are on stage."

Lest anyone think that using smiles to secure a sale happens only in America, evidence shows that countries across the ideological spectrum know the value of a smile. When the British handed over sovereignty of Hong Kong to the Chinese, tourism dropped precipitously. The Hong Kong tourism association responded by encouraging its residents to smile more. Posters picturing celebrities appeared everywhere showing Hong Kong residents how to smile.

France, too, has had its own smiley campaign. The French idea entailed distributing booklets of "smile checks" (*cheques-sourire*) to tourists to use when they received particularly good service in a hotel, restaurant, or museum. Visitors were instructed to inscribe the name of a particularly friendly employee on a smile check and mail it (postage prepaid) to France's tourist office. The rationale was that this would induce service providers to smile more because if enough smile checks were received bearing their names they could win a trip to a chosen foreign country. Even the Russians initiated a smile program in 2004 in which border guards were ordered to smile politely at foreign travelers.

The Worth of a Smile

Quality service is the clarion call of private businesses and public agencies. The service sector is now the largest industry in the United States and projections from the Department of Labor indicate it will continue to be the fastest growing industry for at least another decade. Europe, too, has an expanding service sector. Service occupations are numerous—among them fast food employees, insurance agents, financial planners, bank tellers, health care workers, waitresses and bartenders, front-line hotel employees, airline staff, receptionists, personal assistants, agents, brokers, customer service reps, technical support, and tour directors.

But there seems to be a gap between intention and action. In 2002, *Time* magazine reported that eight of ten Americans believed that unpleasant sales and service encounters were the norm, and nearly half the respondents said that they had walked out of stores because of rude or surly service. Indeed, bad service is cited as the primary reason customers switch from one business to another.

Businesses that aim for service with a smile believe that value is added when customers are happy. But therein lies the rub. Is value added when the smiles are staged, when employees are constantly admonished to get out there with a smile? While strategic smiles may be good for business, are they good for the workers?

After new CEO Phillip Schaengold toured George Washington University Hospital in Washington, D.C., he announced that henceforth there would be service with a smile *or else*. All 1,700 hospital employees were trained in customer-friendly procedures, at the end of which they were required to sign a pledge to uphold standards of service excellence, including the stipulation to greet people with a smile. Failing to do so would result in termination. In China, failure to smile could even get you arrested—or it did for shopkeepers during the 2008 Olympic Games in Beijing.

Do positive displays by employees actually affect the bottom line? For a significant number of people in the hospitality

Smiling generates larger tips

business, the question is not trivial. Some 3 million waiters, waitresses, counter attendants, and bartenders in the United States depend on customer tips, which can represent up to 80 percent of their income. If they smile, their income goes up.

Tipping is the customer's half of the bargain in an unsigned contract in restaurants between diners and servers. For their part, good waiters and waitresses deliver more than food and drink; they deliver hospitality. Complimenting customers on their selections, for example, makes the customer feel good and leads to larger tips. And since they know that happy faces make people feel good, they smile. Indeed, the size of the smile may influence the size of the tip. In one experiment, researchers trained a waitress to show customers either a big smile or a small smile but otherwise to perform the same duties in the same way.

Customers on the receiving end of larger smiles left larger tips; customers receiving smaller smiles responded in kind with small tips.

Picking up a cappuccino on the way to work is as much a part of many people's morning ritual as brushing their teeth. In espresso bars, researchers have found that big smiles also made a big difference. Big toothy grins by baristas led to significantly higher customer satisfaction than smaller social smiles. Moreover, the researchers demonstrated that the big smiles caused the customer to smile more, which in turn made him or her even more satisfied. It is worth noting here that the big smiles were thoroughly intentional, but contagious nonetheless.

Businesses swap smiles for sales. They give customers a recognized "good" with the expectation that customers will hold up their end of the bargain by buying more or returning more often. Social scientists have measured whether this bartering works in everything from selling shoes to savings. In shoe stores, for example, observers noted how much clerks smiled at customers and whether the smiles received translated into more shoes being sold. Smiling was not directly related to shoe sales, but it was associated with more promises by customers to return and greater likelihood of recommending the store to a friend. At hotel reception desks, smiling works up to a point. If the check-in goes smoothly, then genuine smiles by the desk clerk lead to higher customer satisfaction. However, if the check-in process was slow, then positive facial expressions at reception did little to override guests' assessment that the service they received was lackadaisical.

Finally, teller-customer interactions were systematically observed in thirty-nine branch offices of a major bank in a southern region of the United States. Following what is now common practice, researchers observed how frequently tellers smiled at customers, and when customers left the bank, they were asked about their transaction in the bank. By now, this is not surprising news: the more tellers smiled at customers, the more positively customers evaluated the quality of service they had received.

When service is delivered with a smile, the currency is goodwill. And the smiles don't even have to be genuine, at least in some contexts. In the bank teller study, customer satisfaction was affected by how much the teller smiled, but there was no connection between what the tellers actually felt and how much they smiled. Their smiles occurred independently of how pleased they were. But this is not always the case—other studies have shown that only smiles perceived as sincere enhance customer satisfaction.

So, which is it? Should employees use the more-is-better strategy, that is, display lots of big beaming facial expressions without worrying too much about whether they seem genuine? Or should efforts be placed instead into making sure the smiles are sincere? One experiment actually set smile *quantity* against smile *quality* to see which led to more customer satisfaction. The investigators set up a movie rental service on a college campus. It looked like the real thing, complete with customers reviewing DVD cases, monitors playing trailers, display shelves, movie posters, and staff discussing whether a new release should be given a thumbs-up or a thumbs-down. In the experiment, employees (actually trained confederates) varied both how much they smiled at customers and how sincere their smiles were.

You might ask how does one deliberately produce a genuine smile, let alone enact a sincere smile one moment and a superficial smile the next. It's a methodological challenge, to say nothing of an existential dilemma. Researchers of course have ways to deal with the first. For the *superficial* smile condition, confederates were told to modify just their faces, their outward expression. Put a smile there. For the *sincere* smile, they were prompted to dig deep within themselves for real positive feelings and then let their faces reflect those feelings.

Each research subject encountered a person at the counter who showed either a superficial or a sincere smile that was either short-lived or occurred a number of times. Smile quality clearly won over smile quantity in the service satisfaction sweepstakes. When smiles were sincere, satisfaction with the service was significantly higher than when the smiles were just applied to the surface. Customers preferred the clerks who showed genuine smiles over those with pasted-on smiles, regardless of whether they smiled a lot or a little.

This debate between smile quality versus quantity is not yet settled since scientists have yet to determine what makes a smile seem sincere and when it matters. But in the meantime, even smiley faces help generate higher tips. One study showed that the presence of a smiley face drawn on the diners' check significantly increased the size of tips if the server was a waitress. Alas, a smiley face on the check did nothing to increase tips for waiters. I hope for their sake that those auditions work out.

Performance Smiles

The Walt Disney conglomerate probably provides more services with smiles than any other business in the world. Mickey Mouse has smiled across decades of appearances on screen and in costume and even through the period when animators felt the need to round his pointy, little rodent head. And its not just Mickey who is smiling. Disney theme park employees show the same unflagging smiles, whether in the United States, France, or Japan. Disney resorts, hotels, and cruise lines present omnipresent smiles to tourists and convention goers. Disney stores sell merchandise designed to generate smiles in children and adults alike, while Disney business centers teach employees of companies large and small its service with a smile system. And that does not include smiles generated by blockbuster Disney films, television productions, sports teams, franchise operations, CDs, books, magazines, and computer software. In Disney's world, "smiling is elevated to a philosophy of work and life."

Before Disney's "Magic Kingdoms" became a global business, there was Luna Park on Coney Island in New York, with its fantastical onion domes and minarets. Luna Park, America's first theme park, opened on May 16, 1903. Fred Thompson, the park's creator, understood the "cash value of smiles." He imagined Luna Park as a place for families that would generate "billion-dollar smiles," as he planned to take it from coast to coast.

At Disney, the service *is* the smile. In Disney theme parks across the world, each and every employee who has face-to-face contact with visitors must smile. They are required to be upbeat, and any semblance of impatience and irritation must immediately be adjusted with a smile.

When an employee is in a good mood, the spontaneous expression of positive emotions is child's play. In sales, there is an adage that selling starts when the customer says no. In the service industry, the work starts when the worker doesn't feel cheerful. Social scientists have labeled such work *emotion labor*. In her book *The Managed Heart*, Arlie Hochschild defined emotion labor as "the management of feeling to create a publicly observable facial and bodily display." Emotion labor is what employees do when they are required to feel, or to give the impression of feeling, the

Providing service with a smile

kind of emotions that employers want to see and customers are pleased to receive.

Performing Smiles

Managing what one feels and what one shows at work can be done in one of two ways: by *surface acting* or *deep acting*. Surface acting is a lot like putting on a uniform or appropriate attire to go to work. It is all about changing the surface, the appearance of feeling something rather than actually having good feelings about the customer having a good day.

Employees who surface act adopt, suppress, or modify what can be seen or heard—a pleasing smile, a friendly voice, a sympathetic head cant. That warm reception you got this morning from your personal trainer is likely an example of superb surface acting.

Deep acting, in contrast, involves creating or drawing on real feelings rather than merely crafting the appearance of them. One deep acting employee described it this way: "We try to stir up a feeling we wish we had and . . . try to block or weaken a feeling we wish we did not have." Deep acting means genuinely feeling good about being able to help, genuinely feeling delighted when customers find what they want, and genuinely sharing in a customer's pleasure at finding just the right thing. Since the goal in deep acting is to truly experience a desired emotion, it has been described as "faking in good faith."

In the early 1980s, Hochschild attended flight attendant school to observe how new employees become smiling "Deltoids." They began by learning how to surface act—to smile on cue, repeatedly. Smile when passengers are boarding and smile when they are deboarding; smile when passengers indicate what they want to drink or eat; smile when passengers ring the bell, smile when they want to change their seat, smile when they want a place for their suitcase, ask for a pillow, and so on. Some of you may remember when this actually happened on airplanes.

But I digress. Following basic training in surface acting, flight attendants graduated to deep acting. This involved learning how to draw on past experience, on memory, on fantasy, on imagination or whatever it took to generate happy feelings in the here and now. A surface acting flight attendant would deal with an obnoxious passenger by grinning and bearing it. A deep acting flight attendant would instead reimagine the passenger not as obnoxious but as an anxious and scared traveler a long way from home, who could use a little TLC.

But what if the smile itself is in some way flawed? Consider a *New York Times* story about a woman who was unable to find a decent job despite relevant work experience, solid skills, and exemplary work habits. Why? Because she had no teeth. "If she were not poor, she would not have lost her teeth, and if she had not lost her teeth, perhaps she would not have remained poor."

The Costs of Making Nice

A friend of mine recently had surgery at a renowned Boston hospital. In the hospital, he was more than a little cranky. Apparently, the health care workers taking his vitals, bringing meals, and changing his bed didn't smile. His questions about the absent smiles were rhetorical, "Would it hurt them to smile once in while?" and, "What would it cost them to smile?" But the answers are not. According to research on the effects of emotion labor, it sometimes hurts to smile—emotion labor can be an occupational hazard.

Service employees under the gun to smile often report that they cease to feel much of anything on or off the job. Flight attendants use the phrase to "go robot" to describe the deadened emotional state that happens when their private feelings and public behavior are too often out of sync. For service providers, real feelings disappear: "When conditions estrange us from our faces, they sometimes estrange us from feelings as well."

The adolescent protagonist in Carson McCullers's novel *The Heart Is a Lonely Hunter* describes a similar estrangement after long hours of waiting on people. "It was the small of her back and her face that got so tired. Their motto was supposed to be 'Keep on your toes and smile.' Once she was out of the store she had to frown a long time to get her face natural again."

Emotion labor becomes a problem when there is a breach between the feelings a company wants its employees to have and personal feelings that tend to have a mind of their own. Carried on too long, service employees may psychologically withdraw from the job and their own selves. They become cynical about the work they do, lose sleep over it, and may become depressed.

Fortunately, not all emotion laborers experience emotional dissonance. Some actually thrive on being nice to customers. This obviously complicates the simple conclusion that emotion labor is damaging to anyone who does it over the long haul. For social scientists, it has meant examining when emotional labor has adverse consequences and when it does not.

Does it make a difference whether the emotion labor is on the surface or is in the emotional depths? Surface acting might seem to entail less emotional wear and tear since adopting a called-for facial expression would seem to involve less effort. Deep acting would seem more demanding since it requires putting one's whole heart into being friendly. But the empirical evidence shows otherwise. A study involving many service employees found that feigning positive feelings was more emotionally exhausting than digging deep to find the real emotion. It seems that service workers become more, not less, stressed by "faking it."

Who would have thought that faking a smile is more exhausting than adopting Method acting? Konstantin Stanislavsky, the originator of Method acting, could have been commenting on deep acting on the job when he wrote that "The great actor should be full of feeling, and especially he should feel the thing he is portraying. He must feel an emotion not only once or twice while he is studying his part, but to a greater or lesser degree every time he plays it, no matter whether it is the first or the thousandth time." If service workers throw themselves completely into their roles, if they become the Marlon Brandos of the service sector, they may put in more effort but they will not feel alienated; instead, they are likely to feel pride in their accomplishment.

Are Cheerful Service Providers Born or Made?

You've seen them—tour guides, concierges, or maître d's whose smiles snap on and off like a toggle switch. Then there are service providers who do the opposite—their smiles are gracious and genuine. I have a friend who takes people on tours of Mexico and does it in a way that makes clients feel as though they toured with a very knowledgeable companion. I once asked her where all her enthusiasm came from. She said it had to do with her mother. It wasn't that her mother set a great example; actually, she was not an especially good model. Rather, as a five-year-old, my friend was already making tea and bringing it to her mother. She learned that she would be loved if she made her mother happy. Maybe she would be loved if she made others happy, too. However, even those who love helping people have their moments when they need to act. Nonetheless, terrific tour guides never let travelers know that the job can sometimes be a chore.

Many service-oriented establishments would give their eye-teeth to have employees like my friend because the affability is mostly not an act. They derive sustenance and satisfaction from being able to make others happy. In psychological terms, the regulation of positive emotion for such people is *automatic*. They are "born" that way, not in the sense that they pop out of the womb ready to go sing: "Hi, ho, hi, ho. It's off to work we go." Rather, they are inclined to find encounters with others rewarding—an inclination that is likely a self-reinforcing combination of temperament and experience. For others, the regulation of positive emotion is *controlled*, that is, it takes deep acting to make it happen.

One recent study examined automatic and controlled emotion

in a sample of family doctors. Three hundred and forty-five physicians answered questions about how they communicated positive emotion to their patients, how emotionally exhausted they felt, and how satisfying they found the interactions. The doctors' responses were remarkably similar to those of other service providers. The more surface acting they did, the more emotionally exhausted they felt. The more they put on a positive front, the more they felt like they were putting out a lot and getting little in return. This was self-reinforcing, causing interactions with patients to be even more exhausting and unsatisfying. In contrast, those doctors who truly felt positive emotions reported expending less effort with patients and receiving more positive rewards from them.

So, how does a service organization implement service with a smile? Should it set its divining rod on naturally cheerful people, or should it go the instructional route and develop training programs for employees in how to produce smiles on demand?

Some companies clearly opt for a search strategy with face-valid criteria. Holiday Inn, for example, winnowed 5,000 job applicants down to 500 by applying this rule: any candidate who did not smile at least four times during the job interview was automatically out. Greyhound Lines used a similar selection rule: candidates for its customer service center needed to smile at least five times during a fifteen-minute interview to get the job.

Other companies rely more heavily on employee training to produce smiling in their service reps. One successful restaurateur calls this the 5–90–5 rule, which breaks down this way: 5 percent are born good service providers; another 5 percent cannot or will not ever give good service no matter how much training they get; and in between is the 90 percent that can give good and cheerful service if they are provided with the right training.

MIT professor John Van Maanen memorably described Disney employee training as the "smile factory." A Disney education involves total immersion in the Disney philosophy. Trainees hear examples of how other cast members have made guests smile. One alert employee, noticing a child's distress because a broken button was causing her shorts to fall down, whisked the child and accompanying parent off to the Disney store, where a new pair of shorts was provided free of charge. Disney training is deep acting writ large: trainees come to identify with the parks' purpose ("You're here because you care"). By so doing they can expect substantial emotional rewards. Just in case they forget, there are posted reminders: "Do you know where your smile is?"

Some establishments do not screen for cheerful employees or implement training programs to produce smiles but leave it to veteran employees to teach newcomers how to provide friendly service without losing themselves in the act. In fire stations, for instance, novice firefighters ("Booters") learn by observation, hazing, and a few well-placed insults. The first thing they learn is to keep their emotions in check, especially in chaotic and dangerous situations. The second thing they hear is that the public is always watching. This means, for example, that they need to remain cheerful even when a situation requiring their attention is a minor one.

In bars, restaurants, and hospitals, new hires learn from veterans not only how to act but also how to survive emotionally. In law firms, new paralegals learn from those who have been around for a while. In all these industries, a considerable amount of emotion work goes into suppressing anger and frustration in the face of difficult, irascible, and entitled customers and bosses. The ones who survive learn to hold a smile out front and wait to rant until they are out of range.

Buying and Selling Smiles

Lest we forget: customers are not passive bystanders in service encounters or sales situations. They are part of the social transaction. They can be pleasant and appreciative, but they can also be demanding and demeaning. It takes extra emotion labor to deal with the latter. Being able to take a customer's rant with equanimity is no small achievement since the usual course of social relations follows a tit-for-tat strategy. Is it too far-fetched to think about training consumers to smile?

Even though sales and service smiles begin intentionally, with practice and repetition they may become automatic. But whether these smiles have the emotional depth of an automatic teller machine or Pavarotti singing "*Nessun Dorma*" comes down to the qualities in the smile itself. If, in the words of Jonathan Franzen, it is possible to see "the hydraulics" of the smile, then emotion contagion is not going to happen.

Service smiles are produced with purpose. They sometimes verge on the genuine due to considerable practice and serious commitment, but it would be good not to forget that smiles-with-service are a means to an end. The friendly reception you receive upon checking into a hotel may be warm and welcoming, but you are a customer, not cherished company. The context of a smile provides important clues as to whether it is genuinely felt or a superb forgery.

LOYALTY

real men don't smile

On October 3, 1861, nineteen-year-old John Williams enlisted in the Union Army to fight in the American Civil War. Some time later, he was discharged on the grounds of breaking a cardinal Army rule—"he proved to be a woman." Charles Freeman was similarly discharged for "sexual incompatibility" when hospital doctors, treating Freeman for a serious fever, discovered that he was actually she, known formerly as Mary Scaberry.

The number of women who masqueraded as men in the Civil War is unknown. A few were discovered whilst being prepared for burial, during medical examination, or as prisoners of war. For the most part, however, neither their behavior nor their appearance gave them away. They changed their names, donned the uniform (padding and binding where necessary), cut their hair, and learned to smoke, swear, and drink like . . . well, soldiers. This was usually sufficient since physical exams, although theoretically required, were seldom carried out. Following common practice, soldiers slept in their uniforms and bathed in their underwear. If some were thought to look a little too fresh-faced, they were mostly indistinguishable from underage male recruits, of whom there were many. This history teaches one lesson: most of the time we "know" a person's sex not by seeing their genitalia but by inferring what it is from appearance and demeanor. How an individual smiles is a significant part of demeanor and thus has consequences for gender identity and identification.

For the most part, neither behavior nor appearance gave female soldiers in the Civil War away. One imposter, however, Margaret Catherine Murphy, a member of the Ohio Infantry, was found out when she laughed. Her merriment was judged to be unmistakably feminine. Only a woman would laugh like that. Besides laughing in different ways, women and men are assumed to differ in ways too many to mention. When a man is described as "throwing like a girl," the implication is not only that women throw baseballs differently (less well) than men, but that the difference is more deep-seated and immutable than one's clothes or hair length. Gender impostors are eventually exposed, the thinking goes, because women and men have such manifestly different bodies and brains that their authentically gendered selves will out in the end.

But historical facts about real soldiers, not to mention fictional gender imposters, such as *Tootsie*, *Dame Edna*, *Viola*, *M. Butterfly*, and *Mrs. Doubtfire*, are reminders that displays of gender are performances that everyone knows. In real life as well as on stage, most of us know how to do this convincingly.

The popular and scientific press cannot of course stop offering dispatch after dispatch about the ways in which women and men profoundly differ from each other. Talk of sex differences is everywhere and touches on everything from nicotine effects in male and female mice to the ethics of female and male business managers. While scientific reports of sex differences are omnipresent, understanding their causes and grasping the ramifications are not. *Why* do men smile less than women? *Why* is

Sarah Edmond Seeley (left) enlisted in the Union Army as Frank
Thompson (right)

femininity connected with being emotional while manliness is
not? *Why* does it matter so much that we be able to immediately
spot who is female and who is male and think that something is
wrong if we cannot? *What if* femininity and masculinity are independent of femaleness and maleness? As you will see, how much a
person smiles and when and with whom tells us much about how
gender is performed in everyday social encounters.

Smile Like a Lady

The first thing people want to know when a baby is born, even
before confirming that it has ten fingers and ten toes, is whether
it is a boy or a girl. Once the sex is identified, gender expectations click into place, covering everything from how fast or frequently an individual blinks (women should do more) to how
much he or she should invest in a career (women should do less).

Our assumptions about men and women, boys and girls, extend as well to whether emotion should be expressed or suppressed. Gender stereotypes do not just reside tucked away in our brains, but alter our conduct toward everyone, especially babies, often precipitating precisely the behavior we were expecting. This is the way socialization happens.

Parents often describe their baby daughters as softer, finer-featured, smaller, cuter, prettier; sons a mere few hours old are seen as tough little things, ready to take on the world. A recent study showed for probably the hundredth time that parents continue to have clear sex-differentiated perceptions of their newborns. Daughters are perceived to be more affectionate; sons are perceived to be more adventurous.

We do not yet have evidence that girl babies smile more than boy babies. Before long, however, girls begin outsmiling boys. When any sex difference shows up later in development, the social environment has likely played a part in determining or shaping it. In what came to be called the "Baby X" studies, researchers showed how gender expectations generate behavior. Some research participants were told that the infant in the film they were about to watch was a boy while others were told the infant was a girl. In the film, a nine-month-old baby interacts with a Teddy bear, a doll, a buzzer, and a jack-in-the-box. When the adults were questioned about what they thought the baby felt with each object, the infant's assumed sex affected how its emotional reactions were described. For example, the infant believed to be a boy startled in reaction to the jack-in-the-box: "he" was described as angry, whereas "she" was described as fearful.

In a study in which adults interacted with real infants, the sex of the baby was kept from participants or misrepresented to them. The infants were dressed in yellow or green baby suits

(I personally would have preferred something like chocolate brown). Again, expectations provided a lens through which the baby's behavior was interpreted and understood. If the baby smiled, participants guessed it was a girl, regardless of the infant's actual sex. If the baby fretted, subjects were more likely to think it was a boy.

The expectations about which sex smiles and which frowns do not end at childhood, although the size of the smiling difference between the sexes varies across the lifespan. My colleagues and I reviewed studies examining smiling from early teens to elderly adults and found that females smile significantly more than males when they are in their late teens and as young adults. After that, the differences fall off substantially, and they are gone by the time men and women are in their fifties. In short, not surprisingly, at the time in life when females and males are most sexually interested in each other, the males smile very little compared to the females. Smiling is a reliable gender identity marker at precisely the moment that one needs to be reliably marked.

Real Men Don't Smile

Copious studies carried out over several decades have converged on the finding that women smile more than men. That is not to say that the difference is huge or present everywhere you look—and social scientists have looked in lots of places. Researchers have coded the presence of smiling in thousands of photographs in scores of high school and college yearbooks, newspapers and online images, print and electronic advertisements, Facebook pages and annual reports. The finding again and again is that girls and women are more likely than boys and men to smile when their pictures are taken.

Researchers have also examined everyday conversations where people are involved in talking about current events, arguing about politics, collaborating on projects, engaging in getting-acquainted interactions, or simply sitting quietly in a waiting room. And they have examined smiling in the real world—in restaurants, meeting rooms, offices, conferences, on street corners, and in classrooms. Both indoors and out, males are statistically less likely than females to return a smile aimed in their direction, and especially less likely to reciprocate a smile when it comes from another male. So established is this sex difference that social psychologists regard a smile as the default facial expression for females and impassivity as the usual facial display for males.

But before I get ahead of myself, I need to mention a couple of caveats to the pattern that women smile more than men. First, the difference occasionally reverses itself such that in some contexts men smile more than women. More about these situations in a moment. Second, differences among men and among women in how much they smile are often greater than the average difference between men and women.

Muscles, Hormones, and Smiles

A few years back, researchers discovered that the primary smile muscle, the *zygomaticus major* muscle, was significantly thicker in women then in men. That this should be so is not surprising, given that women smile more than men. But a thicker facial muscle does not tell us how it got to be that way. Are women born with a thicker zygomaticus—the muscle which allows them to hit the ground running with a smile fused to their faces—or does the *zygomaticus major* bulk up in women due to all the practice they are encouraged to get? Or might it be that the muscle in some males atrophies from disuse?

A few men are sourpusses a good deal of the time, while others have really great smiles that are turned on frequently. What would account for these differences? Let's start with that quintessential male hormone, testosterone. Men vary amongst themselves in how much testosterone they have coursing through their bodies. Men with high levels tend to be more dominant in their social interactions, are observed to be more combative more of the time, and are more likely to sport tattoos than men with lower average levels of testosterone.

Men with high levels of testosterone are also averse to smiling. This was shown in a wonderfully simple study. After measuring testosterone levels in a sample of men from saliva samples, each man was photographed twice, once with the instruction not to smile, simply to adopt a neutral face, and then again with the simple instruction, "Okay, now smile." The higher the level of a man's testosterone, the less likely he was to give a full smile when asked to do so. In his book *Heroes, Rogues, and Lovers*, Professor James Dabbs indicated that even in the relatively rare cases when men with high testosterone levels smiled when he asked them to, the smiles he did get he described as "wolfish" in character. Interestingly, "wolfish" is the same word used by Dashiell Hammett to describe his tough private detective, Sam Spade, who is said to have yellow-gray eyes and a wolfish grin.

Instead of using the term *wolfish* to describe a particular group of men, psychologists use the term *unrestricted sociosexuality*. Ever since Alfred Kinsey's groundbreaking research on sexuality, investigators have noted that there is a wide spectrum describing people's interest in having sexual relations unencumbered by being in a relationship. At one end of the scale there are men

A "wolfish" smile

with unrestricted sociosexuality who are drawn to having sex free
of emotional attachment. These men report that they have many
current and anticipated sex partners, more one-night stands,
more positive attitudes toward casual sex, and a greater likelihood of having sex outside an existing relationship. Men at the
other end of the scale, those with a more *restricted sociosexuality*,
like sex as much as the next man but prefer to have it within the
bounds of an ongoing intimate relationship.

Personality psychologists speculated that men high in sociosexuality might be more inclined to smile as part of a general
seduction strategy, a smile offensive, as it were. To test this
idea, investigators set up a dating game scenario in the lab.
They brought men one at a time into a room in which an attractive woman interviewed them. Some of these men had scored
at the unrestricted end of the sociosexuality scale while others
were more circumspect with respect to choice of sex partners.
Men high in unrestricted sociosexuality clearly saw the interview as a sexual opportunity and brought the full force of their

grins to make it happen. They smiled significantly more at the attractive female interviewer than did their less single-minded counterparts. It was not that these men were particularly smiley people—they did not smile more with other people. Rather, when presented with a pertinent sexual situation (attractive woman, potential date), their grinning shifted into high gear. As the researchers described it, they were "contact ready"—one of the world's great euphemisms.

Smile Expectations

In Jane Austen's *Pride and Prejudice*, one character advises another that a woman would do better to show more affection than she feels. Boys get the opposite advice. By the time they turn ten, boys in the United States are already practicing "cool"; to do otherwise risks being taken for a wimp. Advice to girls about what expressions they should show differs somewhat, since girls are required to express a range of feelings with their faces while boys basically work on not showing much of anything. The doyenne of etiquette, Emily Post, insisted that females learn how to smile naturally: "A smile should be spontaneous . . . [because] nothing has less allure than a mechanical grimace."

These social rules—women show feeling; men suppress feeling—are there for a reason. When women don't smile or men smile too much, they risk being booed off the social stage. California governor Arnold Schwarzenegger once derided recalcitrant male members in the other political party as "girlie men." The silent film star Rudolph Valentino was scoffed at by men because he smiled too much, although female fans loved his portrayal of the grinning *Sheik*.

So well known are these rules that women anticipate criticism

if they don't smile. In my lab, we asked male and female undergraduates to imagine themselves in a variety of social situations,
and to consider how others would react if they did not smile. A
friend tells you about getting a great job offer; you say congratu-
lations, but say it with a neutral facial expression. We found that
females more than males believe that bystanders will think less
well of them for not responding with a positive facial expression.
When males imagined not smiling in similar circumstances they
thought hardly anyone would notice.

Indeed, one of the most common forms of street catcall-
ing involves men asking women walking down the street why
they're not smiling, or congratulating them for having a pretty
smile. Female dancers, ice skaters, waitresses, and nurses all
are expected to smile; a failure to do so would seem a little like a
failure to do one's job. Objecting to the expectation that women
smile all the time—and thus project an unthreatening, affable,
attractive servility—was one of the issues that helped earn second
wave feminism its reputation as chilly.

One way we know that people are following expressive rules is
because they change when they realize that others are watching. One experiment looked at the facial expressions of men and
women when photographs were taken of them under either posed
or candid conditions. When they posed for the pictures, women
on average smiled more than men. But when their pictures were
taken without their being aware of it, women were found to smile
with the same frequency. When people sense that others are
watching, the men damp down their cheerful expressions and
the women turn up their expressive wattage. Tom Wolfe nicely
captured these gender differences in a scene from his novel *I Am*

Charlotte Simmons: " 'What college do you go to?' and he would say as evenly and tonelessly as possible, 'Dupont,' and then observe the reaction. Some, especially women . . . smile, their faces would brighten . . . while others, especially men, would tense up and fight to keep their faces from revealing how impressed they were."

Being male does not, of course, rule out smiling. In truth, there are occasions when smiling is actually the best way to convey that one's masculinity is firmly in place. When men laugh at fear or smile under duress, the message is that they have everything under control. In his book *Manliness*, Harvard professor Harvey Mansfield declared that true manliness is marked by "confidence in the face of risk." What could be a better expression of confidence than smiling when the going gets tough? Think Bruce Willis's smirk, Clint Eastwood's thin-lipped grin ("Go ahead, make my day!"), Humphrey Bogart's frozen-lip sneer, and John Wayne's laconic smile as he one-handedly spins his rifle. In describing his attempt to imitate Gary Cooper's smile in the western *Vera Cruz*, Sam Shepard wrote: "For days I practiced in the backyard. . . . Sneering. Grinning that grin. Sliding my upper lip over my teeth." It takes a lot of effort and practice to look completely unconcerned.

Ordinary, non-matinée-idol men also smile to demonstrate how unflappable they are. In one study, participants watched some ghastly video clips containing scenes of human dissections, tribal animal sacrifices, and insects devouring each other. Participants either viewed the clips alone or with a male or female stranger. Many men responded by laughing and smiling. In contrast, women's faces frequently displayed repulsion. But back to the men: they smiled the most when a male stranger was in the room with them. Indeed, the presence of another man doubled how much the men smiled compared to when they saw

the disturbing material when they were alone. The male participants were not conscious of changing their behavior, yet it was
clear that they did not want to be caught looking bothered when
another man might see it.

In short, a man smiles to show that he can look terror in the face
and snicker at it. "What, me care?" displays are often seen among
young men on "dares," at horror movies, and on amusement park
rides. It's worth noting that when men are asked to explain why
they do not show much feeling much of the time, many are ada-
mant that they feel things deeply and could express what they feel
if they wanted to, and if there was a good reason to. It's just that
there are few reasons to smile and many for not smiling—which
shows again that men have different smile scripts from women.
Males, especially young adult males, are pleased to report that
they often suppress emotional expression of any kind.

Lest we think that males are unique in suppressing their
smiles, women have also been known to dampen their smiles
if a situation calls for them to show that they are not "typical"
females. For example, female police officers intentionally refrain
from smiling in the company of fellow officers. They know just
as male officers know that smiling could convey a dropping of
guard or loosening of defenses—not something police officers
want to be seen doing. Members of girl gangs who want to be seen
as "macha" also wouldn't be caught dead smiling.

The usual dynamic is that females smile in the company of
others and especially so when the social task is to demonstrate
niceness. Girls and women are more likely than boys and men
to smile when they receive a disappointing gift—a performance
they use their whole lives, along with writing all those thank-you
notes. Depressingly, smiling in the face of disappointment is
something girls learn to show as early as age five.

Masculine Men, Feminine Women, and In-Betweens

For a great number of men, masculinity entails rejecting in themselves anything that could be construed as remotely feminine. In similar fashion, many women see femininity as the exact opposite of masculinity, and so feel they must avoid any semblance of self-sufficiency. Psychologists unfortunately have often abetted this either/or thinking by designing tests of gender identity that have masculinity and femininity opposite to each other. Masculine males and feminine females receive the psychological seal of approval while feminine males and masculine females are labeled abnormal.

The thinking that males and females are polar opposites was typically applied to any psychological disposition. If one sex was emotional, then the other sex was believed to be—in fact, had to be—unemotional. If one sex was brave, then the other was necessarily frightened. Since women were regarded as the emotional sex, men should stay very far away from unseemly displays of emotion. That was the state of things in psychology until Professor Sandra Bem at Cornell University and other psychologists proposed an alternative to the view of masculinity and femininity as opposites. Instead, masculinity and femininity were envisioned as separate and potentially co-existing qualities. Consequently, any individual could manifest traits typically identified as masculine *and* feminine. An individual could be, for instance, both competitive and compassionate, both independent and sociable.

Professor Bem went further, arguing that when an individual incorporated both masculine and feminine attributes, he or she was psychologically healthier and more socially flexible than a person who vowed lifetime fidelity to one domain and forever rejected anything to do with the other one. She called people possessing both sets of traits *androgynous*. Those who stuck with male and masculine, or female and feminine, she termed *sex-typed males* and *sex-typed females*, respectively. The sex-typed man, aligning himself with masculinity, would prohibit or inhibit anything remotely feminine in himself, just as the sex-typed female, completely identified with femininity, would shun anything masculine in herself. Androgynous individuals, being less bound by traditional gender scripts, are more flexible and better able to adapt to situations, possessing as they do a larger repertoire from which to draw.

In my lab, we examined whether differences in gender identity were embodied in facial behavior. Does a person's level of masculinity or femininity literally manifest itself in one's face? We measured subjects' gender identification by asking them to rate how much each of sixty traits described themselves. Some traits were associated with masculinity—"assertive" and "independent"—while others were associated with femininity—"affectionate" and "sympathetic."

We then videotaped participants as they talked. We found that sex-typed males (masculine-identified males) and sex-typed females (feminine-identified females) followed gender scripts to the letter. They showed high numbers of behaviors associated with their own sex and scant behavior linked with the other sex. As expected, feminine females smiled the most; masculine males smiled the least; and the two androgynous groups fell midway and did not differ from each other.

Psychologists now agree that gender is a complex construct, made up of at least three dimensions: sex in the biological sense; sexual orientation in terms of the sex of preferred sexual partners; and gender identity in the psychological sense. In short, gender is more complicated than a simple male/female distinction implies.

When it comes to psychological gender, it is not which sex you are that matters but how strongly you identify with characteristics that society calls "masculine" or "feminine." To the extent that a person sees him- or herself as compassionate, affectionate, and sensitive, that is, identifies with "femininity," then she or he is more likely to smile. Ask not what sex a person is, but rather watch how much they smile.

Transgender Identities

Gender identity is but one of several variations on the purported dichotomy between male and female. Previously, a blend of gender attributes within the same person was frowned on, and in many parts of the world it still is. A female working in a man's job; a man wearing kinky boots; a man taking female hormones or a woman desiring to live as a man; a person of either sex longing to be in the clothes or body of the other sex—all have been seen as requiring psychological intervention to "cure" them. We know now that most of these are normal variations, which, if not always acceptable in a societal sense, are nonetheless understood to be part of the gender spectrum. Even though biology loves variability, many societies deplore it.

Some women, as we saw earlier, impersonated men during the American Civil War. But this was not an anomalous event. Women lived as men in the nineteenth and early twentieth centuries in order to pursue careers not open to them as women. Today, there is more leeway for individuals to dress in the clothes typically worn by the other sex. Psychologists continue to tussle with the question of whether transvestism has to do with sexuality or identity. For example, it is not uncommon for male transvestites to report feeling relaxed when freed, however temporally, of the demands for masculinity attendant on dressing in masculine apparel. Whatever complex factors underlie cross-dressing, it is troubling to some because transvestites challenge the rules that one should be identifiable on the basis of appearance.

Some cross-dressing is done in the light of day and some under the cover of darkness. At the closeted end of the spectrum are heterosexual men who keep their inclination to dress in women's apparel under wraps. Out front in broad daylight, on stage, and in film are female impersonators and drag queens. In "real life," RuPaul is a six foot eight inch bald man, but on stage, he's a knockout as a woman. Drag kings, women impersonating men, tend to be less familiar and make some people less comfortable. And that probably has something to do with the fact the people being parodied by drag kings are men. The performance artist Diane Torr, for example, reminds women as they leave her "guy-for-a-day" workshops to continue to do things they typically would not do as feminine females, like taking up physical space wherever they go and ditching any tendency to smile.

For many, the bending of gender has nothing to do with entertainment and everything to do with trying to piece mind and body together into a whole that makes sense. *Transsexuals* are people who experience an intense and long-standing disconnect between the sex of their bodies and their experience of being of the other sex. An FTM transsexual is a female who is transitioning to a male (called a transsexual man) and an MTF is a male transitioning to a female (called a transsexual woman). For those who choose complete sex reassignment surgery, most are required by law and professional standards to live as the reassigned sex for at least a year before surgery. Cross-dressing is just one of several activities transsexuals undertake during the transition from the

Jennifer Finney Boylas was a he and is now a she

sex they were labeled at birth to the physiological and anatomical sex change they seek.

During the transition period, and often long after, transsexuals work at acquiring the external characteristics and internal attributes of the reassigned sex. It takes attention and practice to acquire the gender-appropriate signs of the reassigned sex and to lose those that have been adopted by or forced on the person since birth. These include grooming, body language, speech patterns, and facial expressions. Non-transgendered people are often amazed at the lengths to which transgendered people will go to fashion a gender credible appearance. For instance, surveys of transsexuals find that many consider getting their demeanor right as important as, if not more important than, sex reassignment surgery, demonstrating how much of our gender identities

are tied up in our gestures, our movements, our physical expressions of attitude. MTFs often work at learning to smile often and
with animation, while FTMs work at squelching the inclination
to smile frequently.

Smiling on the Job

People compose their faces to fit the places where they find or
place themselves. When femininity is expected, count on seeing an abundance of smiles. Consider female figure skaters. The
Russian pairs coach Tamara Moskvina was quoted in the *San
Diego Union-Tribune* as saying of one of her female athletes, "She
was too serious. I told her that half the audience wanted to see her
more feminine . . . they want to see her more smiling. She always
looked at her partner like she was controlling him." Perish that
improperly balanced gender thought!

Then there's cheerleading, currently performed by more
than 3.8 million people in the United States, of whom 97 percent
are female. The perfect cheerleader is perky, peppy, and playful; smiling is as essential to the activity as pom-poms. It was
not always so. Through the nineteenth century and well into the
twentieth, cheerleaders were mostly men, and the required skill
was gymnastic ability. In the 1950s, requirements for cheerleaders changed as the sport transitioned from a primarily male to a
primarily female activity. Once women took over, cheerfulness, a
pleasant disposition, and good manners replaced gymnastic skill
as prerequisites.

Beyond specialized pursuits like figure skating and cheerleading, many real jobs thought to be women's work require the ability
and/or willingness to smile. Women are significantly more likely
than men to be in service and care-giving sectors: receptionists,

nurses, schoolteachers, secretaries, personal assistants, paralegals, and medical assistants.

Certain patterns set apart jobs for women from those thought
to be more appropriate for men. First, jobs in which women
are overwhelmingly represented are not as well paid as those
dominated by men. Second, smiling is frequently a professional
requirement. The fact that occupations slated for women have low
pay and a high cheeriness component has not gone entirely unno-
ticed, and therein lays some contentious research. But before I get
to that, a few words about the work women do and the centrality
of smiling while doing it.

Nurses do a lot of dirty work, and many do it with a smile—or
should. The United Kingdom's National Health Service recently
announced that nurses are to be rated on how kind and friendly
they are to patients. A book on nursing practice put it this way:
"Focus on your delivery of warmth." Smiling is apparently as
essential as being able to reliably read vital signs. It is thought to
be essential because it helps put patients at ease, draws them out
so that vital information can be acquired, enhances compliance
with medical advice, and overrides anonymity. Less pressure is
put on male nurses to smile, since their impassivity is interpreted
as emotional objectivity. Physicians have been advised to smile
more with patients, but for some reason it is not enthusiastically
endorsed by the doctors themselves. This may be because smiling
is so tightly bound up with notions of femininity, and femininity so tightly bound to inferiority, that the idea of smiling makes
doctors feel like they are diminishing their own power.

There is an ironic twist to the smiles of the fictional nurse in
One Flew Over the Cuckoo's Nest. Nurse Ratched smiles a great deal—
but her smiles are not associated with good bedside manners. Ken
Kesey describes how "she has the ability to turn her smile into

whatever expression she wants to use on somebody." Her grimace is a "painted smile [that] twists, stretches to an open snarl." At other times her smile "stretched tight and thin as a red-hot wire," or it went "out before her like a radiator grill."

Teaching is also considered women's work; over 70 percent of the 6.2 million teachers in the United States are female. Parents like to see their children happy at school, and so a teacher's smile is reassuring. One book advised parents who were checking out schools to look for bright clean spaces, a safe and secure environment, and especially for smiling teachers. When teachers appear as characters in children's storybooks, researchers find that although female teachers are shown in many body types and fashions, the feature common to figures we're supposed to recognize as good teachers is that they smile. Some old school educators believe that no good teacher ever smiles before Christmas break. Therein might lie a double bind for female teachers. Smile too much and risk being seen as unprofessional; smile too little and be seen as without care for or interest in children.

Still another underpaid occupation more typically employing women is that of the paralegal. Paralegals or legal assistants help lawyers prepare for closings, hearings, trials, and the like. But the sociologist Jennifer Pierce drew attention to a significant yet unacknowledged (and unpaid) part of the paralegal's job. Paralegals must bolster the emotional stability of the lawyers for whom they work. They take care of the lawyer by boosting his confidence, soothing his anxieties, cheering his achievements, and being pleasant all the time. This includes women lawyers too, at least those that make partner. "Being pleasant not only involves inducing a feeling . . . but also calls for a specific facial display—a smile."

There is little doubt that being affable is part and parcel of the many jobs that women do at higher rates than men. In *Just a Temp*, sociologist Kevin Henson showed that temporary workers, the majority of whom are women, must show outsized cheeriness, a willingness to cooperate and submit. This presents a bit of a problem for male temporary workers. Temps are required to present a demeanor that looks awfully like what women do, but gender scripts simultaneously require men to be masculine. The solution lies with the adage that clothes make the man: dress in a manner that is unambiguously masculine. In many temporary positions, men are required to wear shirts and ties so that all that smiling at least appears within the context of a masculine guise.

As soon as one reverses the usual work patterns or jobs for the sexes, there is an associated shift in the frequency of smiling. Some social roles call for smiling regardless of the gender of those who occupy them. Mothers most often care for the children, but primary caregiving fathers do exist, and they smile noticeably more than fathers who do not stay at home with their kids. Stay-at-home fathers actually smile the same amount as stay-at-home mothers. The role rather than the sex of caregiver is a good predictor of how much they will smile. Put men in roles more often done by women, and lo and behold, we would have more cheerful-looking men (although they probably would earn less than they do otherwise).

Smiles of Love and Lust

Romantic relationships exemplify a large set of facial expressions. Joy and smiling, yes, but also anger and tears. Shall we start at love's beginning? Even before words are spoken, fleeting smiles flicker across faces and are often enough to get the ball rolling. Later, the sight of a new love can provoke a smile that simply cannot be stopped. Smiles burst out during brief and unbidden surges of love in couples who have been together for a long time. Private smiles sent and received across a room at a crowded gathering verify that a special bond doesn't happen everyday. If there is little smiling, doubts may surface about the future of the liaison. And when former smiles begin to look more like smirks, the death knell for a relationship may be at hand.

Smiles of various forms and frequencies are a good way to gauge the state of a union, typically—sometimes terrifyingly— with greater accuracy than the words being spoken. As signals of love, smiles are without peer. It is no surprise that couples who exchange frequent smiles report being more satisfied than couples showing fewer or non-reciprocated smiles. In truth, romantic partners who cannot muster smiles and laughter are the same ones whose accounts begin to diverge about when, how, and even why they got together in the first place.

Satisfied and stable couples do not smile constantly; if they do, something other than their relationship has probably taken center stage. Couples also feel and express impatience, irritation, anger, and pain when in close relationships, but psychologists believe that if there are sufficient positive expressions there is little need for concern. In fact, the respected couples' researcher John Gottman proposed and tested a mathematical equation for the right ratio of smiling to grimacing in a good relationship. He studied thousands of couples and determined that when spouses exceed a ratio of one negative exchange for every five positive exchanges, they are headed for trouble. Other signs of probable fracture include pervasive criticism, contempt, stonewalling, and defensiveness.

Researchers have focused almost exclusively on the communication patterns of heterosexual couples, but Gottman is one of the few who has extended studies of romantic love to gay and lesbian couples. As with straight pairs, he examined interactions in which partners were asked to discuss a conflict in their relationship. Interestingly, he found fewer expressions of negative affect and more humor among gay and lesbian partners than in heterosexual pairs.

Is it love or is it sex? Does the kind of smile reflect the difference? Theories abound among scientists and nonscientists alike as to differences between being in love and being in lust. Some believe that when it comes to true romantic love, it is not possible to have one without the other. Others contend that love and sexual desire could not be more different from each other. Romantic love can take hold without sexual desire and sexual desire can be amply manifest without a shred of romantic love. Social psychologists theorize that deep love and passionate sexual attraction exhibit clearly distinctive experiences and physiology, as well as types of smiles.

For example, researchers asked Caucasian, Asian-American, and Latino heterosexual and monogamous couples to discuss various events in their lives, including their first date and the relationships that preceded the one they were currently in. When the video recordings of the conversations were analyzed, several nonverbal cues distinguished the couples very much in love from those who were very much in lust. The more in love, the more they showed Duchenne smiles in each other's company. On the other hand, people who reported high levels of sexual desire but not a whole lot of love showed fewer Duchenne smiles and a substantial number of other lip actions (e.g., lip bites, lip licks). The researchers interpreted these latter variations as signals that demarcated different kinds of intimacy. Individuals in intimate relationships need to know and convey that they are committed to the relationship. Duchenne smiles communicate the desire to be close; lip actions communicate arousal and passion.

These results may appear at odds with the finding described earlier that men high in sociosexuality smiled a lot while interacting with an attractive woman. Two features differentiate these studies. First, the study associating more smiling with sociosexuality involved only men, while the present study included men and women. Second, the former study grouped all smiles into one batch, while the present study distinguished between types and found that only Duchenne smiles marked couples high in love.

Smile Boycotts

All is not love or lust in the smiles that pass between women and men. Smiles also show up in relationship work mostly done by women. Researchers find that women laugh and smile more often when they are observers, especially when the speaker is male. Studies show too that happily married women and men report comparable levels of commitment but different rates of smiling. This happens because the wives smile and look at their husbands significantly more than their husbands do at them. It's tempting, here, to consider Virginia Woolf's observation that "Women have served all these centuries as looking glasses possessing the magic and delicious power of reflecting the figure of man, at twice its natural size."

Could greater smiling by women even stave off divorce? The intensity of people's smiles in over 1,500 college yearbook photographs was correlated with participants' subsequent marital status. Women who smiled less intensely when they were younger were more likely later to have had a divorce. We can only speculate why this association was found. One guess is that when women follow social scripts that call for them to smile more, everyone is happier because the status quo is maintained. It could also be that happier women smile when they are young and continue to be happier when they are older and married.

Men like to see women smile. Studies have repeatedly demonstrated that they are considerably more attracted to a woman who smiles. Such smiles may signal openness to having sex or simple confirmation that the gender order is operating normally. Indeed, a female character in Raymond Chandler's *Farewell, My Lovely* obliges private detective Philip Marlowe by giving him "a smile he could feel in his hip pocket." Men expect women to smile and women know that men expect them to smile. Social psychologists have demonstrated how easily informal expectations mutate into rules, from "It's nice to see a woman smile," to, "There's something wrong when a woman won't smile."

A few years ago, the Safeway supermarket chain instituted a policy stipulating that employees were henceforth to smile at customers. Not every employee was pleased at the prospect of showing indiscriminate smiles. In fact, several female employees filed a grievance over the smile rule. They complained that they were being propositioned by male shoppers who mistook company-required friendliness for flirting.

Their complaints have a scientific basis. Several studies have found that what a woman intends as being friendly is often construed by men as reflecting sexual interest. Regardless of how little her behavior connotes a desire for sex, men see a woman smile and are inclined to interpret it as flirting. In contrast, when women see a man smiling, they do not tend to see it as a reflection of sexual interest and are more likely to see it as a gracious or supportive gesture.

People want women to smile, and this expectation is frequently

met. What harm can there possibly be in a woman smiling—
besides the occasional misperception by men that her smile
means something other than what it actually does? Alas, even
when it's the last thing she wants to do, a woman is expected to
smile. We have found in our studies that women smile even when
they are being sexually harassed while being interviewed for a
job. These smiles do not reflect pleasure at the unwanted attention but are grin-and-bear-it smiles. The more a woman showed a
"social" smile, the more angry she described being, and the more
sexist she rated the interviewer. Women who were interviewed,
but not harassed, showed few of these grin-and-bear-it smiles
and held a more positive view of the interviewer.

There is more. We took video segments from the interviews,
deleted the sound track, and showed them to business students
who were asked to evaluate the interviewees. Did they seem competent? Would they hire them? Unfortunately for the sexually
harassed applicants who showed the social smiles, the observers rated them as less competent, less bright, and expressed less
interest in hiring them.

We also found that male observers were pretty bad at telling
the difference between women's genuine smiles and deliberate
social smiles, and their errors seem self-serving. More often
than not, men mistook women's social smiles for genuine pleasurable smiles. This does not bode well for women in work or professional contexts. Women are expected to smile and are judged
rather severely if they do not. But if they smile, there is a good
chance it could be misinterpreted as sexual or judged as profes-
sionally inappropriate.

A deliberate smile by someone in an awkward situation is
understandable. But tell that to a potential boss who may regard
it as unprofessional. There is no easy way out of this double bind.

If women smile too much, they are perceived as too feminine, and hence not fit for top-level leadership positions; but if they don't smile enough, questions are raised about their quality as human beings.

It is inconceivable that one man would say to another man he does not know, "Give us a little smile." Yet women and girls regularly hear this from complete strangers. In the *Harvard Law Review*, Cynthia Bowman argued the case that being told to smile by persons unknown infringes on a person's right to go about their business. She labeled this behavior and others in the same category (whistles, catcalls, touching) "street harassment." It is harassment, she contends, because people must be able to assume that they can be in public spaces without having their personal space violated. Whether the woman targeted by the directive to smile complies, ignores, or challenges it is irrelevant. Being directed to do something with one's own body by a stranger is an intrusion, a reminder if you will that women's bodies are too often seen as available to others. The smiles people want to see from women are for their own benefit, not the benefit of the women. It is no wonder then that psychologists have found that street harassment causes emotional reactions from mild aggravation to intense fear.

People are supposed to act their age, and even more strongly to act their gender. Most everyone is happier when others follow gender scripts, even if it is all an act. We expect to see smiling women and non-smiling men unless there are good reasons to the contrary. Each person's task is to learn how to show gender-based expressions and demeanor well enough that it all seems spontaneous and natural. Failure to perform elicits serious consequences—exclusion, derision, or punishment. This is theater of the people, by the people, with each of us as audience and performer.

If it all goes according to plan, then each person becomes their own self-socialization agent. We watch and perform and monitor. Oscar Wilde once declared while a man's face is his autobiography, a woman's face is her work of fiction. He was partly right—the facial expressions of both men and women are works of fiction, but no less true for that. Even if females come prepared to smile more than men, it's impossible to overestimate how much culture, temperament, family upbringing, social roles, and occupational demands affect the frequency with which anyone smiles. Most females and males have the capacity to smile or not, and both sexes have the psychological and physical elasticity to smile however much is called for.

smiles with a foreign accent

Near the end of the four-hour-long opening ceremony for the 2008 Olympic Games in Beijing, still one more legion of performers ran onto the field, this time hoisting enormous photographs of beaming children. The pictures, culled by the Smiling Faces Collection Office, reflected the global response to the Olympics organizing committee's call for pictures of happy-faced children.

From a bird's-eye view, it was a trove of cheerful faces; yet on closer examination, enormous variety was evident. The audience had previously been treated to masses of performers (literally casts of thousands) in identical costumes choreographed to move in perfect unison. Instead, here were photographs of children with idiosyncrasies galore. Ears sticking out here, a front tooth or two missing there, eyes agape or squeezed shut, chin and cheek dimples, and a whole spectrum of colors. But beneath all the diversity the core theme was plain as the nose on your face: children's smiles are universal and unifying.

While it is true that people show welcoming smiles across the planet, smiles do not necessarily unify people across cultural and ethnic divides. Smile at the wrong person in some parts of the world and you are as likely to get in trouble as in the door. Smile too little elsewhere and be seen as unforgivably rude. A smile is more complicated than its pleasantness and universality imply. Each culture puts its own spin on how it does smiles. And there are rules for when and where one is encouraged to or prohibited from smiling. Among Chinese merchants there is a saying that if one cannot smile, then one should not open a store; but in some Muslim countries, smiling at customers is seriously frowned upon, as it might imply sexual interest. Some groups prize the rare smile while others think the infrequent smiles bespeak malcontents. The poet Rupert Brooke said of one English city: "For Cambridge people rarely smile / Being urban, squat, and packed with guile."

In Northern Europe, one does not smile at strangers. Russians and Poles refrain from grinning at unfamiliar people and are suspicious if an unfamiliar person smiles at them. Scandinavians would never think of smiling at a stranger since doing so is seen as invading that person's private space. Consequently, what is considered polite in these places is cold comfort to people from locales where frequent smiling is the norm. Prior to the Winter Olympics in Norway, the *Wall Street Journal* stamped Norwegians as "Frosty Mugs" because they don't smile at people they don't know.

Americans on the other hand are partial to smiling at strangers. Why, for heaven's sake, would one need an excuse or reason to be pleasant? The German philosopher Theodor Adorno was mystified by what he saw in the United States as indiscriminate smiling, grouping it with other suspect American practices like astrology, suburban tract housing, and nicknames. The French, who rarely smile at people they don't know, regard the American tendency to routinely smile as naive, or *mon Dieu*, bourgeois.

French actor Catherine Deneuve with a characteristic French smile

One French cultural theorist, Jean Baudrillard, mocked Americans with this sardonic suggestion: "Smile if you have nothing to say . . . Let this emptiness, this profound indifference shine out spontaneously in your smile."

There is increasing evidence that different countries and even regions within countries have particular smile habits. Travelers are often brought up short when they cross borders and note that people eat, talk, touch, pray, play, sit and—yes—express emotion in odd ways. Since people tend to assume that their own ways of communicating are natural and normal, unfamiliar facial expressions can be perceived as "inscrutable" or "inhospitable."

Small variations in the look of a smile or the use of smiles in different cultural codes can have unexpected consequences. Americans tend to find the smiles of the Japanese hard to read.

Residents of the American South smile more than their Northern counterparts and wonder why Northerners have to be so glum, while Northerners for their part distrust the Southerner's broad grin. Just as languages are spoken with varying inflections and dialects, so too smiles are expressed with culturally specific "accents."

Each culture's way of smiling is spontaneous and unconscious, having been learned so well and done so often. Spontaneous smiles can have predictable consequences "at home" and pass without particular notices. But cross a border, go through Customs, and lo and behold, the consequences of a smile are less predictable and potentially more volatile.

Learning to Smile with the Proper Accent

Many years ago, I was a participant observer in a class in Conversational French taught at Harvard by American scholar of all things French Laurence Wylie. The class was unusual in part because Wylie believed that the best way for people to learn a new language was first through its movements and postures, gestures and facial expressions. So we students would purse our lips and mime a French accent ("Thank 'eaven for leetle girls") and work at adopting a recognizable French shrug. It didn't hurt our improvisations that Wylie served a decent Beaujolais Nouveau along with the lessons. But I get ahead of myself. Two hundred years before Wylie demonstrated how thoroughly speech is nonverbal as well as verbal, Jean-Jacques Rousseau wrote that "Accent is the soul of a language; it gives the feeling and truth to it." He might also have said that facial expressions give feeling and truth to talk, for by the time children begin to speak they already understand that nonverbal communication goes hand-in-hand with words.

Infants are innately ready to chat. More amazing is recent evidence that babies come prepared to learn more than one language. Scientists found that infants as young as four months are able to tell that people speak different languages just from *watching* them talk. In that study, babies looked at a videotape of a speaker saying the same sentence over and over again either in French or in English but with no sound. The babies watched, as babies do, until they were bored, at which point they looked away, which is what babies do. Then a second videotape was run that showed the same person either silently mouthing the same language as before or speaking (again without sound) a different language. The babies fixed their eyes on the person speaking a different language but were not interested in watching the tape that was a repeat of the first one. Scientists interpreted this as showing that the babies knew something novel was happening when a different language was spoken, while the looking away showed they knew when it was the same old thing. In short, they could tell when a different language was introduced—they were able to tell English and French apart just by *watching* (not hearing) someone talk. Infants know that people do not speak by words alone. The face is pitching in as well.

With a few more months under their belts, babies who live in homes where only one language is spoken have lost the capacity to react to the introduction of a new language. Infants from bilingual homes, however, notice when speakers switch languages. They know that French differs from English or Spanish differs from German because exposure to more than one mother tongue is what happens in their world. They still cannot utter a single word themselves, but they are preparing for the time when they will be bilingual.

This is not to say that older children cannot become bilingual or multilingual, for clearly they can and do. It is to say that infants come with brains wired to detect different languages and that this is in part made possible by differences in facial expressions.

Can a smile have an "accent"? Are there aspects of a smile's form, enactment, or timing that reveal a person's origins? Indeed, there are. Different cultural groups imbue their facial expressions with unique inflections even when they are speaking the same language. When French speakers from the Canadian province of Quebec and from the African nation of Gabon were asked to express happiness with their faces, both groups showed the same upward curve of the mouth corners, yet most of the Quebec participants also showed cheek raising and eye-corner wrinkling, something the Gabonese rarely showed.

The tricky thing about reading expressions of emotion in different parts of the world is that while there is marked similarity, societies fine-tune their facial displays with subtle variations. The result is that insiders take the meanings for granted while outsiders are sometimes baffled. Or worse, outsiders believe that since the expressions look basically like they do at home, they mean the same thing and have the same consequences.

Just as spoken accents provide information about whether a person is one of us or one of them, facial accents do so as well. To investigate this possibility, researchers presented hundreds of participants with pictures of people displaying an array of facial expressions. Participants were asked to label the emotion displayed on each face. The finding repeated many times over: participants were significantly better at identifying the expressions of people from their own culture than people from other cultures. Psychologists label this pattern the *in-group advantage effect*.

Moreover, people can identify one of their own just from facial expression even if he or she is in a crowd. Research participants were presented with photographs of gatherings of people drawn from different countries and asked to select any in the group who were from the same region as the participant. The results showed that people are quite good at doing this, *but* only if the face displays something other than a neutral expression. A face needs to show something beyond physical structure or shape or color for people to *recognize* it as familiar. It is rather amazing when you think about it—a still shot of a facial expression caught in midstream is enough to mark a person as a member of one's own group; in short, a facial accent.

The ability to identify one of "us" from their nonverbal behavior holds true even for cultures that share the same language and have similar customs. Americans are able to correctly spot who is American and who is Australian with nothing more than a photo of a smiling face. Again, some facial expression was needed to identify the recognizable facial accent—the American and Australian participants could not pick out the country when faces showed a neutral expression. To be an insider is to have a deeply embedded knowledge about how culturally similar people smile, even though they would be hard-pressed to describe what it is.

Scientists, of course, cannot leave it at that. They want to decipher what makes people see some faces as familiar and others not. One possibility is that people from different cultures focus their attention on different parts of the face. For the Japanese, it is the eyes, while American are more drawn to the lower part of the face. This was demonstrated in a study that compared undergraduates from Ohio State University and Hokkaido University in Japan. The students looked at facial expressions that showed emotion either in the eyes or in the mouth. Some pictures showed faces with happy eyes and a neutral mouth. Others showed faces with smiling mouths and neutral eyes. The final set of faces showed

mixed emotions: crinkly, happy eyes combined with downturned,
sad mouths, or downcast eyes with smiling mouths.

When the Japanese students looked at faces with happy eyes
and neutral mouths, they saw happiness, whereas Americans
didn't see any emotion. But viewing faces with neutral eyes
and a mouth smile, the Americans were much more inclined to
believe the person was happy than the Japanese students were.
And Japanese students rated faces with sad eyes and a neutral
mouth as sadder than the Americans did. When the faces showed
mixed emotions (i.e., happy eyes combined with a sad mouth),
Japanese participants again went with the emotion shown in
the eyes, while the Americans placed their bets on the emotion
expressed in the mouth area. A face with a happy mouth smile
told the Americans that all was well but said nothing to the Japanese observers.

The Chinese also appear to regard the area around a person's
eyes as informative about what feelings lie beneath. One anthro-
pologist examined a large selection of familiar folk tales written in Mandarin Chinese, looking for references to changes in
characters' facial expressions. The investigator found that multiple authors referred to a person's eyes to reflect what he or she
is feeling.

Even simple *emoticons* included in text and e-mail messages
carry facial accents. In the United States, the typical typographi-
cal representation of a smile is the colon followed by a closing
parenthesis, :) or alternatively :-). If the sender wants to insert a
sad face to a message, the emoticon will show the colon followed
by an opening parenthesis, :(or :-(. The change is in the mouth.
Japanese emoticons show changes in the characters for the eyes
but leave the mouth unchanged. The Japanese emoticon for a
happy face is (^_^) and for a sad or crying face (;_;).

It is not surprising, then, that cartoons produced in the United States and Japan reflect these different emphases. Japanese *anime* typically uses fewer facial expressions than American animation, which has led some U.S. film critics to regard it as less sophisticated. The difference is not in sophistication (except perhaps in the critics) but in the stock that different cultures place in how expressive one's face should be. Japanese *anime* (like its people) is less inclined to wear its heart on its face. Rather, "deeply resounding emotion is found instead in a slight twinkle of a character's eye or in an intensely furrowed brow."

Smiling Buddhas Here, Grinning Buddhas There

In India, where Buddha was born some 500 years bce, sculptures and paintings show him with a barely detectable smile, a sign of self-control and enlightenment. In China, however, where Buddha arrived several hundreds of years later, the Buddha has a large grin—so large in fact that he is known in China as the Laughing Buddha. In China, and later in Japan, representations of Buddha show him as a potbellied monk with a round face and bulbous earlobes. According to Zen scholar Conrad Hyers, the grin conveys inexhaustible and cheerful generosity.

Humans, like deities, change when they cross borders—their smiles are often reshaped as they acquire the communication habits of the locals. In Henry James's *The Ambassadors*, Strether is sent to Paris by Mrs. Newsome to bring her son Chad back to Massachusetts. Strether finds Chad considerably changed since he last saw him in the United States. The time in France had "retouched his features, drawn them with a cleaner line . . . it had toned his voice, established his accent, encouraged his smile to more play and his other motions to less."

Prince Charles of England showing the characteristic British smile
with visible lower teeth

If an American were to move to England, they might acquire
a new vocal accent and perhaps a new "British" smile as well.
The American smile pulls the lip corners up at an oblique angle
toward the cheekbones, and if it is large, the movement exposes
the upper teeth. The British smile on the other hand involves
contraction of the risorious muscle that pulls the mouth corners
sideways, which has the effect of pulling the bottom lip downward
to expose the lower teeth.

Culture also has something to say about what makes people
smile. Residents of India and the United States agree that smiling reflects positive feelings, but they differ in what they see as
causing happy feelings. Americans are more likely to attribute
happy feelings to success or achievement. In India, happiness is

more often induced by events that brought individuals together with others.

In *Twelfth Night*, Maria says of Malvolio: "He does smile his face into more lines than is in the new map." Her words are meant to mock Malvolio, yet in likening a smile to a map's coordinates, Shakespeare acknowledged the elasticity of facial expression. At birth, human smiles have the potential to stretch every which way, yet culture steps in and molds that potential into a few locally recognized smiles. A stretch here, some teeth showing there, eye-crinkling elsewhere—now you've got a homegrown smile.

Smiles Rule and Smile Rules

Mark Twain sounded more like a scientist than a storyteller when he asserted that, "any emotion, if it is sincere, is involuntary," while neuroscientist Antonio Damasio sounded more like a humorist when he wrote "we are about as effective at stopping an emotion as we are at preventing a sneeze." Both agree that emotions are a force unto themselves.

Many emotion scientists agree with Twain and Damasio. They believe human beings are preprogrammed, genetically speaking, with a small set of basic emotions, each of which is linked both to a particular facial expression and a unique pattern of neuro-logical and bodily responses. The consequences of emotion are regarded as preset and unstoppable. See an expression, and you will know which emotion caused it. Know what emotion has been triggered, and you know what it will look like.

Not everyone agrees. Ray Birdwhistell, the American anthro-pologist, was one who didn't buy it—asserting on many occasions that there is no such thing as a universal gesture. He granted that anywhere anyone has looked, humans smile, but he argued that

that the meaning is not necessarily the same across the globe. His point was that different cultures assign a different significance to the smile: joy, yes, but also defiance and misery and apprehension, among others, depending on the culture and the context.

On occasion Birdwhistell deliberately manipulated parts of his body to demonstrate a travel case of cultural backgrounds. He would tense the muscles on his scalp to make his hair stand up on end and thus resemble a person from Russia. Or he would lock his shoulders up around his ears and walk in such a way that he was none other than a teenage gang member from northern England. Or he could substantially relax his abdomen muscles to mimic a Bushman from sub-Saharan Africa. He used his body to make the larger point that human bodies are malleable and are molded by culture into forms and actions that seem both recognizable and yet unique. Thus, smiles take on shapes and conventions that fit where they are found rather than coming in one-size-fits-all and means-the-same-everywhere.

So, which is it? Is a smile a sure sign of positive emotion because that is the way our species has evolved, or is the meaning of any particular smile embedded in cultural and social contexts?

Paul Ekman staunchly endorses the first position—that there is a strong and reliable link between an emotion felt and expression displayed. Facial expressions are a necessary and essential part of an emotional response and not tacked on as an afterthought. Happiness will always give rise to a genuine smile.

As I described earlier, Ekman and Friesen compared the spontaneous facial expressions of Japanese and American males as they watched pleasant or unpleasant films. The unpleasant films were truly unpleasant. (You don't want to know.) While the subjects viewed the films alone, their facial expressions were captured on hidden cameras. Analyses showed that Japanese and American participants showed almost the same amounts of disgust and distress on seeing the gory films. Ekman took these findings as strong support for the idea that emotion and facial expressions are the same everywhere.

The study was run a second time with an important variation—another person was placed in the room where subjects watched the films. Now, cultural differences in facial expression were much in evidence. With someone else present, the Japanese subjects actually smiled while watching the unpleasant films and very few showed distress, while the Americans looked very much as they had when no one else was present.

On the surface, this seemed clear evidence for strong cultural differences in the expression of disgust rather than there being a universal expression. Unswayed by the apparent contradiction, Ekman expanded his theory to a *neurocultural theory of emotion*. The *neuro-* part kept the original idea that each emotion spontaneously generates a particular facial expression because biology has set it that way. The *cultural* addition acknowledged that individual cultures might impose guidelines as to when and how the automatically generated expression is to be expressed. These guidelines, known as *display rules*, regulate or fine-tune what actually appears on the face, even though the spontaneous expression would have been there at the start.

Display rules are like that last check you make in the mirror before going out the door, only they occur automatically and without awareness. Adjustments are made to the face so that it is culturally appropriate. Thus, when Japanese subjects viewed the unpleasant film in another person's company, their normal disgust reactions were "adjusted" to emerge as smiles. These smiles didn't reflect delight but rather deep training in a system that values equanimity.

Cultural display rules change the external expression in a variety of ways, including exaggerating, suppressing, masking, or modifying the appearance of the spontaneous facial expression. One culture, for example, might place a high value on covering any negative feeling. So anger would be *masked* with a smile or an expression of detachment. When the Japanese baseball player Hideki Matsui hit a grand-slam home run playing for the New York Yankees in his first game at Yankee Stadium, he didn't smile as he rounded the bases. To do so, in Japanese eyes, would have conveyed disrespect to the pitcher.

In some locales, emotional outbursts, including displays of joy, are suppressed because unadulterated expression is regarded as gauche. Other cultures call for expressions to be enhanced or *intensified* ("It's fabulous, really, really fabulous"). In sum, the neurocultural model holds fast to the idea that emotions cause spontaneous expressions but cultural display rules may step in to alter what the public sees. The rules are rehearsed and practiced until they too become automatic.

We smile automatically on some occasions and intentionally on many others because smiling greases the wheels of our social lives. We hear that a co-worker has just become a new father or gotten a promotion and we smile—not necessarily because that news delights us but because our aim is to let others know that we are team players. Our smiles sometimes have little to do with real emotion and much to do with confirming membership.

Consider social rituals like weddings and funerals. Weddings in Western culture tend to be smile fests, but in other parts of the world, a smiling bride is a rarity if not an outright aberration. At traditional weddings in Pakistan, the convention holds that the bride not smile since such an occasion is solemn. That rule also was in effect during the mass weddings in Seoul, South Korea, conducted by Sun Myung Moon of the Unification Church. Photographs of the event show thousands of young couples not exactly grinning as they were joined in matrimonial bliss.

Smile Consequences in Foreign Places

American children learn to smile at friends and at strangers. Not so in other countries. In one study, a friendly woman smiled at nearly a thousand children in both the United States and Israel and note was made as to whether the children returned the smile. The age range was three to fifteen years. From the toddlers to the teens, the children in Israel were significantly less likely to return the smile than children in the United States.

Israeli adults are no more moved to respond positively to another's smile than are their children. Consider the results of a study that examined the role of emotional displays in cross-cultural negotiations. The negotiators were from Hong Kong and Israel. The Hong Kong negotiators were more inclined to accept offers if they were accompanied by smiles than if they were attended by negative or neutral expressions. However, smiling expressions had no such effect with the Israeli negotiators.

So, smiles make a difference—but not always the same difference in different cultures. Just why this is the case is not yet clear. One factor may reside in the values and worldviews held by different societies. Social psychologists have proposed that societies involved in ongoing conflict, like Israel, tend to be dominated by a collective fear toward outsiders, with the result that their citizens are wary of strangers bearing smiles.

The faith in our *own* people even extends to the beliefs about who smiles the most in general, us or them. People are more likely to believe that members of their in-group smile more than out-group members, regardless of how much each group actually smiles.

Why would Southerners in the United States smile more frequently, or, as Florence King wrote in *Southern Ladies and Gentlemen*, why do they have "a distinctive devilish gleam" to them? Social psychologist Dov Cohen and his colleagues have suggested that all that sweetness and politeness is actually a buffer against latent hostility. Hospitality is part of the effort to keep hostility under control. Moreover, that latent hostility exists because Southern males are more likely than Northern males to subscribe to a *culture of honor*, whose core principle is that insults, affronts, and threats must not go unanswered.

Psychologists decided to look at this North-South divide in the lab. Males from Northern and Southern states were asked to stay in a "waiting room" while the study was prepared. Also in the waiting room was another male, who began to mildly but insistently provoke the participant. The participants believed that the provocateur was a subject like themselves. (He was, in fact, a research assistant trained to be obnoxious.) Males from the North reacted by suggesting that the offending person knock it off, but then pretty much left it at that. Southern males, in contrast, began by being gentlemen, but as the other person's bad behavior continued, their anger ratcheted up to the point of physical confrontation. In the Southern United States, smiles of hospitality are like Kevlar vests, providing protection from attack

for insiders and outsiders alike. Sometimes, however, the niceness gives way and all smiles are off.

Smile Responsibilities

In his 700-page history of American democracy, Harold Laski
wrote that Americans' promiscuous smiling embarrasses many
Europeans. If Europeans have trouble with how much Americans
smile, Americans for their part are often dismayed by how much
the Japanese smile. They are especially confounded when they
see Japanese people smiling in situations that seem grounds for
expressions of chagrin or irritation. While smiling in the face
of disagreeable situations seems hypocritical to Americans, it
makes all the sense in the world to the Japanese, although the
American travel writer Paul Theroux was not sympathetic: "Is
there a Japanese smile that does not seem like an expression of
pain?"

For Americans, an individual's feelings are privileged. They
do not trust people who put on a front. A person who hides what
they really feel is often regarded as a hypocrite. But in other parts
of the world, an individual's feelings must give way to the feelings of others. To use a distinction made by Erving Goffman,
smiles are given *to* others rather than given *off* by the person who
displays them. Smiling in a difficult situation is a voluntary act
intended not to protect the smiler but those who see the smile.

In many Asian countries, a smile does not reflect or even act
as a cover for a person's feelings, but instead is a message about
how he or she wants others to feel. An English writer who made
his home in Japan more than a century ago argued that at its core,
the Japanese smile is a sign of extreme consideration.

From the time they are babies, Japanese children learn not to show distress in public; instead, they learn to smile when they are unhappy. Other people's possible distress is the first concern. American moms encourage their babies to be emotive and expressive, while Japanese mothers focus more on soothing and quieting their babies. The Japanese smiles are acquired through an extensive cultural education and are enacted to make social life predictable and harmonious. That value is more important than honestly expressing what one feels.

Jeanne Tsai, a social psychologist at Stanford University, speculates that culture not only influences what people show on their faces but also affects what they feel in their hearts. In short, cultures differ in the value they give to experiencing some emotions over others. Some emotions are sought—a phenomenon she calls *ideal affect*.

This is how it works. With some exceptions, most humans choose to feel good rather than lousy. You don't need a psychologist to tell you that. It is common knowledge that humans gravitate to what is pleasurable and steer clear of what is painful. Tsai offers a new twist on this basic premise, namely, that what feels good is not the same in all cultures. In some countries, to feel *good* means to feel "up"—excited, enthusiastic, enthralled. For Westerners, feeling good means experiencing states of high positive arousal. Elsewhere, however, to feel good means to feel calm, serene, and at peace. These are considered "low" positive arousal states.

When Tsai and her colleagues asked European-American, Asian-American, and Hong Kong Chinese adults to describe what they most wanted to feel, both American groups reported that they liked feeling "up" (high positive arousal) while the ideal affect for Hong Kong Chinese was to feel calm and peaceful (low positive arousal).

Culture starts to instill these ideal affects early on. To assess how early, experimenters presented three-year-olds with two smiling faces set side by side and asked them which one would they rather be. The faces differed only in the size of the smile. American children, whether of European or Asian descent, were three and a half times more likely than children from Taiwan to want to be the person with the larger, excited smile than the one with the smaller, calmer smile.

How do children absorb the goals endorsed by their culture? It comes from many directions—what they see at home, on TV, and in picture books. In fact, compared to American storybooks, the illustrations of characters in popular Taiwanese storybooks show significantly more calm expressions. The Taiwanese characters are also more likely to be engaged in quiet activities. These divergent representations are even more telling in light of the fact that the storybooks did not differ in how many smiles were shown but rather in how big the smiles were.

What is wondrous about cultural variations in faces and feelings is that—like driving a car—we know how to do it so well that we don't have to think about how we do it. What we feel and what we express seem entirely natural and normal. Culture's programming is so pervasive and subtle that most people are never aware that they received such training. That's just the way things are done. It rises to consciousness only when someone from another country doesn't follow our rules.

Americans and Japanese, Russians and Argentineans may differ in how expressive they are, but they all control their emotions and their faces. As the linguist Edward Sapir wrote many years ago, "we respond to gestures with an extreme alertness and, one might almost say, in accordance with an elaborate and secret code that is written nowhere, known by none, and understood by all."

Cultural Worldviews

Culture includes the ways we do things and the ways we think and feel about things. Having a culture means we have an identity that differentiates "us" from "them." French and English, black and white, East and West.

Social scientists as well as travelers are often struck by how people from the East go about things differently from those who reside in the West. The scientists attribute the differences to how much value each culture places on the individual. The theory is that people in the West emphasize "me" while people in the East stress "we." A "me" orientation, known as *individualism*, regards each person as egocentric, separate, autonomous, self-contained, and independent. Individuals are assumed to possess a set of personal characteristics—thoughts, traits, preferences, motives, goals, attitudes, beliefs, and abilities—that uniquely define them. With a "me" orientation, the person deeply values independence, individual initiative, and self-expression.

In contrast, the Eastern "we" consciousness is referred to as *collectivism*, or *interdependence*. Interdependence regards the person as relational, socially embedded, and interdependent. People with a "we" consciousness value harmonious relationships, group solidarity, sharing, and fulfilling obligations.

These disparate orientations toward the self are said to seep into every psychological crook and cranny, affecting feelings, judgments, and actions. For those with a collectivistic stance, social behavior is largely influenced by the goals, attitudes, and values shared with one's in-group, whereas in individualist cultural contexts, social behavior is largely determined by one's personal goals and attitudes. For example, Americans tend to see themselves as unique and unlike others, while Asians tend to see themselves as more like others.

The East/West difference can even be seen between European-Americans and Asian-Americans. Richard Nisbett at the University of Michigan and his colleagues showed Americans of either Japanese or European descent a video clip of an underwater scene of a few large fish swimming in a seascape containing typical small marine life, plants, and rocks. The task for the subjects was to report what they saw.

By and large, European-Americans focused on the larger, brighter, and faster moving fish. In contrast, the Japanese-Americans began with the context, specifically the non-moving aspects of the scene, such as the color of the water and movement of the plants. Overall, Japanese subjects reported 60 percent more items of context than did the Americans.

The difference between individualist and collectivist perspectives extends also to matters of emotion and its expression. Professor David Matsumoto and his merry band of international collaborators studied 5,361 people from thirty-two countries on five continents. They found that people from countries supporting high individualism were significantly more likely to believe that expressing emotions was a good thing. People from collectivist countries tended to prefer to dampen emotional expressivity so as to take into account the feelings of others.

The difference between "me" and "we" mind-sets also accounts for why people in the West sometimes interpret facial expressions differently than people from the East. Subjects in one study were presented with photographs of a target person surrounded by other people. In one picture, the person of interest was smiling, as were the others in the picture. In a second picture, the target person was smiling as before, but now the people surrounding him were not. In fact, they all looked quite sad. Japanese and American participants were asked to gauge how happy they thought the target person was in both photographs. As predicted, the Japanese participants were more affected by what people around the target person were expressing—in the company of sad-looking people, the target person was seen as less happy than when surrounded by happy-looking people. American participants, on the other hand, zeroed in on the individual each time, and their judgments of his level of happiness were unaffected by the facial expressions shown by others in the group.

Vive la Différence

If number of passports is any indication—over 13 million issued in 2009 in the United States alone—people are eager to travel to foreign places to experience cultures unlike their own. Unfortunately, travel guides rarely provide reference to what expressions or gestures should be observed to avoid the risk of giving offense. Alas, irritation is all too often the response when travelers run up against something other than what they expect. They roll their eyes, shake their heads, and raise their voices at how "the foreigners" are behaving.

Culture is more than rites and rituals, food and fashion—more than established ways of doing things. It is an encompassing mind-set and a useful face-set. Facial expressions and the consequences that flow from them help define how people are to relate to one another.

So, where does the culture of smiles leave us? When traveling, beware (sometimes) of people bearing smiles, because the consequences of a smile may not be the same as back home. It may not reflect delight at with your questions or humor at your jokes, but may instead be a cover for discomfort. Be patient too if at first no one returns your smile. The absence of a smile *now* does not preclude one coming later. Larry Wylie once said of the French that although they may be reluctant to let strangers in and show that by grand displays of facial disinterest, once you are granted entry, they may not let you go.

smile for the camera

The wedding was fantastic. The bride was radiant, the groom uncharacteristically nervous, and the bridesmaids and groomsmen resplendent. The weather could not have been more perfect, or the service, or the reception. The photographs . . . well, the photographs were *not* perfect. In fact, they were terrible. A friend of a friend took the pictures using a wide-angle lens—people's heads and bodies were distorted, and it looked more like a funhouse than a wedding. So Nancy and Richard decided to do it again: to restage the entire wedding, complete with reception. The original wedding might as well not have happened, there being no good photos to show for it. Fortunately, the bride had had the foresight to purchase wedding insurance that covered photographic catastrophes, so five weeks after the original event, they did do it all over again—this time with a professional photographer, having thoroughly reviewed several portfolios beforehand.

Photographs are often people's most valued possessions. Not only do we look *at* them, we also look *into* them. In photographs we see what has been and, as we shall see, what might be. "Remember how she couldn't get the ring on his finger? We really need to get back in touch with them." Through photographs we remember, although sometimes all we remember is the photograph.

And among our most remembered pictures are those of people smiling. But these smiles are among the most deliberate and least revealing expressions people show the world. This, then, is the paradox of smiling for the camera. When a photographer takes aim, subjects intentionally smile in a way that hopefully will look candid. There are repercussions in doing that. Later, when the picture and the event are recalled, the consequences of smiling for the camera keep on going.

Photographs that make it into albums, digital frames, and social network sites show people smiling more than any other facial expression. We grow up smiling for the camera. When someone says, "Okay, everybody smile," groans and grumbles might be heard, but most everyone complies. Even the stretched grins of two-year-olds show that children are initiated into the practice early on. A comment in *The New Yorker* nicely captured this: "A father of our acquaintance looked up from his paper last Sunday morning to find his small son poised a few feet away, aiming a Donald Duck camera at him. 'I'm going to take your picture, Daddy,' the boy said. 'Pretend you're smiling.'"

It is easy to make light of smiling for the camera. True, there is little spontaneity in these smiles, and yes, everyone knows what to do when they hear, "Say cheese." However, smiling for the camera is *not* trivial—it is a deeply embedded social and cultural experience.

In *Shooting War: Photography and the American Experience of Combat*, Susan Moeller showed that the smile ritual is so deeply seated

An early family portrait showing somber faces

in American psyches that the mere presence of press photographers raising their cameras was enough to prompt war-weary soldiers to look up and smile. And during World War II, when prisoner of war Angelo Spinelli aimed his camera at his fellow prisoners, many roused themselves and smiled.

Several factors conspired to make smiling for the camera at first possible and then commonplace. Photographs taken at the end of the nineteenth century and early into the twentieth rarely show people smiling. Faces were held as still and straight as ramrods. Subjects had to keep their bodies and faces motionless for lengthy periods because the slightest movement would cause the image to blur. It was expensive and time-consuming enough to have one's photograph taken, without having to repeat it.

Then along came Kodak. In 1888, George Eastman launched

the first camera intended for the amateur photographer. With it, picture taking became portable and prolific. No long focus time— actually, no need to focus at all. The camera did that. The recreational photographer only needed to push a button to release the shutter. The new box camera allowed pictures to be taken outside the studio into the real world. In 1900, the dollar Brownie camera followed, and with it the brave new world of snapshots, helped along by images of the smiling Kodak girl.

Brave new world indeed. Kodak took the word "snapshots" from a hunting term for a round fired hurriedly and without aim. Other hunting terms were appropriated as well. Amateur photographers were encouraged to "shoot" pictures at events big and small to "capture" precious moments. They were instructed how to "point" and "aim" their cameras. And shoot they did. People snapped shots of weddings, vacations, birthday parties, graduations, celebrations, as well as the new baby, the new puppy, any occasion on which people would be smiling. By the final decade of the twentieth century, according to one calculation, amateur and professional photographers together developed more than 2.5 billion pictures. A recent estimate suggests that Americans alone take about 550 snapshots per second.

Professional photographers tend to steer clear of smiling faces to distinguish their creative endeavors from lowly snapshots. Julia Margaret Cameron's famous photographs showed very dour Victorian women. One reviewer wrote of the faces, "Their poses embody sorrow, resignation, composure, solemnity, and love, determined love, love which will have a hard time of it." One contemporary photographer, Marion Ettlinger, celebrated for her pictures of authors adorning book jackets, actually forbids her subjects to smile for their portraits. "If you're going for the iconic moment," Ettlinger has asserted, "then smiling interferes

with that." My friends who have gone to schools where professional photography is taught are immersed in the no-smile rule
for art photographs. It is interesting, is it not, that when people
take pictures of and for themselves, smiling predominates, but
art photographers assume that the smile is a mask that needs to
be removed.

Passport photos and mug shots are also not known for incan-
descent smiles. Canada, for one, expressly prohibits any trace
of a smile in a passport photo. It's also hard to imagine mug
shot photographers encouraging their arrested subjects to "Say
cheese," but a recent book devoted to police photographs shows
notorious criminals like Al Capone, John Gotti, and Charles
Ponzi looking out with full-faced grins. Such smiles let law
enforcement officials know what they can do with their arrest
warrants.

We Create Family Photos and They Create Us

People want to have pictures and psychologists want to know why.
What are the consequences of taking and viewing photos? The
simple answer, of course, is that pictures capture significant
occasions. Psychologists believe that picture taking does much
more than this. The resulting photographs don't just capture
events, they construct events. Picture taking does not merely set
memory; it resets it again and again. Smiling is factored into the
revisions.

Social psychologist Stanley Milgram (he of the infamous shock
experiments) asked rhetorically: "If we stop two strangers on the
street, ask them to pose momentarily, and take a picture, have
we thereby created through a photograph a bond that previously
did not exist?" Three decades later, a team of Canadian social

psychologists put Milgram's question to empirical test. Pairs of previously unacquainted college students agreed to have their pictures taken. Half of the pairs were photographed, while the other half, who had anticipated that their pictures were going to be taken, were told that the experimenters had enough photos and so they would not be photographed. All the participants were then asked for their impressions of how friendly, attractive, and likable they found the person they were paired with.

If Milgram was right—that the experience of having one's picture taken creates a reality that did not exist prior to the picture being taken—then the pairs who were photographed should experience a different kind of relationship from the pairs who spent the same amount of time together but were not photographed. That is exactly what happened. Photographed twosomes expressed greater connection to and liking for each other than those whose pictures were not taken. The experience of being photographed as a pair constituted a relationship. So, photographs not only mark socially significant occasions but also create them.

Smile Snaps Make Happy Memories

Humans like their glasses half full. They like personal photographs to show happy faces. Pictures make it easier to remember an experience as having been a good one, even if it was far from wonderful at the time. Our psychological makeup contributes to this memory magic. First, left to our own devices, we tend to see things through rose-colored glasses. Second, the relatively high proportion of smiling faces in pictures means that recall is nudged even further in a positive direction.

Abundant psychological studies show that we prefer to look on the bright side of life. In one particular study, a large and varied sample of people was instructed to keep a diary for several months with the stipulation that they record one event each day and that that one event be unique, not routine like having breakfast or driving to work. Participants were also asked to rate each event for how pleasant or unpleasant it was when it happened.

There was clear evidence of a positive bias. Across thousands of events, pleasant ones far outnumbered unpleasant ones. More interesting is what happened next. In a follow-up some three and a half months later, participants again rated the same events. When the original ratings of the unpleasant events were compared with the ratings of the same events later, the second ratings moved toward the brighter side. The events seen as unpleasant when they first happened became on second thought months later significantly less unpleasant. What had once seemed disagreeable was recalled as not so bad after all. The ratings of pleasant events did not change over time. What started out as pleasant stayed that way.

The fact that most of the photographs we keep of family and friends show lots of smiling does not necessarily reflect the actual amount of smiling that occurred at the time. But the pictures encourage the idea that a happy time was had by all. If the family get-togethers were actually not all that happy, at least we have a few photographs to bolster the illusion that on balance those visits were really not so bad.

Not everyone complies with a smile when pictures are being taken. For the picture taker, some cajoling or trickery is required to get everyone to smile so that a "good" picture can be taken. We want the moment to look "natural" even though we may have had to fabricate it.

Except that sometimes it doesn't work. The film *Ordinary People* (1980) shows a family trying to come to terms with the death of a favored son and esteemed older brother. The father, the surviving son, and especially the mother, are having trouble holding it together—cracks start to appear. In one scene, it is Christmas Day. The mother, father, and son, along with visiting grandparents, are straining for normalcy. And what more normal than the annual photo of happy relatives gathered round the Christmas tree? In the usual pre-photo confusion of where people are to stand, the mother in the film, played by Mary Tyler Moore, reflexively moves away from her surviving son and thereby graphically signals her unwillingness be in any picture beside him, let alone a happy one.

Smiles, Obituaries, and Staying in Touch

If all this talk of creating and capturing happy memories on film is getting depressing, not to worry. The emphasis on the bright side of life may be a passing fad, if history is an indication. The fact of the matter is that happiness has not always occupied a privileged position in American life. According to social historians, optimism and cheerfulness have not always been at the forefront of what Americans value in people. Americans in centuries past did not always place being happy at the top of the list of what one should aim for. Rather, two hundred or so years ago the highest regard was reserved for serious and abstemious people, even a bit melancholic. Through the end of the eighteenth century, sensitive people were thought to occupy a higher moral plane than those who seemed sunny and buoyant. This began to shift in the twentieth century. Today, Americans value cheerfulness more than seriousness. It is no wonder that we want our photographs to show lots of smiling.

These days, even obituaries have a sunny side. Probably the

obituary pages are not the first place you might think to go to find signs of cheerfulness, but there are frequent upbeat references to the recently deceased. When newspapers around the world reported the death of England's beloved "Queen Mum" in 2002 at the grand old age of a hundred and one, it was said of her that she would be remembered for her large flowery hats and ready smile. Humorist Art Buchwald was eulogized for his consistent ability to make people smile. Novelist Carol Shields was described as having had a wide warm smile just before she died of breast cancer.

One does not have to be royalty or widely liked to be remembered for one's smile. Obituaries of ordinary people that take up a few lines in local newspapers frequently use the same language. "He enjoyed reading, religion and always had a smile on his face" . . . "He will be remembered for his smile, teachers said of the seventeen-year-old" . . . " 'When she smiled,' her mother said, 'she could melt anybody's heart.' " Even the death of animals has been known to elicit obituaries full of praise for the smiles they showed. In 2004, Kathy, the beloved beluga whale at the New York Aquarium, died at the age of 34. She was described as "the ever-smiling ambassador" of the aquarium, who "brought smiles and gave them."

Even when tragic circumstances surround a person's death, friends and family note the person's ready smile. In late September 2001, *The New York Times* began to publish "Portraits of Grief"—brief accounts of the lives of the people who died in the World Trade Center on 9/11. Attention to a person's smile was a frequent feature. "His memory for customers' names was encyclopedic, but no matter how crowded the bar and no matter how frenzied he was, he would always aim a smile toward the customers he did not know."

Before the obituaries of the victims of 9/11 appeared in the

Flyers of missing people after the events of 9/11 often showed them smiling

newspaper, in fact, almost immediately after the attacks on the World Trade Center, homemade notices went up all over lower Manhattan—on posts, walls, fences, barricades, phone booths, storefronts, and newsstands seeking information about missing individuals. A common feature of many of these flyers was a photograph of the missing person with a smiling expression. The contrast of these smiling pictures with the surrounding destruction and the collective grief could not have been starker.

Social psychologists have recently examined why recollections of people who have died are more positive than thoughts about them when they were alive. In an interesting set of studies, psychologists Dafna Eylon and Scott Allison at the University of Richmond, Virginia, presented research participants with information about a stranger and asked them for their first impressions. This method, termed the *zero-acquaintance procedure*, is

one often used by researchers to investigate first impressions
of a stranger from a few select details. The interesting twist
in this study involved telling some participants that the target
person had died while the other group were not told this. When
the impressions were compared, those who were thought to be
deceased were rated as significantly more likable, competent,
and inspirational than living targets. The famed baseball player
Roger Maris had a similar experience: "It's like obituaries; when
you die they finally give you good reviews."

But why do the good reviews come after a person has died?
According to the authors of *Terror Management Theory*, humans
don't do particularly well when faced with mortality. In fact, it is
the nature of the human condition to experience profound terror
when death becomes salient—a close brush with serious illness
or accident, the news of the death of someone close, or images of
disease and dying.

Terror management theorists propose that we keep terror
at bay by shifting our thinking away from whatever it was that
prompted thoughts of mortality, instead thinking of enduring
values outside ourselves. These values might be embedded in
religious beliefs or ethical principles or a cultural worldview.
The content is not important. When faced with mortality, it is
psychologically settling to step outside the terror of the moment
and think instead about something permanent and important.
"This is what I believe."

We focus on the enduring and the significant because it helps
to ground ourselves emotionally when reminded of the precari-
ousness of life. Recalling a friend's warm smile upon hearing of
her death affirms that social relationships matter and memories
of her don't die.

Fixing Family Photos

Most people have collections of family photos. They may be organized or haphazard, but whatever their order or location, the importance of photographs of family and friends would be hard to overestimate. If a speedy exit is necessary due to fire or some other disaster, one of the first things people think of grabbing is the family album. Serious grieving follows if pictures of family and friends are lost or destroyed. This is in part because the photographs of friends and relatives provide us with cues as to our identities.

> People take pictures of the summer,
> just in case someone thought they had missed it,
> and to prove that it really existed.
> Fathers take pictures of the mothers,
> and the sisters take pictures of the brothers,
> just to show that they love one another.
> —The Kinks, "People Take Pictures of Each Other"

Family albums are actually strikingly similar. From one occasion to the next, from one year to the next, from one family to the next, from one generation to the next, photographs of people with their smile-for-the-camera facial expressions appear to have been cut from the same film stock. The photographic convention for a family picture requires that it be taken straight on and that everyone be included. In the late nineteenth century, Edward Wilson published an instruction manual for how to pose for family pictures. Wilson's advice was to "forget all dolefulness." If you must do something, "whistle Yankee-doodle mentally, or think of some pleasant thing that will enliven your spirits and impress a pleasant look upon your face."

And the family photo album in many instances is not complete without the family pet. Many dog owners point to such pictures as clear evidence that Fido is smiling too. In fact, sociologist Richard Chalfen has studied pet cemeteries in Japan where the majority of gravesites are marked with a photograph of the four-legged companions. The picture is often a close-up of the dog, and, according to Chalfen's Japanese interviewees, smiling.

People usually do not bring out the camera on the occasion of losses, defeats, reversals, and failures. We prefer our permanent records to be positive and upbeat. Anyone can see from this picture what a high-functioning, happy family it is. Such stereotypic family photos give a whole new meaning to Tolstoy's observation that "All happy families resemble one another, but each unhappy family is unhappy in its own way."

If, however, some family pictures need a little fixing up to bring them in line with aspirations, then that is easily done. With digital photography, it is now easy to zap the former spouse right out of family photographs. In a split second, the ex-husband is erased from the vacation to the Grand Canyon. ("I don't remember whether he was there or not.") With a little digital assistance the teenager who glowered in his high school picture comes out smiling. In 1999, the BBC reported that the official family photo of Prince Edward's wedding to Sophie was digitally altered because Prince William did not look happy enough.

Do wedding photographs really reveal anything deeper than occasion and fashion? Do the smiles displayed by newly married couples in their wedding photographs say anything at all about the likelihood of a happy marriage? The *Daily Mirror* in London sent four wedding pictures to social psychologist Dacher Keltner and asked him to predict the outcomes of the resulting marriages. Two of the couples had since divorced while the two others remained happily married. Keltner looked for evidence of telltale genuine Duchenne smiles in the photographs, the same ones previously found to predict happy lives. There it was again. The couples showing upturned mouth corners combined with crinkly eyes were still married. The couples who were photographed without the crinkling around the eyes indicative of real happiness were in fact more likely to be divorced or heading that way.

Fake Smiles and False Memories

While our own pictures are fascinating, we do on occasion have to submit to long-winded narratives that accompany the showing of other people's pictures—the drawn-out story about that funny side trip to where they make socks or the extended exegesis about eating hasty pudding. And remember when we almost missed the boat—you should have been there!

Are the stories true? Are the memories veridical? Psychologists take it as fact that memory is a work in progress, subject to gaps and modifications, and not a single indelible print. In fact, the Harvard psychologist and memory expert Daniel Schacter has argued that forgetting is adaptive. What possible use can there be in remembering every detail? It would only clutter up valuable cognitive space. Our memories save the gist and discard the rest.

So there you are, remembering your niece's wedding from two years ago . . . or was it three? Some details are remembered pretty well; others seem to have dissolved with the flight home. Experts in memory tell us that memories tend to become fuller and fuzzier with time. People "remember" details that were not part of the original event. These extra elements are added to the

Looking at a family photo album and re-creating memories

memory mix. They are borrowed from other weddings—weddings
you went to or heard about or saw at the movies. In short, our
brains show a pronounced inclination to fill in gaps with details
that could reasonably have happened.

Did they really have a flower girl? You might remember there
being one who wasn't actually there because flower girls are often
part of weddings. Then, each time you remember your niece's
wedding, other details might get added that were not part of the
original event because they too could have been part of it. What
really happened and what could have reasonably happened blur
together.

Psychologists call the acquisition of altogether new memories
false memories. In a prototypic false memory, people "recall" an
event that never happened. Psychologists have demonstrated this
process in the lab. Research participants hear a list of related

words (e.g., "bed," "rest," "awake"). A related word, termed a *lure* (e.g., "sleep"), is not presented in the original list. Later, subjects are asked to indicate from a longer list which words they heard or read earlier. Many subjects report that they heard or read the lure word when in fact they had not. It is "remembered" not because it was actually there but because it fits with what was there. The mind fills in between the lines and creates a false memory.

False memories occur even in people with "good" memories. If an image or a word meshes with an individual's preexisting ideas about what things go together, he or she is likely to "remember" it as having been there when it actually never made an appearance.

Consider the following experiment. Research participants were brought to a professor's office and asked to wait there for a minute while the experimenter was occupied with something else. After leaving the office, they were asked to recall as many details as they could about the room they had just left. Fully one third of the subjects recalled seeing books in the office when, in fact, there were none. It was, after all, a professor's office and what do professors have in their offices but books, and lots of them. One "remembers" what *should* have been there.

Photographs appear to be especially fertile ground for the generation of false memories. For example, when people are shown a photograph of part of a scene, they recall having seen a larger expanse of the scene than they actually did. Again, our brains fill in the gaps. The real and the expected intermingle in memory.

In an interesting demonstration of the power of photographs to instill false memories, psychologist Kimberly Wade and her colleagues gave participants photographs of themselves as children, obtained from their families. The subjects looked at the photos and talked about what happened at the time each photo was taken. Although most of the pictures were of events that subjects had experienced as children, one photo was digitally altered to place the subject as a child into the basket of a hot-air balloon. Half of the subjects "remembered" several details about the alleged hot-air balloon ride. The fabricated memory seemed very real even if the experience was not.

In a similar study, college students were asked to talk about three childhood events. Parents of the participants had supplied details about two real events. A third, fictional event was added. Half of the participants were also shown group photos of their classmates at the time when the two real events had occurred. The other half saw no photos. A comparison of the groups showed that the inclusion of the photo taken at the same time as the events occurred, yet unrelated to them, generated twice as many false memories as for those who didn't view any photographs. If memories of events that never happened are brought to life through ersatz photographs, think what memories one might conjure just by looking at the family album.

Networked Smiles

The first easy and low-cost method for taking photographs of oneself was the *photobooth*. The "Photomaton," as it was initially called, opened in 1926 on Broadway in New York City, and spread quickly around the world. For a quarter, you could get eight photos of yourself and possibly one other person squeezed in the booth as you made faces and tried on various expressions for the camera.

Flash forward almost a century. Online social networking sites and Internet dating services mean that more people are taking and showing pictures of themselves and their friends than at any time since the invention of the "image freezing machine." But posting a picture of oneself on a dating site can be a particularly formidable decision because only one photo is allowed. Fortunately, there is no shortage of available advice. At Yahoo's site, people are encouraged not only to use a current picture and one of good quality but one where you are smiling. Match.com suggests that the photo be just of you, and you should be smiling.

By the winter of 2011, Facebook alone had more than half a million active users. Photographs, of course, constitute a major part of Facebook pages, with over 90 percent of personal profiles containing a photograph of the Facebook member. Many posted photographs of friends show *very* happy people. However, most of the cover photographs—that is, self-photos—show the person in a silly or comic pose. Why would people present themselves to a potentially huge audience looking goofy? Perhaps ideas about impression management are changing. A pleasing smile may no longer be enough to convey that one has substantial social capital. Perish the thought, but a goofy face may be the new smile-for-the-camera smile, at least for the college-aged set.

The art critic and photography expert John Berger proposed that "pulling faces" is a way to poke fun at the ritual of smiling for the camera. A goofy face simultaneously conveys that one is popular but is a person who doesn't take all this business seriously. Goofiness as irony—who would have thought?

On networking sites, users are allowed to upload innumerable photos, and they do this with abandon. Moreover, people who previously had little or no interest in taking pictures are now prolific users of cell phone cameras, and they upload their pictures immediately. Many of these photographs exhibit lots of smiling faces.

For the sake of future reputations, a little less spontaneity in choice of which photographs to upload is probably advised. Nonetheless, online smiles might actually set off and sustain chain reactions of smiles. Recent studies show that when one person is in a good mood, a friend of a friend of a friend of that person has a somewhat higher probability of feeling happy, too. Smiling profiles on Facebook show the same effect.

No one could have imagined when the first daguerreotypes appeared on the scene in the mid-nineteenth century that photographs would come to play such a huge part in representing and constructing social lives. Smiling for the camera, once exotic, is now ordinary; once a family affair, now a social performance for hundreds or even thousands of people. Some things, however, stay the same even as the technology becomes more sophisticated. People still want to capture smiles in pictures. To make that easier to achieve, it is now possible to purchase a camera or camcorder which includes a mechanism that reacts specifically to smiling faces and takes a picture at the precise millisecond the smile appears. The photographer can adjust for desired smile size (from barely there to full toothy grin) and the camera takes care of the rest. No need to shout: "Smile for the camera."

Torturers Smile for the Camera

The 2004 torture photographs from Abu Ghraib Prison in Iraq were disturbing on many counts, not least the sight of American soldiers smiling at the people they were torturing. One cannot help but stare at the smiles of specialist Charles Graner and Pfc Lynndie England as they grinned and flashed thumbs-up signs next to the pyramid of naked prisoners they had constructed.

The smiles of the guards were genuine. They were not the diabolical smiles of archetypal villains or the maniacal smiles of madmen, but happy, look-at-us-wild-and-crazy-guys smiles. The problem is that the smiling-for-the-camera in these pictures did not merely record the torture; it was part of the torture. The smiling was as essential to the humiliation of the prisoners as their naked bodies were, stacked like logs or pulled along on a leash. The broadcast of the photographs beyond the prison walls kept the humiliation going. With each viewing by other soldiers, by acquaintances, by the "other side," the humiliation and degradation went on.

Had the guards' facial expressions been the asymmetrical smiles more often known as smirks or sneers, the pictures might have been easier to stomach. But no, these smiles are the genuine article. Evil actions are not necessarily accompanied by malevolent grins. People smile genuinely when they are amused even if what amuses them involves torturing or humiliating someone. That these happy expressions are appalling does not make them fake.

Some facial expressions captured on film at Abu Ghraib display a particular smile type, namely, the proud smile. When people feel proud of what they have done, their heads tilt back slightly, their posture expands, they sometimes raise their arms—all of which is combined with a genuine smile. The thumbs-up salute while holding a prisoner on a leash is a smile that announces: "I am superior." And since viewers tend to mimic the expressions they see in photos, the pictures of the smiling guards are an invitation to others to join in the degradation.

When the photographs at Abu Ghraib made their rounds on television and the Internet, a few commentators drew parallels with the trophy pictures taken by whites at lynchings of blacks in 1930s America. In one photograph from that period, it is possible to see two African-American boys hanging from a tree in the town square. In the foreground, several men and women are turned toward the person taking their picture and they are all smiling. These photographs also made the rounds. At the time they were attached to postcards and sent to friends who had missed the "party." What did they remember? What will the guards at Abu Ghraib remember? What will those smiles say?

exit smiling

Who would have thought that something as friendly and familiar as a smile could turn out to be such so complex and essential? Who would have guessed that this bantamweight expression could pack such a punch? Without smiles, the serious business of having and holding social relationships would not be possible. This does not mean however that the world would be a happier, better place if only everyone would just smile more.

What I hope is now clear is that not all smiles are like rays of sunshine. Smiles are often great disguises—smoke and mirrors—to cover sneaky intentions or hostile feelings. After Hamlet learns that Claudius has killed his father, he understands "That one may smile, and smile, and be a villain!" Smiles also come in handy—facial spin, as it were—to cover predicaments like nervousness or a persistent need to please. Then there are individuals whose constant smiling reflects not affability but an outsized belief in their own importance.

———

Smile Clichés

The world is awash with clichés and beliefs about smiling. Given that this is my final chapter, I feel the need to address a few of them.

Consider the truism that says it takes only a few muscles to smile but more to frown. And that is a good thing because . . . ?

Now mull on the one that says, "We all smile in the same language." Actually, we do not all smile in the same language. There is mounting evidence that cultures imbue their own smiles with unique attributes. Basic human smiles are tuned in ways that make perfect sense to natives, though not necessarily to outsiders. Even when a smile looks entirely familiar, the contexts in which it is used and the consequences it has often differ as one moves from one country to another or from one region to another. The impact of a smile depends on where it is used and the perspective of those who see it—two very important considerations in understanding a smile.

The reasons for cultural variations in smiling are not understood completely, but one function seems plausible: that groups find it useful to know at a glance who is a member and who is a foreigner. Take, for example, the view of some Americans that the smiles of the Japanese are inscrutable. When Japanese people smile, other Japanese people do not find it inexplicable. They know what it means without having to think about it.

Next, there is the cliché, "No one has to learn how to smile." Well, actually, we do. Babies come to birth ready to smile, and over time this initial capacity develops and matures. From research in neuroscience, we understand that repetition of any behavior trains our brains and muscles so it can be performed without the need to think about it. Smiling is no exception. Infants and children try on the smiles they see, and as they do so they learn what they mean from the reactions of others. Thus begins the process of repeating some smile types and dropping others, all the while training the neural system and muscular pathways and making it seem as if those ways of smiling were there all along.

Finally, there are those who believe that spontaneous smiles are genuine and deliberate smiles are fake. At best, this is a rough distinction; at worst, it misses the psychology underlying smiling. What looks like an utterly spontaneous smile may actually be an automatic response that is the result of much repetition. A person may have learned all too well that whenever one feels angry, one smiles. That smile is the automatic response to anger, not a spontaneous display of happy feelings. In fact, the smiler is likely unconscious of the fact and people seeing it may be confused. And it is misguided to assume that an intentional smile cannot be genuine. In a conflict-laden situation, where negativity and retaliation rule, one might intentionally smile as a way to change the tone and possibly the outcome. A smile in the midst of an argument has the potential to open the possibility of reconciliation.

The Future of Smiling

"Nexi" is cute as a button. She has huge blue eyes, porcelain white skin, and an expressive face. When people are with her, they can't help smiling, and when they do, she's right there smiling back at them. When people talk to her, she gives them her undivided attention, and when she speaks, people want to catch every word because she seems to be so accessible.

One other thing about Nexi—she is a robot. In the world of robotics, the more specific term would be *social robot* or *humanoid robot.* But Nexi is not just any social or humanoid robot—she was included in *Time* magazine's list of best inventions of 2008. She (we know it is she because the robot is programmed with a feminine voice) represents the application of human emotion and facial expression to artificial intelligence—an intriguing combination if there ever was one.

Nexi looks like a cross between R2-D2 from *Star Wars* and "Eve" from *WALL-E*, except that Nexi has a highly mobile head and face. She moves around easily on a gyroscopic two-wheeled base. Her neck has four degrees of freedom and her face has movable eyes, eyelids, eyebrows, and mouth. Each eye has a camera and her forehead has a 3D infrared camera. Four separate speakers allow her to vocalize sounds and a microphone is used to detect speech. Her head moves somewhat like a human head, allowing her to nod or shake in a manner suggesting agreement or disagreement.

Scientists specified that a movable head and face features were the bare minimum for a social robot. Nexi's face is designed to display different emotions, and its cameras are programmed to recognize the human facial expressions she sees. I have to confess some reservations about the genuineness of Nexi's expression of happiness. Her smile never makes it to her eyes. It appears that not only do humans have a difficult time deliberately contracting the key muscle (the *obicularis occuli*) involved in a genuine smile, but robots do too. Nexi's face doesn't have a semblance of this muscle.

Fortunately, Nexi does not have to go it alone in the social robot sector. "Einstein" was built with similar social goals but with a different kind of face. Like Nexi, Einstein was intended to be communicative, emotionally expressive, and responsive to human facial displays. Unlike Nexi, the designers of Einstein modeled it to look quite human. Their model was the late great

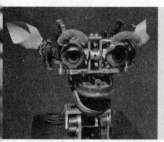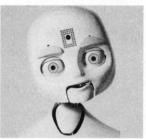

(Left to right) Social robots Kismet, Einstein, and Nexi

Albert Einstein (complete with German accent when it "speaks" English). It has a wild white wig styled like the hair of the original Einstein, along with gray brows and a mustache made from real human hair. Instead of Nexi's bright-white molded shell, Einstein's computerized innards are housed in a skinlike substance called Frubber (face rubber). Frubber approximates the look and feel of human skin—it is soft and supple and can be made to have wrinkles and pouches. Like a human face, Einstein's muscles lie under its surface—thirty-one artificial muscles, to be exact.

When engineers first conceived a robot that could socialize with humans, they knew that it would eventually have to have the ability to be emotive and not merely rational. It would have to have the ability to show a variety of emotions and the ability to accurately recognize human facial expressions as well. Moreover, the scientists recognized that these displays would need to be as natural-looking and -acting as possible since humans react differently to subtle shifts in facial expressions. As you now know, there is no single smile type that can serve all functions in all circumstances. Variations in the form—its composition, duration, intensity, and timing—as well as variations due to culture, gender, status, age, and position, to say nothing of context and previous experience, make a smile. This is a daunting task for the scientists who design social robots.

In less than a decade, social robots have become more human in appearance. The first social robot to garner attention was developed at MIT less than ten years ago by Cynthia Breazeal and her colleagues. "Kismet" had large white eyeballs with blue irises, eyelids made of silver foil, brows made of pieces of brown carpet, twists of pink paper for ears (better to wiggle), and bright red rubber tubing to stand in as lips. Behind those cartoonlike facial features were motors that lifted and arched Kismet's brows and ears, opened and closed its eyes and mouth, bent, straightened, and curled its lips.

As the technology has developed, so too have proposals that smiling robots might also have positive consequences. For example, researchers are hard at work investigating the prospect of using robots to teach autistic children social skills. Given the tendency of these kids to avoid human contact, this is not a farfetched idea. Children with Autism Spectrum Disorder find ordinary social interaction intense and distressing. They avoid eye contact, are unresponsive to smiles, and do not share the same visual point of view with most people. But what if they are introduced to an object that moves and makes faces and is less threatening than a human? Initial results show that robots with facial expressions can engage and hold the attention of autistic kids.

In a recent experiment, a team of Canadian researchers compared the reactions of five-year-old autistic children to a human and a social robot who made the same gestures. Both aimed to get the kids to imitate them. The actions included the facial expressions of joy, sadness, and anger; the body movements of raising arms and pointing at objects; and playing peek-a-boo. Tito, the social robot in this experiment, is a little over two feet tall, wears soft, bright blue, red and yellow clothes, and looks like a cross between Mr. Potato Head and Bart Simpson. The autistic children were more engaged with Tito than with the human. They showed more signs of shared attention with it and imitated more facial expressions from it, especially the smiling ones.

Finally, *embodied agents.* Like social robots, embodied agents show responsive facial expressions, but on two-dimensional inexpensive monitors rather than hyper-expensive robot platforms. Like social robots, embodied agents "interact" with end users, but instead of issuing verbal replies, the animated faces respond immediately to what the user expresses. A recent study evaluated responses to an embodied agent that served as a book reviewer. In addition to assessing various books, the embodied agent either smiled or frowned or was facially neutral while communicating with the user. Results showed that the smiling embodied agent elicited more intention to buy the recommended books and more positive evaluations of the books than the embodied agent who assumed either a straight-faced or a negative demeanor.

This is no longer science fiction: computer scientists accept the idea that robots will have to be social and emotional as well as smart and efficient. They will also need to have a great smile. The goal: being able to offer emotionally expressive robots and socially endowed embodied agents to those who desperately need "social contact." Is this reassuring or terrifying? We have hardly begun to assess the consequences of these kinds of smiles.

It is hard to avoid being affected by seeing someone smile, save perhaps for putting one's head in the sand literally or metaphorically. The fact is, smiles have consequences whether they are intended or inadvertent, conscious or unconscious, and whether they are nice or not. A well-placed smile can completely turn things around, just as the absence of one may affirm that there is nothing left to say.

acknowledgments

Given the considerable time that has transpired between the conception and completion of this book, there are many people who have contributed to it. First, my deep gratitude to the scientists, some mentioned and many not, whose enthusiasm for and skill at research never ceases to inspire. Then there are those who got me moving in the right direction: Paul Bloom for suggesting that I didn't have to commit to anything, that I just talk with his agent, and Laura Green who suggested the title. I am indebted to immediate and extended family for their interest and help, especially my sister Sandra, sister-in-law Cheryl, mother-in-law Peg, and friend Mallory Rich, who read very rough drafts and still enouraged me to stay with it. Thanks too to Rebecca Traister for ideas about writing with zest.

Thanks to friendly colleagues Karen Wynn, Peter Novak, Richard Eibach, Nancy Kuhl, and Richard Deming, and Jack Dovidio, who gave what great colleagues always give—curiosity and animated conversations. I also appreciate the contributions of many students, present and past, especially Marvin Hecht, Julie Woodzicka, Elizabeth Paluck, and Alexandra Sedlovakaya.

I am grateful to good friends who wisely spaced their queries as to how the book was coming: Pat and Bob Willis, Arthur Pinto, Stephen Bohlen, Candace Corvey, Wendy Noyes, Steve Eppler-Epstein, Laura Pesin, Paula Baraket, Nancy Ruther, Karen Dahl, Barbara Chesler, Bob Barker, Charles Rice, Curtis Lee, Larry Miller, Craig Berggren, Christopher Morse, and Jim Stott.

Two people deserve special thanks for helping transform my incipient ideas into a book: my agent, Katinka Matson, was very much in my corner affirming and abetting the project from the beginning; and my editor, Jill Bialosky, who subtly convinced me of the value of revisions.

Finally, how does one acknowledge one person who reads, gives feedback, rereads, edits, and reedits; who attends, listens, understands, and values what you're doing? That would be Megan, and why this book is dedicated to her.

notes

introduction

ix astute U.S. commander: R. Chilcote, "Commander Shows Restraint, Prevents Unnecessary Violence," CNN, 2003, http://www.cnn.com/SPECIALS/2003/iraq/heroes/chrishughes.html.

x a relationship has been found: P. S. Wallace and S. P. Taylor, "Reduction of Appeasement-Related Affect as a Concomitant of Diazepam-Induced Aggression: Evidence for a Link between Aggression and the Expression of Self-Conscious Emotions," *Aggressive Behavior* 35 (2009): 203–12.

x "the face has the only": C. A. Smith and H. S. Scott, "A Componential Approach to the Meaning of Facial Expression," in *The Psychology of Facial Expression*, ed. J. A. Russell and J. M. Fernández-Dols (Cambridge, UK: Cambridge University Press, 1997), p. 229.

xi babies practicing their smiles: Stuart Campbell, *Watch Me Grow: A Unique 3-Dimensional Week-by-Week Look at Your Baby's Behavior and Development in the Womb* (New York: St. Martin's/Griffin, 2004).

xii the *Baseball Register*: E. L. Abel and M. L. Kruger, "Smile Intensity in Photographs Predicts Longevity," *Psychological Science* 21 (2010): 542–44.

xiii such untruths are minor: Sissela Bok, *Lying: Moral Choice in Public and in Private Life* (New York: Pantheon Books, 1978); R. Brown, "Politeness Theory: Exemplar and Exemplary," in *The Legacy of Solomon Asch: Essays in Cognition and Social Psychology*, ed. I. Rock (Hillsdale, NJ: Lawrence Erlbaum Associates, 1990), 23–38.

xiii   separate neural pathways: M. S. Gazzaniga, R. B. Ivry, and G. Mangun, eds., *Fundamentals of Cognitive Neuroscience* (New York: W. W. Norton, 1998).

xiii   individuals have incurred injury: W. Rinn, "Neuropsychology of Facial Expression," in *Fundamentals of Nonverbal Behavior*, ed. R. S. Feldman and B. Rimé (Cambridge, UK: Cambridge University Press, 1991), 3–30.

xiv   evolved in our ancient ancestors: M. J. Owren and J. A. Bachorowski, "Smiling, Laughter, and Cooperative Relationships: An Attempt to Account for Human Expressions of Positive Emotions Based on 'Selfish Gene' Evolution," in *Emotion: Current Issues and Future Development*, ed. T. Mayne and G. A. Bonanno (New York: Guilford Press, 2001), 152–91.

LIFE

smile science

4   "When Farmer Oak smiled": Thomas Hardy, *Far from the Madding Crowd* (London: Smith, Elder & Co., 1874), p. 1.

4   a suitor's facial expressions: Charles Darwin, *The Expression of the Emotions in Man and Animals*, with photographic and other illustrations (1872; London: John Murray, 1921).

4   G.-B.-A. Duchenne de Boulogne: G.-B.-A. Duchenne, *The Mechanism of Human Facial Expression*, trans. R. A. Cuthbertson (1862; New York: Cambridge University Press, 1990).

5   "By the drawing backwards": Darwin, *Expression of the Emotions*, p. 204.

6   "the same curved line": Duchenne, *Mechanism of Human Facial Expression*, p. 72.

7   "She saw herself dancing": Booth Tarkington, *Alice Adams* (Garden City, NY: Doubleday, Page & Co., 1921), p. 64.

8   "The first obeys the will": Duchenne, *Mechanism of Human Facial Expression*, p. 126.

8   "the hydraulics of insincere smiles": Jonathan Franzen, *How to Be Alone: Essays* (New York: Picador, 2003), p. 83.

10   a core element of real emotion: Antonio R. Damasio, *The Feeling of What Happens: Body and Emotion in the Making of Consciousness* (New York: Harcourt, 2000).

10   happily married couples: R. W. Levenson and J. M. Gottman, "Marital

Interaction: Physiological Linkage and Affective Exchange," *Journal of Personality and Social Psychology* 45 (1983): 587–97.

10   Infants . . . smiles: N. A. Fox and R. J. Davidson, "Patterns of Brain Electrical Activity during Facial Signs of Emotion in 10-Month-Old Infants," *Developmental Psychology* 24 (1988): 230–36.

11   sexist jokes: M. LaFrance and J. Woodzicka, "No Laughing Matter: Women's Verbal and Nonverbal Responses to Sexist Humor," in *Prejudice: The Target's Perspective*, ed. J. Swim and C. Stangor (New York: Academic Press, 1998), 61–80.

12   to evaluate a variety of T-shirts: V. Peace, L. Miles, and L. Johnston, "It Doesn't Matter What You Wear: The Impact of Posed and Genuine Expressions of Happiness on Product Evaluation," *Social Cognition* 24 (2006): 137–68.

12   the most scientifically researched facial expression: L. A. Camras, C. Malatesta, and C. E. Izard, "The Development of Facial Expression in Infancy," in *Fundamentals of Nonverbal Behavior*, ed. R. Feldman and B. Rimé (Cambridge, UK: Cambridge University Press, 1991).

12   smiley face buttons: "Creator of Smiley Face Icon Dies at 79," Associated Press, April 13, 2001.

13   "He was appalled again": Graham Greene, *The Power and the Glory* (1939; New York: Penguin Classics, 2003), p. 81.

13   facial composites: P. Ekman and W. V. Friesen, *Unmasking the Face: A Guide to Recognizing Emotions from Facial Clues* (Englewood Cliffs, NJ: Prentice-Hall, 1975; repr. New York: Malor Books, 2003). This reference is to the original.

13   the secondary adversary Hassassin: Dan Brown, *Angels and Demons* (New York: Simon & Schuster, 2009), p. 347.

14   causing dimples to form: J. Pessa et al., "Double or Bifid Zygomaticus Major Muscle: Anatomy, Incidence, and Clinical Correlation," *Clinical Anatomy* 11 (1998): 310–13.

15   "It was a smile": Robert Louis Stevenson, *Treasure Island* (1883; New York: Macmillan, 1922), p. 154.

17   a *miserable* smile: P. Ekman and W. V. Friesen, "Felt, False and Miserable Smiles," *Journal of Nonverbal Behavior* 6 (1988): 238–52.

17   "concern furrows": W. M. Brown, B. Palameta, and C. Moore, "Are There Nonverbal Cues to Commitment? An Exploratory Study Using the Zero-Acquaintance Video Presentation Paradigm," *Evolutionary Psychology* 1 (2003): 42–69.

17   a group of aphasic patients: Oliver Sacks, *The Man Who Mistook His Wife for a Hat* (New York: Simon & Schuster, 1998), p. 80.

18   "In came Mrs. Fezziwig": Charles Dickens, *A Christmas Carol in Prose: Being a Ghost Story of Christmas* (1843; Boston: Little, Brown, 1920), p. 59.

18   *electromyography*: A. J. Fridlund and C. E. Izard, "Electromyographic Studies of Facial Expressions of Emotions and Patterns of Emotions," in *Social Psychophysiology: A Sourcebook*, ed. J. T. Cacioppo and R. E. Petty (New York: Guilford Press, 1983), 243–86.

19   "Well! I've often seen": Lewis Carroll, *Alice's Adventures in Wonderland*. (1865; London: Macmillan and Co., 1913), p. 59.

19   voluntary smiles: G. E. Schwartz, G. L. Ahern, and S. Brown, "Lateralized Facial Muscle Response to Positive and Negative Emotional Stimuli," *Psychophysiology* 16 (1979): 561–71.

19   the *ingratiator's dilemma*: E. E. Jones and T. S. Pittman, "Toward a General Theory of Strategic Self-Presentation," in *Psychological Perspectives on the Self*, vol. 1, ed. J. Suls (Hillsdale, NJ: Lawrence Erlbaum Associates, 1982), 231–62.

20   the more one smiles: Ibid.

20   "indestructible smile": Joseph Heller, *Catch-22: A Novel* (New York: Simon & Schuster, 1961), p. 25.

21   "Having handed them coffee": Doris Lessing, *The Summer before the Dark* (New York: Alfred A. Knopf, 1973), p. 14.

21   The smile "starts": E. Krumhuber, A. S. R. Manstead, and A. Kappas, "Temporal Aspects of Facial Displays in Persona and Expression Perception: The Effects of Smile Dynamics, Head Tilt, and Gender," *Journal of Nonverbal Behavior* 31 (2007): 39–56.

22   a sequence of short smile bursts: U. Hess and R. E. Kleck, "Differentiated Emotion Elicited and Deliberate Emotional Facial Expressions," *European Journal of Social Psychology* 20 (1990): 369–85.

22   "His smiles came": Flannery O'Connor, "Good Country People" (1955), in *The Complete Stories* (New York: Farrar, Straus & Giroux, 1971), p. 288.

22   FACS: Ekman and Friesen, *Unmasking the Face*.

23   student nurses watched: P. Ekman, W. V. Friesen, and M. O'Sullivan, "Smiles When Lying," *Journal of Personality and Social Psychology* 54 (1988): 414–20.

24   "You have to deduce": Lessing, *Summer before the Dark*, p. 3.

24   the *Mona Lisa*: "Behind that Smile," *New Scientist* 188, no. 2530 (2005).

25   "this is how": J. Kincaid, "Girl," *The New Yorker*, June 26, 1978.

out of the mouths of babes

26 "Molly's First Smile": "Baby steals burglar's heart," *Sunday Mirror* (London), May 10, 1998.

27 the "First Laugh Ceremony": J. S. Chisholm, "Learning 'Respect for Everything': Navajo Images of Everything," in *Images of Childhood*, ed. C. P. Hwang, M. E. Lamb, and I. E. Sigel (Mahwah, NJ: Lawrence Erlbaum Associates, 1996), p. 10.

28 by three months, they can initiate: D. N. Stern, "Affect Attunement," in *Frontiers of Infant Psychiatry*, vol. 2, ed. J. D. Call, E. Galenson, and R. T. Tyson (New York: Basic Books, 1984), pp. 3–14.

28 "Sweet babe": William Blake, "A Cradle Song," quoted in Hazel Fellerman, ed., *Poems That Live Forever* (New York: Random House, 1965), p. 246.

28 smiles as *endogenous*: Jerome Kagan, Norbert Herschkowitz, and Elinore Herschkowitz, *A Young Mind in a Growing Brain* (Mahwah, NJ: Lawrence Erlbaum Associates, 2005).

28 Infant smiles: D. S. Messinger et al., "How Sleeping Neonates Smile," *Developmental Science* 5 (2002): 48–54.

29 something sweet to taste: J. E. Steiner, "Facial Expressions of the Neonate Infant Indicating the Hedonics of Food-Related Chemical Stimuli," in *Taste and Development*, ed. J. M. Weiffenbach (Bethesda, MD: U.S. Department of Health, Education, and Welfare, 1977).

30 smiles are *not* due to gas: Daniel G. Freedman, *Human Infancy: An Evolutionary Perspective* (New York: John Wiley and Sons, 1974).

30 observed thirty newborns: R. N. Emde and R. J. Harmon, "Endogenous and Exogenous Smiling Systems in Early Infancy," *Journal of the American Academy of Child Psychiatry* 11 (1972): 177–200.

30 Another study: Freedman, *Human Infancy*.

30 *motor smiles*: Maurice Merleau-Ponty, *The Primacy of Perception*, ed. James M. Edie (1945; Evanston, IL: Northwestern University Press, 1964).

30 How could one argue: C. E. Izard, "The Generality-Specificity Issue in Infants' Emotion Responses," *Infancy* 6 (2004): 417–23.

31 Somewhat later, a baby's smile: L. A. Camras, "Expressive Development and Basic Emotions," *Cognition and Emotion* 6 (1992): 269–84; A. Fogel and E. Thelan, "Development of Early Expressive and Communicative Action: Reinterpreting the Evidence from a Dynamic Systems Perspective," *Developmental Psychology* 23 (1987): 747–61.

32   as children start to manage: C. Z. Malatesta and C. E. Izard, "The Ontogenesis of Human Social Signals: From Biological Imperative to Symbol Utilization," in *The Psychobiology of Affective Development*, ed. N. A. Fox and R. J. Davidson (Mahwah, NJ: Lawrence Erlbaum Associates, 1984), 161–205; L. Alan Sroufe, *Emotional Development* (New York: Cambridge University Press, 1995).

32   Scientists who believe: Alan J. Fridlund, *Human Facial Expression: An Evolutionary View* (San Diego, CA: Academic Press, 1994).

33   One study observed: R. D. Phillips and V. A. Sellitto, "Preliminary Evidence on Emotions Expressed by Children during Solitary Play," *Play and Culture* 3 (1990): 79–90.

33   other investigators tantalized: R. A. Spitz and K. M. Wolf, "The Smiling Response: A Contribution to the Ontogenesis of Social Relations," *General Psychology Monograph* 34 (1946): 57–125.

33   Perhaps literally having clout: M. Virginia Wyly, *Infant Assessment* (Boulder, CO: Westview Press, 1997).

33   they smile significantly more: Fox and Davidson, "Patterns of Brain Electrical Activity."

34   they are able to imitate: A. N. Meltzoff and M. K. Moore, "Imitation, Memory and the Representation of Persons," *Infant Behavior and Development* 17 (1994): 83–94.

34   the link between: Camras, "Expressive Development and Basic Emotions."

34   Jerome Kagan . . . proposed: Jerome Kagan, *Galen's Prophecy: Temperament in Human Nature* (New York: Basic Books, 1994).

34   "emotion would not be emotion": B. Parkinson, "Untangling the Appraisal-Emotion Connection," *Personality and Social Psychology Review* 1 (1997): 62.

35   When three-year-olds are given: T. M. Field and T. A. Walden, "Production and Discrimination of Facial Expressions by Preschool Children," *Child Development* 53 (1982): 1299–1311.

36   babies who are blind: S. Fraiberg, "Blind Infants and Their Mothers: An Examination of the Sign System," in *Before Speech: The Beginning of Interpersonal Communication*, ed. M. Bullowa (New York: Cambridge University Press, 1979), 159–70.

36   infant smiles make mothers: Sarah Blaffer Hrdy, *Mothers and Others: The Evolutionary Origins of Mutual Understanding* (Cambridge, MA: Harvard University Press, 2009).

36   Infants are more likely to smile: S. S. Jones and T. Ragg, "Smile Production in Older Infants: The Importance of a Social Recipient for the Facial Signal," *Child Development* 60 (1989): 811–18.

36   bowlers: R. E. Kraut and R. E. Johnston, "Social and Emotional Messages of Smiling: An Ethological Approach," *Journal of Personality and Social Psychology* 13 (1979): 1539–53.

37   Olympic athletes: J. M. Fernández-Dols and M. A. Ruiz-Belda, "Are Smiles a Sign of Happiness?: Gold Medal Winners at the Olympic Games," *Journal of Personality and Social Psychology* 69 (1995): 1113–19.

37   the same thing happens: S. S. Jones and H. W. Hong, "How Some Infant Smiles Get Made," *Infant Behavior and Development* 28 (2005): 194–205.

37   the factors responsible: L. P. Lipsitt, "Critical Conditions in Infancy," *American Psychologist* 34 (1979): 973–80.

38   the *play* smile: D. S. Messinger, A. Fogel, and K. L. Dickson, "All Smiles Are Positive, But Some Smiles Are More Positive than Others," *Developmental Psychology* 37 (2001): 642–53.

38   the *social* smile: M. Lewis, "The Self-Conscious Emotions: Embarrassment, Shame, Pride and Guilt," in *The Handbook of Emotions*, 2nd ed., ed. M. Lewis and J. M. Haviland-Jones (New York: Guilford Press, 2000), 623–36.

38   They set their sights: Emde and Harmon, "Endogenous and Exogenous Smiling Systems"; P. R. Zelazo and M. J. Komer, "Infant Smiling to Nonsocial Stimuli and the Recognition Hypothesis," *Child Development* 42 (1971): 1327–39.

39   One speculation: M. J. Konner, "Biological Bases of Social Development," in *Social Competence in Children*, ed. M. W. Kent and J. E. Rolf (Hanover, NH: University of Vermont Press, 1979).

40   "payment for services": K. S. Robson, "The Role of Eye-to-Eye Contact in Maternal-Infant Attachment," *Journal of Child Psychology and Child Psychiatry and Allied Disciplines* 8 (1967): 15.

40   shows telltale signs: M. Venezia et al., "The Development of Anticipatory Smiling," *Infancy* 6 (2004): 397–406.

41   *Coy* smiles: V. Reddy, "Coyness in Early Infancy," *Developmental Science* 3 (2000): 186–92.

42   that mothers increase the attention: P. H. Wolff, "Observation on Newborn Infants," *Psychosomatic Medicine* 21 (1959): 110–18.

42   this smile innocently: René A. Spitz, *The First Year of Life* (New York: International Universities Press, 1965).

42 they learn the difference: R. Kahana-Kalman and A. S. Walker-Andrews, "The Role of Person Familiarity in Young Infants' Perception of Emotional Expressions," *Child Development* 72 (2001): 352–69.

43 from a non-smiling baby: M. Gerhold et al., "Early Mother-Infant Interaction as a Precursor to Childhood Social Withdrawal," *Child Psychiatry and Human Development* 32 (2002): 277–93; P. H. Leiderman, "The Critical Period Hypothesis Revisited: Mother to Infant Social Bonding in the Neonatal Period," in *Early Developmental Hazards: Predictors and Precautions*, ed. F. D. Horowitz (Boulder, CO: Westview Press, 1978).

43 Premature babies: E. Elmer and G. S. Gregg, "Developmental Characteristics of Abused Children," *Pediatrics* 40 (1967): 596–602.

43 an expressionless baby: K. Lyons-Ruth et al., "Infants at Social Risk: Relations among Infant Maltreatment, Maternal Behavior and Infant Attachment Behavior," *Developmental Psychology* 23 (1987): 223–32.

43 born to depressed or unresponsive mothers: T. M. Field, "Infants of Depressed Mothers," *Infant Behavior and Development* 18 (1995): 1–13.

43 proto-conversations: M. C. Bateson, "The Interpersonal Context of Infant Vocalization," *Quarterly Progress Report of the Research Laboratory of Electronics* 100 (1971): 170–76.

44 They are a game: J. S. Watson, "Smiling, Cooing, and the Game," *Merrill-Palmer Quarterly* 18 (1972): 323–39.

44 The more mothers reciprocate: S. L. Olson, J. E. Bates, and K. Bayles, "Early Antecedents of Childhood Impulsivity: The Role of Parent-Child Interaction, Cognitive Competence, and Temperament," *Journal of Abnormal Child Psychology* 18 (1990): 317–34; E. Waters, J. Wippman, and L. A. Sroufe, "Attachment, Positive Affect and Competence in the Peer Group: Two Studies in Construct Validation," *Child Development* 50 (1979): 821–29.

44 social referencing: Saul Feinman, ed., *Social Referencing and the Social Construction of Reality in Infancy* (New York: Plenum, 1992).

44 a "visual cliff": J. F. Sorce et al., "Maternal Emotional Signaling: Its Effect on the Visual Cliff Behavior of 1-Year-Olds," *Developmental Psychology* 21 (1985): 195–200.

45 two closed boxes: B. M. Repacholi, "Infants' Use of Attentional Cues to Identify the Referent of another Person's Emotional Expression," *Developmental Psychology* 34 (1998): 1017–25.

46 children tend to see the "wild things": Maurice Sendak, *Where the Wild Things Are* (New York: Harper & Row, 1963).

46   seeing "a woman slap": David Sedaris, *Holidays on Ice* (Milan: Mondadori, 2003), p. 18.

47   *display rules*: P. Ekman and W. V. Friesen, "The Repertoire of Nonverbal Behavior: Categories, Origins, Usage and Coding," *Semiotica* 1 (1969): 49–98.

47   the *mistaken gift paradigm*: C. Saarni, "Children's Understanding of Display Rules for Expressive Behavior," *Developmental Psychology* 15 (1979): 424–39.

47   adults often act this way: J. Haidt, "The Emotional Dog and Its Rational Tail: A Social Intuitionist Approach to Moral Judgment," *Psychological Review* 108 (2001): 814–34.

48   These justifications: J. Gnepp and D. L. R. Hess, "Children's Understanding of Verbal and Facial Display Rules," *Developmental Psychology* 22 (1986): 103–8.

48   when children grasp: P. L. Harris and D. Gross, "Children's Understanding of Real and Apparent Emotion," in *Developing Theories of Mind*, ed. J. W. Astington, P. L. Harris, and D. R. Olson (New York: Cambridge University Press, 1988).

48   Children are asked: T. L. Spinrad, C. A. Stifter, and N. Donelan-McCall, "Mothers' Regulation Strategies in Response to Toddlers' Affect: Links to Later Emotion Self-Regulation," *Social Development* 13 (2004): 40–55.

50   as an impression management system: R. Banerjee and N. Yuill, "Children's Explanations for Self-Presentational Behaviour," *European Journal of Social Psychology* 29 (1999): 105–11.

50   "His smile was": John Updike, "Gesturing" (1974) in *The Early Stories: 1953–1975* (New York: Alfred A. Knopf, 2003).

51   have behavior problems: P. M. Cole, C. Zahn-Waxler, and K. D. Smith, "Expressive Control during a Disappointment: Variations Related to Preschoolers' Behavior Problems," *Developmental Psychology* 30 (1994): 835–46.

51   unpopular children: D. J. McDowell and R. D. Park, "Differential Knowledge of Display Rules for Positive and Negative Emotions: Influences from Parents, Influences on Peers," *Social Development* 9 (2000): 415–32.

51   the refusal to put on: Erving Goffman, *The Presentation of Self in Everyday Life* (Garden City, NY: Doubleday, 1959).

the indispensable smile

52 "He smiled, understandingly": F. Scott Fitzgerald, *The Great Gatsby* (1925; New York: Charles Scribner's Sons, 1953), p. 48.

53 We see smiles: L. Miles, "Who Is Approachable?" *Journal of Experimental Social Psychology* 45 (2009): 262–66.

53 It can be correctly identified: F. Smith and P. G. Schyns, "Smile through Your Fear and Sadness: Transmitting and Identifying Facial Expression Signals over a Range of Viewing Distances," *Psychological Science* 20 (2009): 1202–8.

54 In one study: H. T. Reis et al., "What Is Smiling Is Beautiful and Good," *European Journal of Social Psychology* 20 (1990): 259–67.

54 Viewing either one: J. P. O'Doherty et al., "Temporal Difference Models and Reward-Related Learning in the Human Brain," *Neuron* 28 (2003): 329–37.

54 the *halo effect*: T. P. Mottet, S. A. Beebe, and P. C. Raffeld, "The Effects of Student Verbal and Nonverbal Responsiveness on Teachers' Liking of Students and Willingness to Comply with Student Requests," *Communication Quarterly* 52 (2004): 27–38.

55 *subliminal priming*: K. C. Berridge and P. Winkielman, "What is an Unconscious Emotion? The Case for Unconscious 'Liking,'" *Cognition and Emotion* 17 (2003): 181–211.

55 a photo of their smiling supervisor: M. B. Baldwin, S. E. Carrell, and D. F. Lopez, "Priming Relationship Schemas: My Advisor and the Pope are Watching Me from the Back of my Mind," *Journal of Experimental Social Psychology* 26 (1990): 435–54.

55 a neutral face comes across: T. Sweeny et al., "Within-Hemifield Perceptual Averaging of Facial Expressions Predicted by Neural Averaging," *Journal of Vision* 9 (2009): 1–11.

56 literally contagious: U. Dimberg, M. Thunberg, and K. Elmehed, "Unconscious Facial Reactions to Emotional Facial Expressions," *Psychological Science* 11 (2000): 86–89.

56 Three degrees of happiness: J. H. Fowler and N. A. Christakis, "Dynamic Spread of Happiness in a Large Social Network: Longitudinal Analysis over 20 Years in the Framingham Heart Study," *British Medical Journal* 337 (2008): 1–9.

56 BBC television: Cited in G. Underwood, "Subliminal Perception on TV," *Nature* 370 (1994): 103–10.

57   "When Milly smiled": Henry James, *The Wings of the Dove* (1902; London: Penguin Classics, 2008), p. 108.

57   "It is only shallow": Oscar Wilde, *The Picture of Dorian Gray* (1891; Charleston, SC: Bibliolife, 2008), p. 30.

58   Unconsciously absorbed smiles: Dimberg, Thunberg, and Elmehed, "Unconscious Facial Reactions."

59   used virtual reality: Miles, "Who Is Approachable?"

59   belongingness: R. Baumeister and M. R. Leary, "The Need to Belong: Desire for Interpersonal Attachments as a Fundamental Human Motive," *Psychological Bulletin* 117 (1995): 497–529.

59   Social rejection hurts: N. I. Eisenberger, M. D. Lieberman, and K. D. Williams, "Does Rejection Hurt? An fMRI Study of Social Exclusion," *Science* 302 (2003): 290–92.

60   a smiling face: C. N. DeWall, J. K. Manner, and D. A. Rouby, "Social Exclusion and Early-Stage Interpersonal Perception: Selective Attention to Signs of Acceptance," *Journal of Personality and Social Psychology* 96 (2009): 729–41.

60   To get at this: C. L. Pickett, W. L. Gardner, and M. Knowles, "Getting a Clue: The Need to Belong and Enhanced Sensitivity to Social Cues," *Personality and Social Psychology Bulletin* 30 (2004): 1095–1107.

60   Relationship expert: J. M. Gottman, *The Relationship Cure: A 5-Step Guide to Strengthening Your Marriage, Family, and Friendships* (New York: Crown Publishing, 2002).

61   "She looked at him": Milan Kundera, *The Book of Laughter and Forgetting* (New York: HarperPerennial, 1996), p. 29.

61   humans are hardwired: G. MacDonald and M. R. Leary, "Why Does Social Exclusion Hurt? The Relationship between Social and Physical Pain," *Psychological Bulletin* 131 (2005): 202–23.

61   "The half-caught smile": Hilda (H. D.) Doolittle, *Collected Poems, 1912–1944* (1931; New York: AMS Press, 1986), p. 212.

62   that people think: K. Lander and S. Metcalfe, "The Influence of Positive and Negative Facial Expression on Face Familiarity," *Memory* 15 (2007): 63–69.

62   smiled more at a stranger: S. M. Andersen, I. Reznik, and L. M. Manzella, "Eliciting Transient Affect, Motivation, and Expectancies in Transference: Significant-Other Representations and the Self in Social Relations," *Journal of Personality and Social Psychology* 71 (1996): 1108–29.

62   "They gave each other": Ring Lardner, "The Big Town" (1920) in *Selected Stories* (New York: Penguin Classics, 1997), p. 335.

62   his job as a taxi driver: R. Granatstein, "Taxi Drivers Live in Constant Fear," *Toronto Sun*, March 16, 1998, p. 5.

62   how taxi drivers: Diego Gambetta and Heather Hamil, *Streetwise: How Taxi Drivers Establish Customers' Trustworthiness* (New York: Russell Sage Foundation, 2005).

63   In one study: M. A. Hecht and M. LaFrance, "License or Obligation to Smile: The Effect of Power and Sex on Amount and Type of Smiling," *Personality and Social Psychology Bulletin* 24 (1998): 1332–42.

64   Economist Robert Frank: Robert H. Frank, *Passions within Reason: The Strategic Role of the Emotions* (New York: W. W. Norton, 1988).

64   unselfish people: W. M. Brown and C. Moore, "Smile Asymmetries and Reputation as Reliable Indicators of Likelihood to Cooperate: An Evolutionary Analysis," in *Advances in Psychology Research* 11, ed. S. P. Shohov (New York: Nova Science Publishers, 2002), pp. 59–78.

64   two-person games of trust: K. L. Schmidt et al., "Movement Differences between Deliberate and Spontaneous Facial Expressions: *Zygomaticus Major* Action in Smiling," *Journal of Nonverbal Behavior* 30 (2006): 37–52.

65   authentic smiles: Krumhuber, Manstead, and Kappas, "Temporal Aspects of Facial Displays."

65   "Some change of countenance": Jane Austen, *Emma* (1815; Boston: Little, Brown, 1902), p. 150.

65   a person's habitual facial expressions: C. Z. Malatesta, M. J. Fiore, and J. Messina, "Affect, Personality, and Facial Expressive Characteristics of Older Individuals," *Psychology and Aging* 1 (1987): 64–69.

67   Johann Kaspar Lavater provided: See Ellis Shookman, ed., *The Faces of Physiognomy: Interdisciplinary Approaches to Johann Caspar Lavater* (New York: Camden, 1993).

67   contended that phrenology: F. J. Gall, *On the Functions of the Brain and of Each of Its Parts: On the Origin of the Moral Qualities and Intellectual Faculties of Man, and the Conditions of Their Manifestation* (Boston: Marsh, Capen & Lyon, 1835; repr. 2010).

67   yearbook photos at Mills College: D. Keltner and L. A. Harker, "Expressions of Positive Emotion in Women's College Yearbook Pictures and Their Relationship to Personality and Life Outcomes," *Journal of Personality and Social Psychology* 80 (2001): 112–24.

68   even in mourning: G. A. Bonanno and D. Keltner, "Facial Expressions

of Emotion and the Course of Bereavement," *Journal of Abnormal Psychology* 106 (1997): 126–37.

68   when people feel social support: S. L. Master et al., "A Picture's Worth:
      Partner Photographs Reduce Experimentally Induced Pain," *Psychological Science* 20 (2009): 1316–18.

68   a group of nuns: D. D. Danner, D. Snowdon, and W. V. Friesen, "Positive Emotions in Early Life and Longevity: Findings from the Nun
      Study," *Journal of Personality and Social Psychology* 80 (2001): 804–13.

69   Positive emotion: B. Fredrickson, "Cultivating Positive Emotions to
      Optimize Health and Well-Being," *Prevention and Treatment* 3 (2000);
      A. Papa and G. Bonanno, "Smiling in the Face of Adversity: The Interpersonal and Intrapersonal Functions of Smiling," *Emotion* 8 (2008):
      1–12.

70   These psychologists measured: K. M. Prkachin and B. E. Silverman,
      "Hostility and Facial Expression in Young Men and Women: Is Social
      Regulation More Important than Negative Affect?" *Health Psychology*
      21 (2002): 33–39.

70   "The robb'd that smiles": William Shakespeare, *Othello*, Act I, scene
      III, in *The Oxford Shakespeare: The Complete Works*, 2nd ed., ed. John
      Jowett, William Montgomery, Gary Taylor, and Stanley Wells (Oxford,
      UK: Oxford University Press, 2005).

71   *weak ties*: M. Granovetter, "The Strength of Weak Ties," *American Journal of Sociology* 78 (1973): 1360–80.

72   A Miss Manners column: Nicholas Tavuchis, *Mea Culpa: A Sociology of
      Apology and Reconciliation* (Stanford, CA: Stanford University Press,
      1991), p. 28.

72   "Margot was vexed": Vladimir Nabokov, *Laughter in the Dark* (1938; New
      York: New Directions, 1960), p. 186.

72   "I mean if a boy's": J. D. Salinger, *The Catcher in the Rye* (1951; New York:
      Bantam Books, 1984), p. 14.

73   An embarrassed smile: D. Keltner and B. N. Buswell, "Embarrassment: Its Distinct Form and Appeasement Functions," *Psychological
      Bulletin* 122 (1997): 250–70.

missing smiles, frozen smiles

77   Moebius syndrome: Jonathan Cole, *About Face* (Cambridge, MA: MIT
      Press, 1999).

77   Autism Spectrum Disorder: R. Clark, P. Winkielman, and D. N.

McIntosh, "Autism and the Extraction of Emotion from Briefly Presented Facial Expressions: Stumbling at the First Step of Empathy," *Emotion* 8 (2008): 803–9.

77 People whose facial expressions: L. Tickle-Degnen and K. Doyle-Lyons, "Practitioners' Impressions of Patients with Parkinson's Disease: The Social Ecology of the Expressive Mask," *Social Science and Medicine* 58 (2004): 603–14.

77 the "Ghost Sickness": Chisholm, "Learning 'Respect for Everything.'"

78 their ability to empathize: M. Stel and A. van Knippenberg, "The Role of Facial Mimicry in the Recognition of Affect," *Psychological Science* 19 (2008): 984–85.

78 Our brains come prepared: R. Campbell, "The Neuropsychology of Lip Reading," *Philosophical Transactions of the Royal Society: Biological Sciences* 335 (1992): 39–45.

79 "God hath given you": William Shakespeare, *Hamlet*, Act III, scene I, in *The Oxford Shakespeare: The Complete Works*, 2nd ed., ed. John Jowett, William Montgomery, Gary Taylor, and Stanley Wells (Oxford, UK: Oxford University Press, 2005).

80 "the body's capacity to embody emotion": Tickle-Degnen and Doyle-Lyons, "Practitioners' Impressions."

80 It is not a surprise: G. Nijhof, "Parkinson's Disease as a Problem of Shame in Public Appearance," *Sociology of Health and Illness* 15 (2008): 193–205.

80 a study with married couples: T. Deshefy-Longhi, *Nonverbal Communication Accuracy in Couples Living with Parkinson Disease* (PhD diss., School of Nursing, Yale University, 2008).

81 "Moebians": Cole, *About Face*.

82 detected telltale signs: J. L. Adrien et al., "Blind Ratings of Early Symptoms of Autism Based on Family Home Movies," *Journal of the American Academy of Child and Adolescent Psychiatry* 33 (1993): 617–25.

82 *autistic aloneness*: L. Kanner, "Autistic Disturbances of Affective Contact," *Nervous Child* 2 (1943): 217–50.

83 When autistic children look: M. Dapretto et al., "Understanding Emotions in Others: Mirror Neuron Dysfunction in Children with Autism Spectrum Disorders," *Nature and Neuroscience* 9 (2006): 27–30.

83 "I need to rely": Temple Grandin, *Thinking in Pictures: And Other Reports from My Life with Autism* (New York: Doubleday, 1995).

84 the first face transplant: J. M. Dubernard et al., "Outcomes 18 Months

after the First Human Partial Face Transplantation," *New England Journal of Medicine* 357 (2007): 2451–60.

84 "He had a smile": Eric Ambler, *Journey into Fear*, in *Intrigue: The Great Spy Novels of Eric Ambler* (New York: Alfred A. Knopf, 1943), p. 79.

84 "He was a man": G. K. Chesterton, *The Ball and the Cross* (1910; Digireads .com Publishing, 2009), p. 20.

85 They can even detect: C. Nelson and M. De Haan, "A Neurobehavioral Approach to the Recognition of Facial Expressions in Infancy," in *The Psychology of Facial Expression*, ed. J. A. Russell and J. M. Fernández-Dols (New York: Cambridge University Press, 1997), 176–204.

85 women at home raising: M. Weissman, "Advances in Psychiatric Epidemiology: Rates and Risks for Major Depression," *American Journal of Public Health* 77 (1987): 445–51.

86 Depressed mothers: Field, "Infants of Depressed Mothers."

86 When the key adult: T. Striano, P. A. Brennan, and E. J. Vanman, "Maternal Depressive Symptoms and 6-Month-Old Infants' Sensitivity to Facial Expressions," *Infancy* 3 (2002): 115–26; M. Hernandez-Reif et al., "Happy Faces Are Habituated More Slowly by Infants of Depressed Mothers," *Infant Behavior and Development* 29 (2006): 131–35.

87 "In this sad world of ours": Abraham Lincoln, "Letter to Fanny McCullough, December 23, 1862," in *Lincoln Addresses and Letters*, ed. Charles W. Moores (New York: American Book Company, 1914).

87 developmental milestones: A. M. Cornish et al., "Postnatal Depression and Infant Cognitive and Motor Development in the Second Postnatal Year: The Impact of Depression Chronicity and Infant Gender," *Infant Behavior and Development* 28 (2005): 407–17.

87 *still-face procedure*: A. Gianino and E. Z. Tronick, "The Mutual Regulation Model: The Infant's Self and Interactive Regulation and Coping and Defensive Capacities," in *Stress and Coping Across Development*, ed. T. M. Field, P. McCabe, and N. Schneiderman (Hillsdale, NJ: Lawrence Erlbaum Associates, 1988), 47–68; G. A. Moore, J. F. Cohn, and S. B. Campbell, "Infant Affective Responses to Mother's Still Face at 6 Months Differentially Predict Externalizing and Internalizing Behaviors at 18 Months," *Developmental Psychology* 37 (2001): 706–14.

89 *indiscriminate friendliness*: S. W. Parker, C. A. Nelson, Bucharest Early Intervention Project Core Group, "The Impact of Early Institutional Rearing on the Ability to Discriminate Facial Expressions of Emotion," *Child Development* 76 (2005): 54–72.

89 read several facial expressions: G. Margolin and E. B. Gordis, "Children's Exposure to Violence in the Family and Community," *Current Directions in Psychological Science* 13 (2004): 152–55; A. S. Walker-Andrews, "Perceiving Social Affordances: The Development of Emotional Understanding," in *The Development of Social Cognition and Communication*, ed. B. D. Homer and C. S. Tamis-LeMonda (Mahwah, NJ: Lawrence Erlbaum Associates, 2005), 93–116.

89 Abused preschoolers: S. D. Pollak et al., "Recognizing Emotion in Faces: Developmental Effects of Child Abuse and Neglect," *Developmental Psychology* 36 (2000): 679–88.

89 Fathers, too, can show: H. Orvaschel, G. Walsh-Allis, and W. Ye, "Psychopathology in Children of Parents with Recurrent Depression," *Journal of Abnormal Child Psychology* 16 (1988): 17–28.

89 *positivity suppression*: T. Jacob and S. L. Johnson, "Sequential Interactions in the Parent-Child Communications of Depressed Fathers and Depressed Mothers," *Journal of Family Psychology* 15 (2001): 38–52.

90 Depressed adults: I. H. Gotlib and M. E. Beatty, "Negative Responses to Depression: The Role of Attributional Style," *Cognitive Therapy and Research* 9 (1985): 91–103.

91 *flat affect*: D. M. Sloan et al., "Looking at Facial Expressions: Dysphoria and Facial EMG," *Biological Psychology* 60 (2002): 79–90.

91 "drive-by smiling": C. Kotchemidova, "From Good Cheer to 'Drive-By Smiling': A Social History of Cheerfulness," *Journal of Social History* 39 (2005): 5–37.

93 "The sovereign voluntary path": William James, *The Principles of Psychology* (1890; New York: Dover, 1950), p. 201.

93 *facial feedback hypothesis*: D. N. McIntosh, "Facial Feedback Hypothesis: Evidence, Implications and Directions," *Motivation and Emotion* 20 (1996): 121–47; R. Tourangeau and P. C. Ellsworth, "The Role of the Facial Response in the Experience of Emotion," *Journal of Personality and Social Psychology* 37 (1979): 1519–31.

93 a woman with complete facial paralysis: J. M. Keillor et al., "Emotional Experience and Perception in the Absence of Facial Feedback," *Journal of the International Neuropsychological Society* 8 (2002): 130–35.

94 one of the first researchers: J. D. Laird, "Self-Attribution of Emotion: The Effects of Expressive Behavior on the Quality of Emotional Experience," *Journal of Personality and Social Psychology* 29 (1974): 475–86.

95 devised another ingenious way: R. Strack, L. L. Martin, and S. Stepper, "Inhibiting and Facilitating Conditions of the Human Smile: A

Non-Obtrusive Test of the Facial Feedback Hypothesis," *Journal of Personality and Social Psychology* 54 (1988): 768–77.

95   Other investigators borrowed: T. A. Ito et al., "The Influence of Facial Feedback on Race Bias," *Psychological Science* 17 (2006): 256–63.

95   parallel golf tees: R. J. Larsen, M. Kasimatis, and K. Frey, "Facilitating the Furrowed Brow: An Unobtrusive Test of the Facial Feedback Hypothesis Applied to Unpleasant Affect," *Cognition and Emotion* 6 (1992): 321–38.

96   complete suppression of all facial expression: A. Kappas, F. Bherer, and M. Theriault, "Inhibiting Facial Expressions: Limitations to the Voluntary Control of Facial Expressions of Emotion," *Motivation and Emotion* 24 (2000): 259–70.

96   strong feelings can leak: J. J. Gross and R. W. Levenson, "Hiding Feelings: The Acute Effects of Inhibiting Negative and Positive Emotion," *Journal of Abnormal Psychology* 106 (1997): 95–105.

96   Inexpressivity: E. A. Butler et al., "The Social Consequences of Expressive Suppression," *Emotion* 3 (2003): 48–67.

97   heard to complain: Martin Scorcese, cited in A. Hill, "Actors Warned to Keep Off the Botox," *The Observer* (London), February 9, 2003, http://www.guardian.co.uk/uk/2003/feb/09/film.filmnews.

99   "She shook hands": Henry James, *The Portrait of a Lady* (1881; Boston: Houghton Mifflin, 1909), p. 271.

99   Chronic social anxiety: E. A. Heerey and A. Kring, "Interpersonal Consequences of Social Anxiety," *Journal of Abnormal Psychology* 116 (2007): 125–34.

99   interviews with women who had a documented history: G. A. Bonanno et al., "When the Face Reveals What Words Do Not: Facial Expressions of Emotion, Smiling, and the Willingness to Disclose Childhood Sexual Abuse," *Journal of Personality and Social Psychology* 83 (2008): 94–110.

99   "He had a mouth as stiff": Marion Meade, *Buster Keaton: Cut to the Chase* (New York: HarperCollins, 1995).

LIES

two-faced smiles

103   Bernard Goetz: M. Gladwell, "In a Different New York, a Different Goetz Trial," *Washington Post*, April 21 1996, p. A01. See also *Washington Post*, January 4, 1985; April 28, 1987; and June 17, 1987.

104 "They exchanged": Quoted in Marshall Pugh, *The Chancer* (New York: Hutchinson, 1959), p. 92.

107 how context affects: M. G. Cline, "The Influence of Social Context on the Perception of Faces," *Journal of Personality* 2 (1956): 142–58.

108 a recent British study: B. C. Jones et al., "Integrating Gaze Direction and Expression in Preferences for Attractive Faces," *Psychological Science* 17 (2006): 588–91.

108 Lev Kuleshov: *Kuleshov on Film: The Writings of Lev Kuleshov*, ed. and trans. Ronald Levaco (Berkeley: University of California Press, 1974).

109 mixed messages: H. S. Friedman, "The Interactive Effects of Emotion and Verbal Messages on Perceptions of Affective Meaning," *Journal of Experimental Social Psychology* 15 (1979): 453–69; M. R. DiMatteo et al., "Predicting Patient Satisfaction from Physicians' Nonverbal Communication Skills," *Medical Care* 18 (1980): 367–87.

109 mixed messages . . . in marriage: P. Noller, "Channel Consistency and Inconsistency in the Communication of Married Couples," *Journal of Personality and Social Psychology* 43 (1982): 732–41.

110 distract with your smile: J. B. Bavelas et al., *Equivocal Communication* (Newbury Park, CA: Sage Publications, 1990).

110 when you are working: J. L. Robinson and H. A. Demaree, "Physiological and Cognitive Effects of Expressive Dissonance," *Brain and Cognition* 63 (2007): 70–78.

110 the blatant expression of prejudice: E. J. Vanman et al., "The Modern Face of Prejudice and Structural Features That Moderate the Effect of Cooperation on Affect," *Journal of Personality and Social Psychology* 73 (1997): 941–59.

111 Those with lots of experience: J. Richeson and J. N. Shelton, "Thin Slices of Racial Bias," *Journal of Nonverbal Behavior* 29 (2006): 75–86.

111 All that smiling: J. D. Vorauer and C. Turpie, "Disruptive Effects of Vigilance on Dominant Group Members' Treatment of Outgroup Members: Choking versus Shining under Pressure," *Journal of Personality and Social Psychology* 87 (2004): 384–99.

111 a joking message: D. Bugental, J. W. Kaswan, and L. R. Love, "Perception of Contradictory Meanings Conveyed by Verbal and Nonverbal Channels," *Journal of Personality and Social Psychology* 16 (1970): 647–60.

112 asked all sorts of people: B. M. DePaulo et al., "Lying in Everyday Life," *Journal of Personality and Social Psychology* 8 (1996): 969–95.

112   And the ability to come up: R. W. Byrne and N. Corp, "Neocortex Size
       Predicts Deception Rate in Primates," *Philosophical Transactions of the
       Royal Society: Biological Sciences* 271 (2004): 1693–99.

112   children engage in: P. Newton, V. Reddy, and R. Bull, "Children's
       Everyday Deception and Performance on False-Belief Tasks," *British
       Journal of Developmental Psychology* 18 (2000): 297–317; V. Reddy, "Get-
       ting Back to the Rough Ground: Deception and 'Social Living,'" *Phil-
       osophical Transactions of the Royal Society: Biological Sciences* 362 (2007):
       621–37.

113   Freud, for one: See Sigmund Freud, *Dora: An Analysis of a Case of Hyste-
       ria* (New York: Simon & Schuster, 1905), p. 69.

113   "One can lie": Friedrich Wilhelm Nietzsche, *Beyond Good and Evil* (1917;
       Chicago: H. Regnery Co., 1949), p. 131.

113   Deception is *not* reliably revealed: B. M. DePaulo, J. J. Lindsay, and
       B. E. Malone, "Cues to Deception," *Psychological Bulletin* 129 (2003):
       74–118.

113   rely on flawed theories: Aldert Vrij, *Detecting Lies and Deceit: The Psy-
       chology of Lying and the Implications for Professional Practice* (Chichester,
       UK: John Wiley and Sons, 2000).

114   more deliberate smiles than truth tellers: D. Biland et al., "The Effect
       of Lying on Intentional Versus Unintentional Facial Expressions,"
       European Review of Applied Psychology 58 (2008): 65–73.

115   *Duper's delight*: Paul Ekman, *Telling Lies: Clues to Deceit in the Market-
       place, Politics, and Marriage* (New York: W. W. Norton, 1992).

115   For each smile: P. Gosselin, M. Beaupre, and A. Boissonneault, "Per-
       ception of Genuine and Masking Smiles in Children and Adults: Sen-
       sitivity to Traces of Anger," *Journal of Genetic Psychology* 163 (2002):
       58–72.

116   "but the latter": Nathanial Hawthorne, *The Scarlet Letter* (1850; New
       York: Penguin Classics, 2003), p. 148.

116   *micromomentary facial expressions*: E. A. Haggard and K. S. Isaacs,
       "Micromomentary Facial Expressions as Indicators of Ego Mecha-
       nisms in Psychotherapy," in *Methods of Research in Psychotherapy*, ed.
       L. A. Gottschalk and A. H. Auerbach (New York: Appleton-Century-
       Crofts, 1966), 154–65.

116   the "truth bias": DePaulo, Lindsay, and Malone, "Cues to Deception."

117   "Cunning and deceit": Niccolò Machiavelli, *The Prince and the Discourses*
       (1513), trans. Luigi Ricci (New York: Random House, 1950), p. 318.

117   a Machiavellian worldview: Richard Christie and Florence L. Geis, *Studies in Machiavellianism* (New York: Academic Press, 1970).

117   a little Machiavellianism: D. S. Wilson, D. Near, and R. Miller, "Machiavellianism: A Synthesis of the Evolutionary and Psychological Literatures," *Psychological Bulletin* 119 (1998): 285–99.

118   a study of U.S. presidents: D. K. Simonton, "Presidential Personality: Biographical Use of the Gough Adjective Check List," *Journal of Personality and Social Psychology* 51 (1986): 149–60.

118   Machiavellians possess: P. Cherulnik et al., "Impressions of High and Low Machiavellian Men," *Journal of Personality* 49 (1981): 388–400.

118   "The distinction between": Donald Barthelme, *Sixty Stories* (1966; New York: Penguin, 2003), p. 25.

118   Con artists: E. Hankiss, *Social Traps* (Warsaw: Wiedza Powszechna, 1986).

118   "hidden by an amazing smile": R. D. Hare, "Psychopaths and Their Nature: Implications for Mental Health and Criminal Justice Systems," in *Psychopathy: Antisocial, Criminal and Violent Behavior*, ed. T. Millon et al. (New York: Guilford Press, 1998), p. 190.

119   the "most hideous": R. Holmes, "Voltaire's Grin," *New York Review of Books* 42 (1995): 49.

119   "smiled in an unfriendly": Brett Helquist [Lemony Snicket], *The Bad Beginning*, A Series of Unfortunate Events, vol. 1 (New York: Harper Collins, 2001), p. 95.

119   the *derisive . . . smile*: Darwin, *Expression of the Emotions*, p. 288.

119   Fake smiles: J. M. Gottman, *What Predicts Divorce?* (Mahwah, NJ: Lawrence Erlbaum Associates, 1994).

119   much that goes by the name: Michael Billig, *Laughter and Ridicule: Towards a Social Critique of Humour* (London: Sage Publications, 2006).

119   "Jeer pressure": L. M. Janes and J. Olson, "Jeer Pressure: The Behavioral Effects of Observing Ridicule of Others," *Personality and Social Psychology Bulletin* 26 (2000): 474–84.

120   fraternities . . . tease: D. Keltner et al., "Teasing in Hierarchical and Intimate Relations," *Journal of Personality and Social Psychology* 75 (1998): 1231–47.

120   even babies . . . tease: T. Striano and A. Vaish, "Seven- to 9-Month-Old Infants Use Facial Expressions to Interpret Others' Actions," *British Journal of Developmental Psychology* 24 (2006): 753–60.

121   "Happiness is": Ambrose Bierce, *The Unabridged Devil's Dictionary* (1935; Athens: University of Georgia Press, 2002), p. 106.

121   Insight into the nature of schadenfreude: R. H. Smith et al., "Envy and
       Schadenfreude," *Personality and Social Psychology Bulletin* 22 (1996):
       158–68; W. W. van Dijk et al., "When People Fall from Grace: Reconsid-
       ering the Role of Envy in Schadenfreude," *Emotion* 6 (2006): 156–60.

122   the ability to empathize: S. G. Shamay-Tsoory, Y. Tibi-Elhanany, and
       J. Aharon-Peretz, "The Green-Eyed Monster and Malicious Joy: The
       Neuroanatomical Bases of Envy and Gloating (Schadenfreude)," *Brain*
       130 (2007): 1663–78.

122   When people share: B. G. Englis, K. B. Vaughan, and J. T. Lanzetta,
       "Conditioning of Counter-Empathetic Emotional Responses," *Journal
       of Experimental Social Psychology* 18 (1981): 375–84.

smile politics

124   "From now on": Gore Vidal, *The Best Man* (New York: Dramatists Play
       Service, 1960).

126   presidents in the early days: R. J. Ellis, "The Joy of Power: Changing
       Conceptions of the Presidential Office," *Presidential Studies Quarterly*
       33 (2003): 269–90.

126   Calvin Coolidge: D. K. Goodwin, "A Simple Smile Helped Coolidge Win
       the Presidency," *American Journalism Review* 22 (2000): 21.

127   "Tall as a plow horse": Robert Dallek, *Lone Star Rising: Lyndon Johnson
       and His Times, 1908–1960* (New York: Oxford University Press, 1991),
       p. 162.

127   "It would be a sorrowful": B. Obama, "What I see in Lincoln's Eyes,"
       Time, June 26, 2005, p. 74, http://www.time.com/time/printout/0,88
       16,1077287,000.html.

128   "A mass leader": R. Stengel, "Mandela: His 8 Lessons of Leadership,"
       Time, July 21, 2008, http://www.time.com/time/printout/0,8816,182146
       7,00.html.

128   "Charisma": C. Camic, "The Making of a Method," *American Sociologi-
       cal Review* 52 (1987): 421–39.

128   defines "charisma": Joseph Roach, *It* (Ann Arbor: University of Michi-
       gan Press, 2007).

128   Three telltale traits: R. J. House, "A Theory of Charismatic Leader-
       ship," in *Leadership: The Cutting Edge*, ed. J. G. Hunt and L. L. Larson
       (Carbondale: Southern Illinois University Press, 1977), 189–207;
       J. A. Conger and R. N. Kanungo, "Charismatic Leadership in Organ-

izations: Perceived Behavioral Attributes and Their Measurement,"
Journal of Organizational Behavior 15 (1994): 439–52.

129   ACT: H. S. Friedman, M. R. DiMatteo, and A. Taranta, "A Study of the
Relationship between Individual Differences in Nonverbal Expressiveness and Factors of Personality and Social Interaction," *Journal of
Research in Personality* 14 (1980): 351–64; H. S. Friedman, L. M. Prince,
and M. R. Riggio, "Understanding and Assessing Nonverbal Expressiveness: The Affective Communication Test," *Journal of Personality
and Social Psychology* 39 (1980): 333–42.

130   "style becomes substance": Joe McGinniss, *The Selling of the President,
1968* (New York: Pocket Books, 1970), p. 23.

131   an appealing videostyle: Lynda Lee Kaid and Anne Johnston, *Videostyle
in Presidential Campaigns: Style and Content of Televised Political Advertising* (Westport, CT: Frederick Praeger, 2001).

131   Marshall McLuhan predicted: Marshall McLuhan and Quentin Fiore,
The Medium is the Massage (New York: Random House, 1967).

131   *visual quotes*: Roger D. Masters, *The Nature of Politics* (New Haven, CT:
Yale University Press, 1989).

132   In earlier times: J. B. Thompson, "The New Visibility," *Theory, Culture
and Society* 22 (2005): 31–51.

132   political image bites: Maria E. Grabe and Erik P. Bucy, *Image Bite
Politics: News and the Visual Framing of Elections* (New York: Oxford University Press, 2009).

132   Bill Clinton once complained: Dick Morris, *Behind the Oval Office: Winning the Presidency in the Nineties* (New York: Random House, 1997).

132   If a politician smiles: V. Ottati, N. Terkildsen, and C. Hubbard, "Happy
Faces Elicit Heuristic Processing in a Televised Impression Formation
Task: A Cognitive Tuning Account," *Personality and Social Psychology
Bulletin* 23 (1997): 1144–57.

133   Politicians ought not: Nelson Polsby, Aaron Wildavsky, and David
Hopkins, *Presidential Elections: Strategies and Structures of American Politics* (Lanham, MD: Rowman & Littlefield, 2007).

134   alarm bells: E. P. Bucy and J. E. Newhagen, "The Emotional Appropriateness Heuristic: Processing Televised Presidential Reactions to the
News," *Journal of Communication* 49 (1999): 61–69.

134   In his memoirs: Charles de Gaulle, *The Complete War Memoirs of Charles
de Gaulle*, vol. 1, *The Call to Honour* (1954; New York: Carroll & Graf,
1998).

134   several studies show: G. A. Van Kleef, C. K. W. Dreu, and A. S. R.

Manstead, "The Interpersonal Effects of Anger and Happiness in Negotiations," *Journal of Personality and Social Psychology* 86 (2004): 57–76.

135   Angry displays: R. D. Masters and D. Sullivan, "Nonverbal Behavior and Leadership: Emotion and Cognition in Political Attitudes," in *Explorations in Political Psychology*, ed. S. Iyengar and W. McGuire (Durham, NC: Duke University Press, 1993), 150–82.

135   a television spot: Kathleen Hall Jamieson, *Packaging the Presidency: A History and Criticism of Presidential Campaign Advertising* (New York: Oxford University Press, 1996).

136   what traits they want: G. V. Caprara, C. Barbaranelli, and P. G. Zimbardo, "When Parsimony Subdues Distinctiveness: Simplified Public Perceptions of Politicians' Personality," *Political Psychology* 23 (2002): 77–95.

136   "thin slices": N. Ambady and R. Rosenthal, "Thin Slices of Expressive Behavior as Predictors of Interpersonal Consequences: A Meta-Analysis," *Psychological Bulletin* 111 (1992): 256–74.

136   subjects were shown pictures: A. Todorov et al., "Inferences of Competence from Faces Predict Election Outcomes," *Science* 308 (2005): 1623–26.

137   Citizens who lean: D. R. Carney et al., "The Secret Lives of Liberals and Conservatives: Personality Profiles, Interaction Styles, and the Things They Leave Behind," *Political Psychology* 29 (2008): 807–40.

137   "very happy": P. Taylor, C. Funk, and P. Craighill, "Are We Happy Yet?" Pew Research Center, 2006, http://pewresearch.org/assets/social/pdf/AreWeHappyYet.pdf (accessed August 19, 2007), p. 16.

137   Robert Frost's definition: Jay Parini, *Robert Frost: A Life* (New York: Macmillan, 2000), p. 416.

137   New findings: N. O. Rule and N. Ambady, "Democrats and Republicans Can Be Differentiated from Their Faces" (poster presented at the annual meeting of the Association of Psychological Science, Boston, MA, May 29, 2010).

138   Many people find: D. Keltner, D. H. Gruenfeld, and C. Anderson, "Power, Approach, and Inhibition," *Psychological Bulletin* 110 (2003): 265–84.

138   The *silent bared teeth (SBT) display*: J. Van Hooff, "A Comparative Approach to the Phylogeny of Laughter and Smiling," in *Non-Verbal Communication*, ed. R. A. Hinde (Cambridge, UK: Cambridge University Press, 1972), 209–37.

139 human smiling: Konrad Lorenz, *King Solomon's Ring: New Light on Animal Ways* (1961; New York: Routledge, 2002).

139 Deferential humans often briefly: Keltner et al., "Teasing in Hierarchical and Intimate Relations."

140 on how dominant they looked: C. F. Keating et al., "Culture and the Perception of Dominance from Facial Expression," *Journal of Personality and Social Psychology* 40 (1981): 615–26.

140 Black porters: Jack Santino, *Miles of Smiles, Years of Struggle: Stories of Black Pullman Porters* (Urbana: University of Illinois Press, 1991).

140 likened porters' smiles: B. Mergen, "The Pullman Porter: From 'George' to Brotherhood," *South Atlantic Quarterly* 75 (1974): 224–35.

141 "Instead of speaking": Charlotte Brontë, *Jane Eyre* (1847; New York: Century, 1906), p. 140.

142 Communication: S. Preuschoft, "'Laughter' and 'Smile' in Barbary Macaques (*Macaca sylvanus*)," *Ethology* 91 (1992): 220–36.

143 For example, rhesus macaques: J. D. Flack and F. de Waal, "Context Modulates Signal Meaning in Primate Communication," *Proceedings of the National Academy of Sciences* 104 (2007): 1581–86.

143 Social psychologists define "power": See Keltner, Gruenfeld, and Anderson, "Power, Approach, and Inhibition."

144 observers knew a dominant person: J. Chiao et al., "Knowing Who's Boss: fMRI and ERP Investigations of Social Dominance Perception," *Group Processes and Intergroup Relations* 11 (2008): 201–14.

144 higher up on the socioeconomic ladder: M. W. Kraus and D. Keltner, "Signs of Socioeconomic Status," *Psychological Science* 20 (2009): 99–104.

145 we designed an experiment: Hecht and LaFrance, "License or Obligation to Smile."

service with a smile

147 advertisers had learned: W. L. Larned, "The Smile That Sells Goods," *Printers' Ink*, November 30, 1911, pp. 3–8.

148 " . . . it's not what you do" . . . "He's a man": Arthur Miller, *Death of a Salesman* (1949; New York: Penguin Classics, 1998), pp. 65, 111.

149 Welfare recipients are instructed: R. Schmidt, "A New Wrinkle in Welfare Reform," *Chronicle of Higher Education*, April 23, 1999, p. A42.

149 Female ice skaters: J. Green, "The Making of an Ice Princess," *New York Times*, December 18, 2005, sect. 6, p. 51.

149 The Professional Golf Association: M. Aitken, "European Tour Crying Out for More Shiny, Happy People," *The Scotsman*, May 11, 2004, p. 32.

149 telemarketers: V. Belt, R. Richardson, and J. Webster, "Women, Social Skill and Interactive Service Work in Telephone Call Centres," *New Technology, Work and Employment* 17 (2002): 20–34.

149 Research has in fact shown: V. V. Tartter, "Happy Talk: Perceptual and Acoustic Effects of Smiling on Speech," *Perceptual Psychophysiology* 27 (1980): 24–27.

149 Highway toll takers: "Heard in the Halls; Toll-Taker Bonus: Paid for Smiling," *Patriot Ledger*, May 16, 1998.

149 A railway company in Japan: Peter Cheese, "Japan Railway Monitoring Employees to Ensure They Smile," *The Economist*, September 14, 2009.

149 Adoption agency Web sites: R. Kelley, "Show Them a 'Take Me Home' Face: Enlisting the Camera in the Adoption Quest," *New York Times*, March 21, 2005, p. A1.

149 starving children: D. Kennedy, "Selling the Distant Other: Humanitarianism and Imagery," *Journal of Humanitarian Assistance*, http://jha.ac/2009/02/28/selling-the-distant-other-humanitarianism-and-imagery.

149 book jacket photographs: J. Marshall, "The Write Pose: Authors Can Think of a Lot of Things—but Not How to Get Out of Those Darn Book-Jacket Shots," *Seattle Post-Intelligencer*, February 1, 1996.

150 The advice to supply: Jennifer L. Pierce, *Gender Trials: Emotional Lives in Contemporary Law Firms* (Berkeley: University of California Press, 1995).

150 Hong Kong: P. Kwong and D. Miscevic, "Globalization and Hong Kong's Future," *Journal of Contemporary Asia* 32 (2002): 323–37.

150 "smile checks": C. Endy, "Rudeness and Modernity: The Reception of American Tourists in Early Fifth Republic France," *French Politics, Culture and Society* 21 (2003)": 55–86.

151 bad service: A. M. Ryan and R. F. Ployhart, "Customer Service Behavior," in *Handbook of Psychology*, vol. 12, *Industrial and Organizational Psychology*, ed. W. C. Borman, C. Walter, and D. R. Ilgen (New York: John Wiley and Sons, 2003), 377–97.

151 George Washington University Hospital: T. Hudson, "Service with a Smile, or Else," *Hospitals and Health Networks* 72 (January 20, 1998): 62.

151   during the 2008 Olympic Games: M. Magnier, "As Olympics Loom, Bei-
      jing Outlaws Bad Manners," *Los Angeles Times*, January 14, 2007, p. 18.

152   Complimenting customers: J. S. Seiter and E. Dutson, "The Effect of
      Compliments on Tipping Behavior in Hairstyling Salons," *Journal of
      Applied Social Psychology* 37 (2007): 1999–2007.

152   the size of the tip: K. L. Tidd and J. D. Lochard, "Monetary Significance
      of the Affiliative Smile: A Case for Reciprocal Altruism," *Bulletin of the
      Psychonomic Society* 11 (1978): 344–46.

153   baristas: P. B. Barger and A. A. Grandey, "Service with a Smile and
      Encounter Satisfaction: Emotional Contagion and Appraisal Mecha-
      nisms," *Academy of Management Journal* 49 (2006): 1229–38.

152   In shoe stores: W. C. Tsai, "Determinants and Consequences of
      Employee Displayed Positive Emotions," *Journal of Management* 27
      (2001): 497–512.

153   At hotel reception desks: A. A. Grandey et al., "Is That Smile for Real?
      Reaction to Inauthenticity in Service Settings" (paper presented at the
      annual meeting of the Academy of Management, Denver, CO, 2002).

153   branch offices of a major bank: S. D. Pugh, "Service with a Smile: Emo-
      tional Contagion in the Service Encounter," *Academy of Management
      Journal* 44 (2001): 1018–27.

154   a movie rental service: T. Henig et al., "Are All Smiles Created Equal?
      How Emotional Contagion and Emotion Labor Affect Service Rela-
      tionships," *Journal of Marketing* 70 (2006): 58–73.

155   a smiley face on the check: B. Rind and P. Bordia, "Effect on Restaurant
      Tipping of Male and Female Servers Drawing a Happy, Smiling Face on
      the Backs of Customer Checks," *Journal of Applied Social Psychology* 26
      (1996): 218–25.

156   "smiling is elevated": Y. Altman, "A Theme Park in a Cultural Strait-
      jacket: The Case of Disneyland Paris, France," *Managing Leisure* 1
      (1995): 43–56.

156   Luna Park: Woody Register, *The Kid of Coney Island: Fred Thompson and
      the Rise of American Amusements* (New York: Oxford University Press,
      2003).

156   "the management of feeling": Arlie Russell Hochschild, *The Managed
      Heart* (Berkeley: University of California Press, 1983), p. 7.

157   *surface acting*: Ibid.

158   "We try to stir up": Ibid., p. 43.

158   "faking in good faith": A. Rafaeli and R. I. Sutton, "Expression of

Emotion as Part of the Work Role," *Academy of Management Review* 12 (1987): 32.

158   "If she were not poor": D. K. Shipler, "A Poor Cousin of the Middle Class," *New York Times Magazine*, January 18, 2004.

159   "When conditions estrange": Hochschild, *Managed Heart*, p. 90.

159   "It was the small of her back": Carson McCullers, *The Heart Is a Lonely Hunter* (Boston: Houghton Mifflin, 1940), p. 351.

159   Carried on too long: P. K. Adelmann, "Emotional Labor as a Potential Source of Job Stress," in *Organizational Risk Factors for Job Stress*, ed. S. L. Sauter and L. R. Murphy (Washington, DC: American Psychological Association, 1995), 371–81.

160   thrive on being nice: S. M. Kruml and D. Geddes, "Catching Fire Without Burning Out: Is There an Ideal Way to Perform Emotion Labor?" in *Emotions in the Workplace: Research, Theory, and Practice*, ed. N. M. Ashkanasy, C. E. J. Härtel, and W. J. Zerbe (Westport, CT: Quorum Books, 2000).

160   by "faking it": Ashkanasy, Härtel, and Zerbe, eds., *Emotions in the Workplace*; D. Zapf, "Emotion Work and Psychological Well-Being. A Review of the Literature and Some Conceptual Considerations," *Human Resource Management Review* 12 (2002): 237–68.

160   "The great actor": Constantin Stanislavski, *An Actor Prepares*, trans. E. R. Hapgood (New York: Theatre Arts, 1936), p. 13.

160   likely to feel pride: A. A. Grandey, "When 'The Show Must Go On': Surface Acting and Deep Acting as Determinants of Emotional Exhaustion and Peer-Rated Service Delivery," *Academy of Management Journal* 46 (2003): 86–96; A. J. Morris and D. C. Feldman, "Managing Emotions in the Workplace," *Journal of Managerial Issues* 9 (1997): 257–74.

161   terrific tour guides: L. Holyfield, "Manufacturing Adventure: The Buying and Selling of Emotions," *Journal of Contemporary Ethnography* 28 (1999): 3–32.

161   the regulation of positive emotion: J. J. Gross, "The Emerging Field of Emotion Regulation: An Integrative Review," *Review of General Psychology* 2 (1998): 271–99.

162   a sample of family doctors: E. B. Larson and X. Yao, "Clinical Empathy as Emotional Labor in the Patient-Physician Relationship," *Journal of the American Medical Association* 293 (2005): 1100–1106.

162   Holiday Inn: M. Gardner, "When Service Means More than a Smile," *Christian Science Monitor*, October 7, 1993, p. 7.

162   the 5–90–5 rule: Ari Weinzweig, *Zingerman's Guide to Good Eating* (Boston: Houghton Mifflin, 2003).

163   the "smile factory": J. Van Maanen, "The Smile Factory: Work at Disneyland," in *Reframing Organizational Culture*, ed. P. J. Frost et al. (Newbury Park, CA: Sage Publications, 1991).

163   In fire stations: C. Scott and K. K. Myers, "The Socialization of Emotion: Learning Emotion Management at the Fire Station," *Journal of Applied Communication* 33 (2007): 67–92.

164   customers are not passive: A. A. Grandey and A. L. Brauburger, "The Emotion Regulation behind the Customer Service Smile," in *Emotions in the Workplace: Understanding the Structure and Role of Emotions in Organizational Behavior*, ed. R. G. Lord, R. J. Klimoski, and R. Kanfer (San Francisco, CA: Jossey-Bass, 2003), 260–94.

LOYALTY

real men don't smile

167   "he proved to be": DeAnne Blanton and Lauren M. Cook, *They Fought Like Demons: Women Soldiers in the American Civil War* (Baton Rouge: Louisiana State University Press, 2002), p. 112.

168   Margaret Catherine Murphy: Ibid., p. 238.

170   Parents often describe: J. Z. Rubin, F. J. Provenzano, and Z. Luria, "The Eye of the Beholder: Parents' Views on Sex of Newborns," *American Journal of Orthopsychiatry* 44 (1974): 512–19.

170   parents continue to have: K. H. Hildebrandt, D. A. Vogel, and M. A. Lake, "Parents' Gender-Stereotyped Perceptions of Newborns: The Eye of the Beholder Revisited," *Sex Roles* 33 (1995): 687–701.

170   girls begin outsmiling boys: C. P. Ellsworth, D. W. Muir, and S. M. Hains, "Social Competence and Person-Object Differentiation: An Analysis of the Still-Face Effect," *Developmental Psychology* 29 (1993): 63–73.

170   "Baby X" studies: J. Condry and S. Condry, "Sex Differences: A Study of the Eye of the Beholder," *Child Development* 47 (1976): 812–19.

170   the sex of the baby: E. Nagy, E. Nemeth, and P. Molnar, "From Unidentified to 'Misidentified' Newborn: Male Bias in Recognition of Sex," *Perception and Motor Skills* 90 (2000): 102–4.

171   varies across the lifespan: M. LaFrance, M. A. Hecht, and E. L. Paluck, "The Contingent Smile: A Meta-analysis of Sex Differences in Smiling," *Psychological Bulletin* 129 (2003): 305–34.

171   women smile more than men: Ibid.

171   girls and women are more likely: J. Hyde, "The Gender Similarities Hypothesis," *American Psychologist* 60 (2005): 581–92.

172   the *zygomaticus major* muscle: R. W. McAlister, E. M. Harkness, and J. J. Nicoll, "An Ultrasound Investigation of Lip Levator Musculature," *European Journal of Orthodontics* 20 (1998): 713–20.

173   testosterone: J. M. Dabbs and M. G. Dabbs, *Heroes, Rogues, and Lovers: Testosterone and Behavior* (New York: McGraw-Hill, 2001); J. M. Dabbs, "Testosterone, Smiling and Facial Appearance," *Journal of Nonverbal Behavior* 21 (1997): 45–54.

173   "wolfish": Dabbs and Dabbs, *Heroes, Rogues, and Lovers.*

173   yellow-gray eyes: Robert L. Gale, ed., *A Dashiell Hammett Companion* (Santa Barbara, CA: Greenwood Publishing, 2000).

173   *unrestricted sociosexuality:* J. Simpson, S. Gangestad, and M. Biek, "Personality and Nonverbal Social Behavior: An Ethological Perspective of Relationship Initiation," *Journal of Experimental Social Psychology* 29 (1993): 434–61.

174   a dating game scenario: Ibid.

175   boys . . . already practicing "cool": M. Polce-Lynch et al., "Gender and Age Patterns in Emotional Expression, Body Image, and Self-Esteem: A Qualitative Analysis," *Sex Roles* 38 (1998): 1025–48.

176   We found that: M. LaFrance, "Pressure to Be Pleasant: Effects of Sex and Power on Reactions to Not Smiling," *International Review of Social Psychology* 2 (1998): 95–108.

176   under either posed or candid conditions: J. A. Hall et al., "Status, Gender, and Nonverbal Behavior in Candid and Posed Photographs: A Study of Conversations between University Employees," *Sex Roles* 44 (2001): 677–92.

177   "What college": Tom Wolfe, *I Am Charlotte Simmons* (New York: Picador, 2005) p. 6.

177   "confidence in the face of risk": Harvey C. Mansfield, *Manliness* (New Haven, CT: Yale University Press, 2006), p. 23.

177   "For days I practiced": Sam Shepard, *Motel Chronicles* (San Francisco, CA: City Lights, 1982), p. 14.

177   ghastly video clips: M. Ansfield, "Smiling When Distressed: When a Smile is a Frown Turned Upside Down," *Personality and Social Psychology Bulletin* 33 (2007): 673–75.

178   when men are asked: J. J. Gross and O. P. John, "Mapping the Domain of Emotional Expressivity: Multi-Method Evidence for a Hierarchical

Model," *Journal of Personality and Social Psychology* 74 (1998): 170–91; J. J. Gross and O. P. John, "Individual Differences in Two Emotion Regulation Processes: Implications for Affect, Relationships, and Well-Being," *Journal of Personality and Social Psychology* 85 (2003): 348–62.

178 not "typical" females: B. McElhinny, "Challenging Hegemonic Masculinities: Female and Male Police Officers Handling Domestic Violence," in *Gender Articulated: Language and the Socially Constructed Self*, ed. K. Hall and M. Bucholtz (New York: Routledge, 1995), 217–43.

178 Members of girl gangs: N. Mendoza-Denton, "Fighting Words: Latina Girls, Gangs, and Language Attitudes," in *Speaking Chicanas*, ed. D. L. Galindo and N. Gonzalez-Vasquez (Tucson: University of Arizona Press, 1999).

178 a disappointing gift: T. L. Davis, "Gender Differences in Masking Negative Emotions: Ability or Motivation?" *Developmental Psychology* 31 (1995): 660–67.

179 That was the state of things: S. L. Bem, "The Measurement of Psychological Androgyny," *Journal of Consulting and Clinical Psychology* 42 (1974): 155–62.

180 we examined whether: M. LaFrance and B. Carmen, "The Nonverbal Display of Psychological Androgyny," *Journal of Personality and Social Psychology* 7 (1980): 36–49.

181 Women lived as men: Marjorie Garber, *Vested Interests: Cross-Dressing and Cultural Anxiety* (New York: Routledge, 1992).

181 whether transvestism has to do: Charlotte A. Suthrell, *Unzipping Gender: Sex, Cross-Dressing and Culture* (Oxford, UK: Berg Publishers, 2004).

182 Diane Torr: D. Torr and J. Czyzselska, "Drag Kings and Subjects," *Journal of Lesbian Studies* 2 (1998): 235–38.

182 *Transsexuals*: Matt Kailey, *Just Add Hormones: An Insider's Guide to the Transsexual Experience* (Boston: Beacon Press, 2005).

184 "She was too serious": M. Zeigler, "Pair Au Contraire: Zimmerman and Ina Broke the Ice during Restaurant Chatfests," *San Diego Union-Tribune*, February 9, 2002.

184 cheerleading: A. Adams and P. Bettis, "Commanding the Room in Short Skirts: Cheering as the Embodiment of Ideal Girlhood," *Gender and Society* 17 (2003): 73–89.

185 Certain patterns set apart: P. N. Cohen and M. L. Huffman, "Individuals, Jobs, and Labor Markets: The Devaluation of Women's Work," *American Sociological Review* 68 (2003): 443–63.

185   "Focus on your delivery": Julia Balzer-Riley, *Communication in Nursing*, 4th ed. (St. Louis, MO: C. V. Mosby, 2000), p. 206.

185   Physicians: M. M. Lill and T. J. Wilkinson, "Judging a Book by Its Cover: Descriptive Survey of Patients' Preferences for Doctors' Appearance and Mode of Address," *British Medical Journal* 331 (2005): 1524–27.

185   "she has the ability": Ken Kesey, *One Flew Over the Cuckoo's Nest* (1962; New York: Penguin Classics, 2007), p. 42.

186   "painted smile": Ibid., p. 5.

186   "stretched tight": Ibid., p. 87.

186   "out before her": Ibid., p. 85.

186   Teaching: A. M. Trousdale, "Teacher as Gatekeeper—Schoolteachers in Picture Books for Young Children," in *Images of Schoolteachers in Twentieth-Century America—Paragons, Polarities, Complexities*, ed. P. B. Joseph and G. E. Burnaford (New York: St. Martin's Press, 1994), 195–214.

186   "Being pleasant not only": J. L. Pierce, "Emotional Labor among Paralegals," *Annals of the American Academy of Political and Social Science* 56 (1999), p. 130.

187   temporary workers: Kevin D. Henson, *Just a Temp* (Philadelphia: Temple University Press, 1996).

187   Stay-at-home fathers: T. Field, "Interaction Behaviors of Primary versus Secondary Caretaker Fathers," *Developmental Psychology* 14 (1978): 183–84.

188   couples who have been together: P. R. Shaver, H. J. Morgan, and S. Wu, "Is Love a Basic Emotion?" *Personal Relationships* 3 (2005): 81–96.

188   couples who exchange: J. M. Gottman, "Psychology and the Study of Marital Processes," *Annual Review of Psychology* 49 (1998): 169–97; Gottman, *Relationship Cure.*

189   gay and lesbian couples: Gottman, *Relationship Cure.*

189   Is it love: G. C. Gonzaga et al., "Romantic Love and Sexual Desire in Close Relationships," *Emotion* 6 (2006): 163–79.

190   women laugh and smile more: R. Provine, "Laughter Punctuates Speech: Linguistic, Social and Gender Contexts of Laughter," *Ethology* 95 (1993): 291–98.

190   the wives smile and look: C. C. Weisfeld and M. A. Stack, "When I Look into Your Eyes: An Ethological Analysis of Gender Differences in Married Couples' Nonverbal Behaviors," *Psychology, Evolution and Gender* 4 (2002): 125–47.

190 "Women have served": Virginia Woolf, *A Room of One's Own* (1930; New York: Houghton Mifflin, 2005), p. 35.

190 Could greater smiling: M. J. Hertenstein et al., "Smile Intensity in Photographs Predicts Divorce Later in Life," *Motivation and Emotion* 33 (2009): 99–105.

191 Men like to see women smile: M. R. Cunningham, "Measuring the Physical in Physical Attractiveness: Quasi-Experiments on the Socio-biology of Female Facial Beauty," *Journal of Social and Personality Psychology* 50 (1986): 925–35.

191 "a smile he could feel": Raymond Chandler, *Farewell, My Lovely* (New York: Alfred A. Knopf, 1940; repr. New York: Vintage Crime/Black Lizard, 1992), p. 124. Page reference is to the 1992 edition.

191 what a woman intends as being friendly: A. Abbey and C. Melby, "The Effect of Non-Verbal Cues on Gender Differences in Perceptions of Sexual Intent," *Sex Roles* 15 (1986): 283–98.

192 women smile even when they are being sexually harassed: J. A. Wood-zicka and M. LaFrance, "The Effects of Subtle Sexual Harassment on Women's Performance in a Job Interview," *Sex Roles* 53 (2005): 67–77; C. G. Bowman, "Street Harassment and the Informal Ghettoization of Women," *Harvard Law Review* 106 (1993): 517–80.

smiles with a foreign accent

195 welcoming smiles: I. Eibl-Eibesfeldt, "Similarities and Differences between Cultures in Expressive Movements," in *Nonverbal Communication*, ed. R. A. Hinde (London: Cambridge University Press, 1972), 297–314.

196 in some Muslim countries: A. Rafaeli and R. I. Sutton, "The Expression of Emotion in Organizational Life," *Research in Organizational Behavior* 11 (1989): 1–42.

196 "For Cambridge people": Rupert Brooke, *The Collected Poems of Rupert Brooke: With a Memoir* (Charleston, SC: Bibliolife, 2009), p. 163.

196 In Northern Europe: Larry P. Nucci, Geoffrey B. Saxe, and Elliot Turiel, eds., *Culture, Thought, and Development* (Mahwah, NJ: Lawrence Erlbaum Associates, 2000).

196 "Frosty Mugs": R. Thurow and L. Lescaze, "Frosty Mugs: Winter Olympics Hosts Are Known for Skiing, Not Sunny Disposition," *Wall Street Journal* (Eastern edition), January 17, 1994, p. A1.

196 Adorno was mystified: T. Adorno, *The Culture Industry: Selected Essays on Mass Culture* (London: Routledge, 1991; repr. 2001).

197 "Smile if you have nothing": Jean Baudrillard, *America* (New York: Verso Press, 1989), p. 34.

198 a class in Conversational French: Laurence Wylie and Rick Stafford, *Beaux Gestes: A Guide to French Body Talk* (Cambridge, MA: Undergraduate Press, 1977).

198 "Accent is the soul": Jean-Jacques Rousseau, quoted in T. Edwards, *A Dictionary of Thoughts: Being a Cyclopedia of Laconic Quotations from the Best Authors of the World, Both Ancient and Modern* (London: Cassell Publishing Company, 1908).

199 Scientists found that infants: W. M. Weikum et al., "Visual Language Discrimination in Infancy," *Science* 25 (2007): 1159.

200 When French speakers from the Canadian: H. A. Elfenbein et al., "Toward a Dialect Theory: Cultural Differences in the Expression and Recognition of Posed Facial Expressions," *Emotion* 7 (2007): 131–46.

200 the *in-group advantage effect*: H. A. Elfenbein and N. Ambady, "Is There an In-Group Advantage in Emotion?" *Psychological Bulletin* 128 (2002): 243–49.

201 American and Australian participants: A. A. Marsh, H. A. Elfenbein, and N. Ambady, "Separated by a Common Language: Nonverbal Accents and Cultural Stereotypes about Americans and Australians," *Journal of Cross-Cultural Psychology* 38 (2007): 284–301.

201 One possibility is that people: M. Yuki, W. W. Maddux, and T. Masuda, "Are the Windows to the Soul the Same in the East and West? Cultural Differences in Using the Eyes and Mouth as Cues to Recognize Emotions in Japan and the United States," *Journal of Experimental Social Psychology* 43 (2006): 303–11.

202 familiar folk tales: Z. Ye, "The Chinese Folk Model of Facial Expressions," *Culture & Psychology* 10 (2004): 197–222.

202 Even simple *emoticons*: A. Pollack, "Happy in the East (^_^) or Smiling in the West :-)," *New York Times*, August, 12, 1996, p. D5.

203 "deeply resounding emotion": S. Price, "Cartoons from another Planet: Japanese Animation as Cross-Cultural Communication," *Journal of American and Comparative Cultures* 24 (2001): 163.

203 the Laughing Buddha: Conrad Hyers, *The Laughing Buddha: Zen and the Comic Spirit* (Boston: Longwood Academic, 1991).

203 had "retouched his features": Henry James, *The Ambassadors* (1903; Oxford, UK: Oxford University Press, 2008), p. 164.

204 a new "British" smile: J. Harlow, "The Smile That Says Where You're From," *Sunday Times* (London), February 20, 2005.

204   In India, happiness: D. Keltner and J. Haidt, "Social Functions of Emo-
      tions," in *Emotions: Current Issues and Future Directions*, ed. T. Mayne
      and G. Bonanno (New York: Guilford Press, 2001), 192–213.

205   "He does smile": William Shakespeare, *Twelfth Night*, Act III, scene II,
      in *The Oxford Shakespeare: The Complete Works*, 2nd ed., ed. John Jowett,
      William Montgomery, Gary Taylor, and Stanley Wells (Oxford, UK:
      Oxford University Press, 2005).

205   "we are about as effective": Damasio, *Feeling of What Happens*, p. 49.

205   one who didn't buy it: Ray L. Birdwhistell, *Kinesics and Context* (Phila-
      delphia: University of Pennsylvania Press, 1970).

206   compared the spontaneous: Ekman and Friesen, "The Repertoire of
      Nonverbal Behavior."

208   When . . . Hideki Matsui: J. Curry, "Matsui's Hello: One Colossal Grand
      Slam," *New York Times*, April 9, 2003.

209   mass weddings in Seoul: "Big Wedding: 20,000 Gather for Mass Nup-
      tials," Associated Press, October 13, 2009.

209   children in both the United States and Israel: I. E. Alexander and E.
      Y. Babad, "Returning the Smile of the Stranger: Within Culture and
      Cross-cultural Comparisons of Israeli and American Children,"
      Genetic Psychology Monographs 103 (1981): 31–77.

210   wary of strangers: M. Jarymowicz and D. Bar-Tal, "The Dominance of
      Fear over Hope in the Life of Individuals and Collectives," *European
      Journal of Social Psychology* 36 (2006): 367–92.

210   members of their in-group: M. G. Beaupre and U. Hess, "In My Mind,
      We All Smile: A Case of In-Group Favoritism," *Journal of Experimental
      Social Psychology* 39 (2003): 371–7.

210   "a distinctive devilish gleam": Florence King, *Southern Ladies and Gen-
      tlemen* (New York: Stein & Day, 1975; repr. New York: St. Martin's Press,
      1993), p. 76. Page reference is to the 1993 edition.

210   all that sweetness: D. Cohen et al., "'When You Call Me That, Smile!' How
      Norms for Politeness, Interaction Styles, and Aggression Work Together
      in Southern Culture," *Social Psychology Quarterly* 62 (1999): 257–75.

210   a *culture of honor*: Richard E. Nisbett and Dov Cohen, *Culture of Honor:
      The Psychology of Violence in the South* (Boulder, CO: Westview Press,
      1996).

211   Americans' promiscuous smiling: Harold J. Laski, *American Democ-
      racy: A Commentary and an Interpretation* (New York: Viking Press,
      1948).

211   "Is there a Japanese smile": Paul Theroux, *The Happy Isles of Oceania* (New York: G. P. Putnam's Sons, 1992), p. 361.

211   smiles are given *to*: Goffman, *Presentation of Self*.

211   the Japanese smile: Robert L. Gale, ed., *A Lafcadio Hearn Companion* (Westport, CT: Greenwood Publishing, 2001).

212   Japanese mothers focus more: W. Caudill and H. Weinstein, "Maternal Care and Infant Behavior in Japan and America," *Psychiatry* 32 (1969): 12–43.

212   *ideal affect*: J. L. Tsai, B. Knutson, and H. H. Fung, "Cultural Variation in Affect Valuation," *Journal of Personality and Social Psychology* 90 (2006): 288–307.

212   what feels good: J. L. Tsai et al., "Learning What Feelings to Desire: Socialization of Ideal Affect through Children's Storybooks," *Personality and Social Psychology Bulletin* 33 (2007): 17–30.

213   they all control their emotions: D. Matsumoto et al., "Mapping Expressive Differences around the World: The Relationship between Emotional Display Rules and Individualism versus Collectivism," *Journal of Cross-Cultural Psychology* 39 (2008): 55–74.

213   "we respond to gestures": Edward Sapir, *Selected Writings of Edward Sapir: Language, Culture and Personality*, ed. David G. Mandelbaum (Berkeley: University of California Press, 1984), p. 556.

214   *individualism . . . collectivism*: Geert Hofstede, *Culture's Consequences: International Differences in Work-Related Values* (Beverly Hills, CA: Sage Publications, 1980).

215   a video clip of an underwater scene: T. Masuda and R. E. Nisbett, "Culture and Change Blindness," *Cognitive Science* 30 (2007): 381–99.

215   studied 5,361 people: Matsumoto et al., "Mapping Expressive Differences."

215   Subjects in one study: T. Masuda et al., "Placing the Face in Context: Cultural Differences in the Perception of Facial Emotion," *Journal of Personality and Social Psychology* 94 (2008): 365–81.

smile for the camera

219   Through photographs we remember: Susan Sontag, *On Photography* (New York: Farrar, Straus & Giroux, 1973).

219   "A father of our acquaintance": Quoted in B. Roueche, "Pose," *The New Yorker*, June 24, 1950.

219   the smile ritual: Susan D. Moeller, *Shooting War: Photography and the American Experience of Combat* (New York: Basic Books, 1989).

220   prisoner of war Angelo Spinelli: S. Curley, "Life Behind Barbed Wire: The Secret World War II Photographs of Prisoner of War Angelo M. Spinelli," *Journal of American Culture* 27 (2004): 343–44.

221   more than 2.5 billion pictures: M. Calvey, "Printer-Giant HP Thinks It Oughta Be in Pictures," *San Francisco Business Times*, September 29, 1997, http://cgi.amcity.com/sanfrancisco/stories/092997/focus4 .html.

221   550 snapshots: Geoffrey Batchen, *Forget Me Not: Photography and Remembrance* (New York: Princeton Architectural Press, 2004).

221   "Their poses embody": Phyllis Rose, "Milkmaid Madonnas: An Appreciation of Cameron's Portraits of Women," in *Julia Margaret Cameron's Women*, ed. Sylvia Wolf (New Haven, CT: Yale University Press, 1999), p. 17.

221   "If you're going": M. Ettlinger, radio interview with Terry Gross, *Fresh Air*, NPR, December 12, 2002.

222   mug shot photographers: Raynal Pellicer, *Mug Shots: An Archive of the Famous, Infamous, and Most Wanted* (New York: Abrams/Putnam, 2009).

222   "If we stop": S. Milgram, "The Image-Freezing Machine," in *The Individual in a Social World: Essays and Experiments*, ed. Stanley Milgram (Reading, MA: Addison-Wesley, 1977), p. 350.

223   Photographed twosomes: M. Burgess, M. Enzle, and M. Morry, "The Social Psychological Power of Photography: Can the Image-Freezing Machine Make Something Out of Nothing?" *European Journal of Social Psychology* 30 (2000): 613–30.

223   a large and varied sample: W. R. Walker, J. J. Skowronski, and C. P. Thompson, "Life Is Pleasant—And Memory Helps to Keep It That Way!" *Review of General Psychology* 7 (2003): 203–10.

225   We want the moment: Pierre Bourdieu, *Photography: A Middle-Brow Art*, trans. Shaun Whiteside (Stanford, CA: Stanford University Press, 1990).

225   Americans in centuries past: Kotchemidova, "From Good Cheer to 'Drive-By Smiling.'"

226   Kathy, the beloved beluga: A. Newman, "Kathy the Beluga, 34, Is Dead; Brought Smiles, and Gave Them," *New York Times*, April 10, 2004.

226   "His memory for customers' names": N. M. Christian et al., "A Nation Challenged: Portraits of Grief," *New York Times*, September 27, 2001.

227   recollections are more positive: D. Eylon and S. T. Allison, "The 'Frozen in Time' Effect in Evaluations of the Dead," *Personality and Social Psychology Bulletin* 21 (2005): 1708–17.

228   "It's like obituaries": R. Maris, "Roger Maris Quotes," *Baseball Almanac*, www.baseball-almanac.com.

228   humans don't do: S. Solomon, J. Greenberg, and T. Pyszczynski, "The Cultural Animal: Twenty Years of Terror Management Theory and Research," in *Handbook of Experimental Existential Psychology*, ed. J. Greenberg, S. L. Koole, and T. Pyszczynski (New York: Guilford Press, 2004).

228   Recalling a friend's warm smile: G. Holst-Warhaft, "Remembering the Dead: Laments and Photographs," *Comparative Studies of South Asia, Africa and the Middle East* 25 (2005): 152–60.

229   "forget all dolefulness": E. L. Wilson, "To My Patrons" (1871), in *Photography: Essays and Images*, ed. B. Newhall (New York: MoMA, 1980), 129–33.

230   pet cemeteries in Japan: R. Chalfen, "Celebrating Life after Death: The Appearance of Snapshots in Japanese Pet Gravesites," *Visual Studies* 18 (2003): 144–56.

230   Prince William: "Smile! William Photo Touched Up," BBC, June 21, 1999, available at http://news.bbc.co.uk/2/hi/uk_news/374584.stm.

230   sent four wedding pictures: S. Mayes, "A Psychologist Says He Can Tell Which Marriages Will Last from the Wedding Couple's Smiles . . . Can You?" *Daily Mirror* (London), February 8, 2001, pp. 29–30.

232   *false memories*: Daniel L. Schacter, *Searching for Memory: The Brain, the Mind, and the Past* (New York: Basic Books, 1996).

233   Research participants were brought: W. F. Brewer and J. C. Treyens, "Role of Schemata in Memory for Places," *Cognitive Psychology* 13 (1981): 207–30.

233   a photograph of part of a scene: H. Intraub et al., "Boundary Extension for Briefly Glimpsed Photographs: Do Common Perceptual Processes Result in Unexpected Memory Distortions?" *Journal of Memory and Language* 35 (1996): 118–34.

233   photographs of themselves as children: K. A. Wade et al., "A Picture Is Worth a Thousand Lies: Using False Photographs to Create False Childhood Memories," *Psychonomic Bulletin and Review* 9 (2002): 597–603.

234   three childhood events: D. S. Lindsay et al., "True Photographs and False Memories," *Psychological Science* 15 (2004): 149–54.

234 the *photobooth*: Nakki Goranin, *American Photobooth* (New York: W. W. Norton, 2008).

235 Facebook alone: A. Acquisti and R. Gross, *Imagined Communities: Awareness, Information Sharing and Privacy on The Facebook*, Proceedings of the 6th Workshop on Privacy Enhancing Technologies (Cambridge, UK: 2006).

235 "pulling faces": Quoted in Gunther Kress, ed., *Communication and Culture* (Sydney: University of New South Wales Press, 1998).

235 upload innumerable photos: D.-H. Lee, "Women's Creation of Camera Phone Culture," *Fibreculture*, issue 6 (2005), available at http://journal .fibreculture.org/issue6/issue6_donghoo.html.

235 chain reactions of smiles: Fowler and Christakis, "Dynamic Spread of Happiness."

237 the proud smile: J. L. Tracy and R. W. Robins, "Show Your Pride: Evidence for a Discrete Emotion Expression," *Psychological Science* 15 (2004): 194–97.

237 the trophy pictures taken: S. Henderson, "Disregarding the Suffering of Others: Narrative, Comedy, and Torture," *Literature and Medicine* 24 (2005): 181–208.

exit smiling

239 "That one may smile, and smile": Shakespeare, *Hamlet*, Act I, scene V.

240 repetition of any behavior trains our brains: D. A. Terry and P. L. Pirtle, "Learning to Smile: The Neuroanatomical Basis for Smile Training," *Journal of Esthetic and Restorative Dentistry* 13 (2001): 20–27.

241 "Nexi": S. del Moral, D. Pardo, and C. Angulo, "Social Robot Paradigms: An Overview," *Bio-Inspired Systems: Computational and Ambient Intelligence: Lecture Notes in Computer Science* 5517 (2009): 773–80.

242 "Einstein" was built: M. Harvey, "Is Einstein Robot Too Human? Everything's Relative," *The Times* (London), February 27, 2009.

243 Frubber: Yoseph Bar-Cohen, David Hanson, and Adi Marom, *The Coming Robot Revolution: Expectations and Fears about Emerging Intelligent, Humanlike Machines* (New York: Springer, 2009).

244 "Kismet": C. Breazeal, "Emotion and Sociable Humanoid Robots," *International Journal of Human Computer Studies* 59 (2003): 119–55.

244 researchers are hard at work: B. Robins et al., "Robot-Mediated Joint Attention in Children with Autism: A Case Study in Robot-Human

Interaction," *Interaction Studies* 5 (2004): 161–98; A. Duquette, F. Michaud, and H. Mercier, "Exploring the Use of a Mobile Robot as an Imitation Agent with Children with Low-Functioning Autism," *Autonomous Robots* 24 (2008): 147–57.

245 *embodied agents*: L. I. Gong, "When a Talking-Face Computer Agent Is Half-Human and Half-Humanoid: Human Identity and Consistency Preference," *Human Communication Research* 33 (2007): 163–93.

references

Abbey, A., and C. Melby. "The Effect of Non-Verbal Cues on Gender Differences in Perceptions of Sexual Intent." *Sex Roles* 15 (1986): 283–98.

Abel, E. L., and M. L. Kruger. "Smile Intensity in Photographs Predicts Longevity." *Psychological Science* 21 (2010): 542–44.

Acquisti, A., and R. Gross. *Imagined Communities: Awareness, Information Sharing and Privacy on The Facebook.* Proceedings of the 6th Workshop on Privacy Enhancing Technologies. Cambridge, UK: 2006.

Adams, A., and P. Bettis. "Commanding the Room in Short Skirts: Cheering as the Embodiment of Ideal Girlhood." *Gender and Society* 17 (2003): 73–89.

Adelmann, P. K. "Emotional Labor as a Potential Source of Job Stress." In *Organizational Risk Factors for Job Stress,* edited by S. L. Sauter and L. R. Murphy, 371–81. Washington, DC: American Psychological Association, 1995.

Adorno, T. *The Culture Industry: Selected Essays on Mass Culture.* 1991. London: Routledge, 2001.

Adrien, J. L., P. Lenoir, J. Marineau, A. Perot, L. Hameury, D. Larmande, and D. Sauvage. "Blind Ratings of Early Symptoms of Autism Based on Family Home Movies." *Journal of the American Academy of Child and Adolescent Psychiatry* 33 (1993): 617–25.

Aitken, M. "European Tour Crying Out for More Shiny, Happy People." *The Scotsman,* May 11, 2004, p. 32.

Alexander, I. E., and E. Y. Babad. "Returning the Smile of the Stranger: Within Culture and Cross-cultural Comparisons of Israeli and American Children." *Genetic Psychology Monographs* 103 (1981): 31–77.

Altman, Y. "A Theme Park in a Cultural Straitjacket: The Case of Disneyland Paris, France." *Managing Leisure* 1 (1995): 43–56.

Ambady, N., and R. Rosenthal. "Thin Slices of Expressive Behavior as Predictors of Interpersonal Consequences: A Meta-Analysis." *Psychological Bulletin* 111 (1992): 256–74.

Ambler, Eric. *Journey into Fear.* In *Intrigue: The Great Spy Novels of Eric Ambler.* New York: Alfred A. Knopf, 1943.

Andersen, S. M., I. Reznik, and L. M. Manzella. "Eliciting Transient Affect, Motivation, and Expectancies in Transference: Significant-Other Representations and the Self in Social Relations." *Journal of Personality and Social Psychology* 71 (1996): 1108–29.

Ansfield, M. "Smiling When Distressed: When a Smile is a Frown Turned Upside Down." *Personality and Social Psychology Bulletin* 33 (2007): 673–75.

Ashkanasy, N. M, C. E. J. Härtel, and W. Zerbe, eds. *Emotions in the Workplace: Research, Theory, and Practice.* Westport, CT: Quorum, 2000.

Austen, Jane. *Emma.* 1815. Boston: Little, Brown, 1902.

———. *Pride and Prejudice.* 1813. New York: Charles Scribner's Sons, 1865.

"Baby Steals Burglar's Heart." *Sunday Mirror* (London), May 10, 1998.

Baldwin, M. B., S. E. Carrell, and D. F. Lopez. "Priming Relationship Schemas: My Advisor and the Pope are Watching Me from the Back of my Mind." *Journal of Experimental Social Psychology* 26 (1990): 435–54.

Balzer-Riley, Julia. *Communication in Nursing.* 4th ed. St. Louis, MO: C. V. Mosby, 2000.

Banerjee, R., and N. Yuill. "Children's Explanations for Self-Presentational Behaviour." *European Journal of Social Psychology* 29 (1999): 105–11.

Bar-Cohen, Yoseph, David Hanson, and Adi Marom. *The Coming Robot Revolution: Expectations and Fears about Emerging Intelligent, Humanlike Machines.* New York: Springer, 2009.

Barger, P. B., and A. A. Grandey. "Service with a Smile and Encounter Satisfaction: Emotional Contagion and Appraisal Mechanisms." *Academy of Management Journal* 49 (2006): 1229–38.

Barthelme, Donald. *Sixty Stories.* 1966. New York: Penguin, 2003.

Batchen, Geoffrey. *Forget Me Not: Photography and Remembrance.* New York: Princeton Architectural Press, 2004.

Bateson, M. C. "The Interpersonal Context of Infant Vocalization." *Quarterly Progress Report of the Research Laboratory of Electronics* 100 (1971): 170–76.

Baudrillard, Jean. *America.* New York: Verso Press, 1989.

Baumeister, R., and M. R. Leary. "The Need to Belong: Desire for Interpersonal

Attachments as a Fundamental Human Motive." *Psychological Bulletin* 117 (1995): 497–529.

Bavelas, J. B., A. Black, N. Chovil, and J. Mullett. *Equivocal Communication.* Newbury Park, CA: Sage Publications, 1990.

Beaupre, M. G., and U. Hess. "In My Mind, We All Smile: A Case of In-Group Favoritism." *Journal of Experimental Social Psychology* 39 (2003): 371–77.

"Behind that Smile." *New Scientist* 188, no. 2530 (2005).

Belt, V., R. Richardson, and J. Webster. "Women, Social Skill and Interactive Service Work in Telephone Call Centres." *New Technology, Work and Employment* 17 (2002): 20–34.

Bem, S. L. "The Measurement of Psychological Androgyny." *Journal of Consulting and Clinical Psychology* 42 (1974): 155–62.

Berger, J. *Ways of Seeing.* London: British Broadcasting Company, 1977.

Berridge, K. C., and P. Winkielman. "What is an Unconscious Emotion? The Case for Unconscious 'Liking.'" *Cognition and Emotion* 17 (2003): 181–211.

Bierce, Ambrose. *The Unabridged Devil's Dictionary.* 1935. Athens: University of Georgia Press, 2002.

"Big Wedding: 20,000 Gather for Mass Nuptials." Associated Press, October 13, 2009.

Biland, D., J. Py, J. Allione, S. Demarchi, and J. C. Abric. "The Effect of Lying on Intentional Versus Unintentional Facial Expressions." *European Review of Applied Psychology* 58 (2008): 65–73.

Billig, Michael. *Laughter and Ridicule: Towards a Social Critique of Humour.* London: Sage Publications, 2006.

Birdwhistell, Ray L. *Kinesics and Context.* Philadelphia: University of Pennsylvania Press, 1970.

Birnbaum, M. G. *Taking Goffman on a Tour of Facebook: College Students and the Presentation of Self in a Mediated Digital Environment.* PhD diss., Department of Sociology, University of Arizona, 2008.

Blanton, DeAnne, and Lauren M. Cook. *They Fought Like Demons: Women Soldiers in the American Civil War.* Baton Rouge: Louisiana State University Press, 2002.

Bok, Sissela. *Lying: Moral Choice in Public and in Private Life.* New York: Pantheon Books, 1978.

Bonanno, G. A., and D. Keltner. "Facial Expressions of Emotion and the Course of Bereavement." *Journal of Abnormal Psychology* 106 (1997): 126–37.

Bonanno, G. A., D. Keltner, J. Noll, F. W. Putnam, P. K. Trickett, and J. LeJeune.

"When the Face Reveals What Words Do Not: Facial Expressions of Emotion, Smiling, and the Willingness to Disclose Childhood Sexual Abuse." *Journal of Personality and Social Psychology* 83 (2008): 94–110.

Bourdieu, Pierre. *Photography, A Middle-Brow Art.* Translated by Shaun Whiteside. Stanford, CA: Stanford University Press, 1990.

Bowman, C. G. "Street Harassment and the Informal Ghettoization of Women." *Harvard Law Review* 106 (1993): 517–80.

Breazeal, C. "Emotion and Sociable Humanoid Robots." *International Journal of Human Computer Studies* 59 (2003): 119–55.

Brewer, W. F., and J. C. Treyens. "Role of Schemata in Memory for Places." *Cognitive Psychology* 13 (1981): 207–30.

Brontë, Charlotte. *Jane Eyre.* 1847. New York: Century, 1906.

Brooke, Rupert. *The Collected Poems of Rupert Brooke: With a Memoir.* Charleston, SC: Bibliolife, 2009.

Brown, Dan. *Angels and Demons.* New York: Simon & Schuster, 2009.

Brown, R. "Politeness Theory: Exemplar and Exemplary." In *The Legacy of Solomon Asch: Essays in Cognition and Social Psychology,* edited by I. Rock, 23–38. Hillsdale, NJ: Lawrence Erlbaum Associates, 1990.

Brown, W. M., and C. Moore. "Smile Asymmetries and Reputation as Reliable Indicators of Likelihood to Cooperate: An Evolutionary Analysis." In *Advances in Psychology Research* 11, edited by S. P. Shohov, 59–78. New York: Nova Science Publishers, 2002.

Brown, W. M., B. Palameta, and C. Moore. "Are There Nonverbal Cues to Commitment? An Exploratory Study Using the Zero-Acquaintance Video Presentation Paradigm." *Evolutionary Psychology* 1 (2003): 42–69.

Bucy, E. P., and J. E. Newhagen. "The Emotional Appropriateness Heuristic: Processing Televised Presidential Reactions to the News." *Journal of Communication* 49 (1999): 61–69.

Bugental, D., J. W. Kaswan, and L. R. Love. "Perception of Contradictory Meanings Conveyed by Verbal and Nonverbal Channels." *Journal of Personality and Social Psychology* 16 (1970): 647–60.

Burgess, M., M. Enzle, and M. Morry. "The Social Psychological Power of Photography: Can the Image-Freezing Machine Make Something Out of Nothing?" *European Journal of Social Psychology* 30 (2000): 613–30.

Butler, E. A., B. Egloff, F. H. Wilhelm, N. C. Smith, E. A. Erickson, and J. J. Gross. "The Social Consequences of Expressive Suppression." *Emotion* 3 (2003): 48–67.

Byrne, R. W., and N. Corp. "Neocortex Size Predicts Deception Rate in

Primates." *Philosophical Transactions of the Royal Society: Biological Sciences* 271 (2004): 1693–99.

Calvey, M. "Printer-Giant HP Thinks It Oughta Be in Pictures." *San Francisco Business Times*, September 29, 1997. http://cgi.amcity.com/sanfrancisco/stories/092997/focus4.html.

Camic, C. "The Making of a Method." *American Sociological Review* 52 (1987): 421–39.

Campbell, R. "The Neuropsychology of Lip Reading." *Philosophical Transactions of the Royal Society: Biological Sciences* 335 (1992): 39–45.

Campbell, Stuart. *Watch Me Grow: A Unique 3-Dimensional Week-by-Week Look at Your Baby's Behavior and Development in the Womb.* New York: St. Martin's/Griffin, 2004.

Camras, L. A. "Expressive Development and Basic Emotions." *Cognition and Emotion* 6 (1992): 269–84.

Camras, L. A., C. Malatesta, and C. E. Izard. "The Development of Facial Expression in Infancy." In *Fundamentals of Nonverbal Behavior*, edited by R. Feldman and B. Rimé. Cambridge, UK: Cambridge University Press, 1991.

Caprara, G. V., C. Barbaranelli, and P. G. Zimbardo. "When Parsimony Subdues Distinctiveness: Simplified Public Perceptions of Politicians' Personality." *Political Psychology* 23 (2002): 77–95.

Carney, D. R., J. T. Jost, G. Gosling, and J. Potter. "The Secret Lives of Liberals and Conservatives: Personality Profiles, Interaction Styles, and the Things They Leave Behind." *Political Psychology* 29 (2008): 807–40.

Carroll, Lewis. *Alice's Adventures in Wonderland.* 1865. London: Macmillan and Co., 1913.

Caudill, W., and H. Weinstein. "Maternal Care and Infant Behavior in Japan and America." *Psychiatry* 32 (1969): 12–43.

Chalfen, R. "Celebrating Life after Death: The Appearance of Snapshots in Japanese Pet Gravesites." *Visual Studies* 18 (2003): 144–56.

Chandler, Raymond. *Farewell, My Lovely.* 1940. New York: Vintage Crime/Black Lizard, 1992.

Cheese, Peter. "Japan Railway Monitoring Employees to Ensure They Smile." *The Economist*, September 14, 2009.

Chekhov, Anton Pavlovich. *The Bishop and Other Stories.* 1902. Translated by Constance Garnett. Charleston, SC: Bibliolife, 2007.

Cherulnik, P., J. H. Way, S. Ames, and D. B. Hutto. "Impressions of High and Low Machiavellian Men." *Journal of Personality* 49 (1981): 388–400.

Chesterton, G. K. *The Ball and the Cross*. 1910. Digireads.com Publishing, 2009.

Chiao, J., R. B. Adams Jr., P. U. Tse, L. Lowenthal, J. A. Richeson, and N. Ambady. "Knowing Who's Boss: fMRI and ERP Investigations of Social Dominance Perception." *Group Processes and Intergroup Relations* 11 (2008): 201–14.

Chilcote, R. "Commander Shows Restraint, Prevents Unnecessary Violence." CNN, 2003. http://www.cnn.com/SPECIALS/2003/iraq/heroes/chrishughes.html.

Chisholm, J. S. "Learning 'Respect for Everything': Navajo Images of Everything." In *Images of Childhood*, edited by C. P. Hwang, M. E. Lamb, and I. E. Sigel, 167–84. Mahwah, NJ: Lawrence Erlbaum Associates, 1996.

Christian, N. M., et al. "A Nation Challenged: Portraits of Grief." *New York Times*, September 27, 2001.

Christie, Richard, and Florence L. Geis. *Studies in Machiavellianism*. New York: Academic Press, 1970.

Clark, R., P. Winkielman, and D. N. McIntosh. "Autism and the Extraction of Emotion from Briefly Presented Facial Expressions: Stumbling at the First Step of Empathy." *Emotion* 8 (2008): 803–9.

Cline, M. G. "The Influence of Social Context on the Perception of Faces." *Journal of Personality* 2 (1956): 142–58.

Cohen, D. "Cultural Variation: Considerations and Implications." *Psychological Bulletin* 127 (2001): 451–71.

Cohen, D., and A. K. Leung. "The Hard Embodiment of Culture." *European Journal of Social Psychology* 39 (2009): 1278–89.

Cohen, D., J. Vandello, S. Puente, and A. Rantilla. "'When You Call Me That, Smile!' How Norms for Politeness, Interaction Styles, and Aggression Work Together in Southern Culture." *Social Psychology Quarterly* 62 (1999): 257–75.

Cohen, P. N., and M. L. Huffman. "Individuals, Jobs, and Labor Markets: The Devaluation of Women's Work." *American Sociological Review* 68 (2003): 443–63.

Cole, Jonathan. *About Face*. Cambridge, MA: MIT Press, 1999.

———. "Empathy Needs a Face." *Journal of Consciousness Studies* 8 (2001): 12–25.

Cole, P. M., C. Zahn-Waxler, and K. D. Smith. "Expressive Control during a Disappointment: Variations Related to Preschoolers' Behavior Problems." *Developmental Psychology* 30 (1994): 835–46.

Condry, J., and S. Condry. "Sex Differences: A Study of the Eye of the Beholder." *Child Development* 47 (1976): 812–19.

Conger, J. A., and R. N. Kanungo. "Charismatic Leadership in Organizations: Perceived Behavioral Attributes and Their Measurement." *Journal of Organizational Behavior* 15 (1994): 439–52.

Cornish, A. M., C. A. McMahon, J. A. Ungerer, B. Barnett, N. Kowalenko, and C. Tennant. "Postnatal Depression and Infant Cognitive and Motor Development in the Second Postnatal Year: The Impact of Depression Chronicity and Infant Gender." *Infant Behavior and Development* 28 (2005): 407–17.

Coyne, J. C. "Depression and the Response of Others." *Journal of Abnormal Psychology* 85 (1976): 28–40.

"Creator of Smiley Face Icon Dies at 79." Associated Press, April 13, 2001.

Cunningham, M. R. "Measuring the Physical in Physical Attractiveness: Quasi-Experiments on the Sociobiology of Female Facial Beauty." *Journal of Social and Personality Psychology* 50 (1986): 925–35.

Curley, S. "Life Behind Barbed Wire: The Secret World War II Photographs of Prisoner of War Angelo M. Spinelli." *Journal of American Culture* 27 (2004): 343–44.

Curry, J. "Matsui's Hello: One Colossal Grand Slam." *New York Times*, April 9, 2003.

Dabbs, J. M. "Testosterone, Smiling and Facial Appearance." *Journal of Nonverbal Behavior* 21 (1997): 45–54.

Dabbs, J. M., and M. G. Dabbs. *Heroes, Rogues, and Lovers: Testosterone and Behavior.* New York: McGraw-Hill, 2001.

Dallek, Robert. *Lone Star Rising: Lyndon Johnson and His Times, 1908–1960.* New York: Oxford University Press, 1991.

Damasio, Antonio R. *The Feeling of What Happens: Body and Emotion in the Making of Consciousness.* New York: Harcourt, 2000.

Danner, D. D., D. Snowdon, and W. V. Friesen. "Positive Emotions in Early Life and Longevity: Findings from the Nun Study." *Journal of Personality and Social Psychology* 80 (2001): 804–13.

Dapretto, M., M. S. Davies, J. H. Pfeifer, A. A. Scott, M. Sigman, S. Y. Bookheimer, and M. Iacoboni. "Understanding Emotions in Others: Mirror Neuron Dysfunction in Children with Autism Spectrum Disorders." *Nature and Neuroscience* 9 (2006): 27–30.

Darwin, Charles. *The Expression of the Emotions in Man and Animals,* with photographic and other illustrations. 1872. London: John Murray, 1921.

Davis, J. I. *The Connection between Facial Expression and Emotional Expression.* PhD diss., Columbia University, 2008.

Davis, T. L. "Gender Differences in Masking Negative Emotions: Ability or Motivation?" *Developmental Psychology* 31 (1995): 660–67.

de Gaulle, Charles. *The Complete War Memoirs of Charles de Gaulle.* Vol. 1, *The Call to Honour.* 1954. New York: Carroll & Graf, 1998.

del Moral, S., D. Pardo, and C. Angulo. "Social Robot Paradigms: An Overview." *Bio-Inspired Systems: Computational and Ambient Intelligence: Lecture Notes in Computer Science* 5517 (2009): 773–80.

DePaulo, B. M., D. A. Kashy, S. E. Kirkendol, M. M. Wyer, and J. A. Epstein. "Lying in Everyday Life." *Journal of Personality and Social Psychology* 8 (1996): 969–95.

DePaulo, B. M., J. J. Lindsay, and B. E. Malone. "Cues to Deception." *Psychological Bulletin* 129 (2003): 74–118.

Deshefy-Longhi, T. *Nonverbal Communication Accuracy in Couples Living with Parkinson Disease.* PhD diss., School of Nursing, Yale University, 2008.

DeWall, C. N., J. K. Manner, and D. A. Rouby. "Social Exclusion and Early-Stage Interpersonal Perception: Selective Attention to Signs of Acceptance." *Journal of Personality and Social Psychology* 96 (2009): 729–41.

Dickens, Charles. *A Christmas Carol in Prose: Being a Ghost Story of Christmas.* 1843. Boston: Little, Brown, 1920.

DiMatteo, M. R., A. Taranta, H. S. Friedman, and L. M. Prince. "Predicting Patient Satisfaction from Physicians' Nonverbal Communication Skills." *Medical Care* 18 (1980): 367–87.

Dimberg, U., M. Thunberg, and K. Elmehed. "Unconscious Facial Reactions to Emotional Facial Expressions." *Psychological Science* 11 (2000): 86–89.

Dodd, D. K., B. L. Russell, and C. Jenkins. "Smiling in School Yearbook Photos: Gender Differences from Kindergarten to Adulthood." *Psychological Record* 49 (1999).

Doolittle, Hilda (H. D.). *Collected Poems.* 1931. New York: AMS Press, 1986.

Dubernard J. M., B. Lengelé, E. Morelon, S. Testelin, L. Badet, C. Moure, J.-L. Beziatet, S. Dakpé, et al. "Outcomes 18 Months after the First Human Partial Face Transplantation." *New England Journal of Medicine* 357 (2007): 2451–60.

Duchenne, G.-B.-A. *The Mechanism of Human Facial Expression.* 1862. Translated by R. A. Cuthbertson. New York: Cambridge University Press, 1990.

Duquette, A., F. Michaud, and H. Mercier. "Exploring the Use of a Mobile Robot as an Imitation Agent with Children with Low-Functioning Autism." *Autonomous Robots* 24 (2008): 147–57.

Eagly, Alice H., and Linda L. Carli. *Through the Labyrinth: The Truth about How Women Become Leaders*. Boston: Harvard Business School Press, 2007.

Eibl-Eibesfeldt, I. "Similarities and Differences between Cultures in Expressive Movements." In *Nonverbal Communication*, edited by R. A. Hinde, 297–314. London: Cambridge University Press, 1972.

Eisenberger, N. I., M. D. Lieberman, and K. D. Williams. "Does Rejection Hurt? An fMRI Study of Social Exclusion." *Science* 302 (2003): 290–92.

Ekman, P. *Telling Lies: Clues to Deceit in the Marketplace, Politics, and Marriage*. New York: W. W. Norton, 1992.

Ekman, P., and W. V. Friesen. "Felt, False and Miserable Smiles." *Journal of Nonverbal Behavior* 6 (1988): 238–52.

———. "The Repertoire of Nonverbal Behavior: Categories, Origins, Usage and Coding." *Semiotica* 1 (1969): 49–98.

———. *Unmasking the Face: A Guide to Recognizing Emotions from Facial Clues*. Englewood Cliffs, NJ: Prentice-Hall, 1975. Reprint, New York: Malor Books, 2003.

Ekman, P., W. V. Friesen, and M. O'Sullivan. "Smiles When Lying." *Journal of Personality and Social Psychology* 54 (1988): 414–20.

Elfenbein, H. A., and N. Ambady. "Is There an In-Group Advantage in Emotion?" *Psychological Bulletin* 128 (2002): 243–49.

Elfenbein, H. A., M. Beaupre, M. Levesque, and U. Hess. "Toward a Dialect Theory: Cultural Differences in the Expression and Recognition of Posed Facial Expressions." *Emotion* 7 (2007): 131–46.

Ellis R. J. "The Joy of Power: Changing Conceptions of the Presidential Office." *Presidential Studies Quarterly* 33 (2003): 269–90.

Ellsworth, C. P., D. W. Muir, and S. M. Hains. "Social Competence and Person-Object Differentiation: An Analysis of the Still-Face Effect." *Developmental Psychology* 29 (1993): 63–73.

Elmer, E., and G. S. Gregg. "Developmental Characteristics of Abused Children." *Pediatrics* 40 (1967): 596–602.

Emde, R. N., and R. J. Harmon. "Endogenous and Exogenous Smiling Systems in Early Infancy." *Journal of the American Academy of Child Psychiatry* 11 (1972): 177–200.

Emde, W. "Inductive Learning of Characteristic Concept Descriptions." In *Proceedings of the Fourth International Workshop on Inductive Logic Programming*, edited by S. Wrobel, 1–70. *GMD-Studien* 237 (1994).

Endy, C. "Rudeness and Modernity: The Reception of American Tourists in

Early Fifth Republic France." *French Politics, Culture and Society* 21 (2003): 55–86.

Englis, B. G., K. B. Vaughan, and J. T. Lanzetta. "Conditioning of Counter-Empathetic Emotional Responses." *Journal of Experimental Social Psychology* 18 (1981): 375–84.

Ettlinger, M. Radio interview with Terry Gross. *Fresh Air*, NPR, December 12, 2002.

Eylon, D., and S. T. Allison. "The 'Frozen in Time' Effect in Evaluations of the Dead." *Personality and Social Psychology Bulletin* 21 (2005): 1708–17.

Feinman, Saul, ed. *Social Referencing and the Social Construction of Reality in Infancy*. New York: Plenum, 1992.

Fellerman, Hazel, ed. *Poems That Live Forever*. New York: Random House, 1965.

Fernández-Dols, J. M., and M. A. Ruiz-Belda. "Are Smiles a Sign of Happiness?: Gold Medal Winners at the Olympic Games." *Journal of Personality and Social Psychology* 69 (1995): 1113–19.

Field, T. M. "Infants of Depressed Mothers." *Infant Behavior and Development* 18 (1995): 1–13.

———. "Interaction Behaviors of Primary versus Secondary Caretaker Fathers." *Developmental Psychology* 14 (1978): 183–84.

Field, T. M., and T. A. Walden. "Production and Discrimination of Facial Expressions by Preschool Children." *Child Development* 53 (1982): 1299–1311.

Fitzgerald, F. Scott. *The Great Gatsby*. 1925. New York: Charles Scribner's Sons, 1953.

Flack, J. D., and F. de Waal. "Context Modulates Signal Meaning in Primate Communication." *Proceedings of the National Academy of Sciences* 104 (2007): 1581–86.

Fogel, A., and E. Thelan. "Development of Early Expressive and Communicative Action: Reinterpreting the Evidence from a Dynamic Systems Perspective." *Developmental Psychology* 23 (1987): 747–61.

Fowler, J. H., and N. A. Christakis. "Dynamic Spread of Happiness in a Large Social Network: Longitudinal Analysis over 20 Years in the Framingham Heart Study." *British Medical Journal* 337 (2008): 1–9.

Fox, N. A., and R. J. Davidson. "Patterns of Brain Electrical Activity during Facial Signs of Emotion in 10-Month-Old Infants." *Developmental Psychology* 24 (1988): 230–36.

Fraiberg, S. "Blind Infants and Their Mothers: An Examination of the Sign System." In *Before Speech: The Beginning of Interpersonal Communication*, edited by M. Bullowa, 159–70. New York: Cambridge University Press, 1979.

Frank, Robert H. *Passions within Reason: The Strategic Role of the Emotions*. New York: W. W. Norton, 1988.

Franzen, Jonathan. *How to Be Alone: Essays*. New York: Picador, 2003.

Fredrickson, B. "Cultivating Positive Emotions to Optimize Health and Well-Being." *Prevention and Treatment* 3 (2000).

Freedman, Daniel G. *Human Infancy: An Evolutionary Perspective*. New York: John Wiley and Sons, 1974.

Freud, Sigmund. *Dora: An Analysis of a Case of Hysteria*. New York: Simon & Schuster, 1905.

Fridlund, A. J. *Human Facial Expression: An Evolutionary View*. San Diego, CA: Academic Press, 1994.

Fridlund, A. J., and C. E. Izard. "Electromyographic Studies of Facial Expressions of Emotions and Patterns of Emotions." In *Social Psychophysiology: A Sourcebook*, edited by J. T. Cacioppo and R. E. Petty, 243–86. New York: Guilford Press, 1983.

Friedman, H. S. "The Interactive Effects of Emotion and Verbal Messages on Perceptions of Affective Meaning." *Journal of Experimental Social Psychology* 15 (1979): 453–69.

Friedman, H. S., M. R. DiMatteo, and A. Taranta. "A Study of the Relationship between Individual Differences in Nonverbal Expressiveness and Factors of Personality and Social Interaction." *Journal of Research in Personality* 14 (1980): 351–64.

Friedman, H. S., L. M. Prince, and M. R. Riggio. "Understanding and Assessing Nonverbal Expressiveness: The Affective Communication Test." *Journal of Personality and Social Psychology* 39 (1980): 333–42.

Gale, Robert L., ed. *A Dashiell Hammett Companion*. Santa Barbara, CA: Greenwood Publishing, 2000.

———, ed. *A Lafcadio Hearn Companion*. Westport, CT: Greenwood Publishing, 2001.

Gall, Franz Josef. *On the Functions of the Brain and of Each of Its Parts: On the Origin of the Moral Qualities and Intellectual Faculties of Man, and the Conditions of Their Manifestation*. Boston: Marsh, Capen & Lyon, 1835. Reprint, 2010.

Gambetta, Diego, and Heather Hamil. *Streetwise: How Taxi Drivers Establish Customers' Trustworthiness*. New York: Russell Sage Foundation, 2005.

Garber, Marjorie. *Vested Interests: Cross-Dressing and Cultural Anxiety*. New York: Routledge, 1992.

Gardner, M. "When Service Means More than a Smile." *Christian Science Monitor*, October 7, 1993.

Gazzaniga, M. S., R. B. Ivry, and G. Mangun, eds. *Fundamentals of Cognitive Neuroscience*. New York: W. W. Norton, 1998.

Gerhold, M., M. Laucht, C. Texdorf, M. H. Schmidt, and G. Esser. "Early Mother-Infant Interaction as a Precursor to Childhood Social Withdrawal." *Child Psychiatry and Human Development* 32 (2002): 277–93.

Gianino, A., and E. Z. Tronick. "The Mutual Regulation Model: The Infant's Self and Interactive Regulation and Coping and Defensive Capacities." In *Stress and Coping across Development*, edited by T. M. Field, P. McCabe, and N. Schneiderman, 47–68. Hillsdale, NJ: Lawrence Erlbaum Associates, 1988.

Gladwell, M. "In a Different New York, a Different Goetz Trial." *Washington Post*, April 21, 1996, p. A01.

Gnepp, J., and D. L. R. Hess. "Children's Understanding of Verbal and Facial Display Rules." *Developmental Psychology* 22 (1986): 103–8.

Goffman, Erving. "The Nature of Deference and Demeanor." In *Interaction Ritual: Essays on Face-to-Face Behavior*, 47–53. Garden City, NY: Doubleday, 1967.

———. *The Presentation of Self in Everyday Life*. Garden City, NY: Doubleday, 1959.

Gong, L. I. "When a Talking-Face Computer Agent Is Half-Human and Half-Humanoid: Human Identity and Consistency Preference." *Human Communication Research* 33 (2007): 163–93.

Gonzaga, G. C., R. A. Turner, D. Keltner, B. Campos, and M. Altemus. "Romantic Love and Sexual Desire in Close Relationships." *Emotion* 6 (2006): 163–79.

Goodwin, D. K. "A Simple Smile Helped Coolidge Win the Presidency." *American Journalism Review* 22 (2000): 21.

Goranin, Nakki. *American Photobooth*. New York: W. W. Norton, 2008.

Gosselin, P., M. Beaupre, and A. Boissonneault. "Perception of Genuine and Masking Smiles in Children and Adults: Sensitivity to Traces of Anger." *Journal of Genetic Psychology* 163 (2002): 58–72.

Gotlib, I. H., and M. E. Beatty. "Negative Responses to Depression: The Role of Attributional Style." *Cognitive Therapy and Research* 9 (1985): 91–103.

Gottman, J. M. "Psychology and the Study of Marital Processes." *Annual Review of Psychology* 49 (1998): 169–97.

———. *The Relationship Cure: A 5-Step Guide to Strengthening Your Marriage, Family, and Friendships*. New York: Crown Publishing, 2002.

——. *What Predicts Divorce?* Mahwah, NJ: Lawrence Erlbaum Associates, 1994.

Grabe, Maria E., and Erik P. Bucy. *Image Bite Politics: News and the Visual Framing of Elections.* New York: Oxford University Press, 2009.

Granatstein, R. "Taxi Drivers Live in Constant Fear." *Toronto Sun*, March 16, 1998, p. 5.

Grandey, A. A. "When 'The Show Must Go On': Surface Acting and Deep Acting as Determinants of Emotional Exhaustion and Peer-Rated Service Delivery." *Academy of Management Journal* 46 (2003): 86–96.

Grandey, A. A., and A. L. Brauburger. "The Emotion Regulation behind the Customer Service Smile." In *Emotions in the Workplace: Understanding the Structure and Role of Emotions in Organizational Behavior*, edited by R. G. Lord, R. J. Klimoski, and R. Kanfer, 260–94. San Francisco, CA: Jossey-Bass, 2003.

Grandey, A. A., G. Fisk, A. Mattila, and L. Sideman. "Is That Smile for Real? Reaction to Inauthenticity in Service Settings." Paper presented at the annual meeting of the Academy of Management, Denver, CO, 2002.

Grandin, Temple. *Thinking in Pictures: And Other Reports from My Life with Autism.* New York: Doubleday, 1995.

Granovetter, M. "The Strength of Weak Ties." *American Journal of Sociology* 78 (1973): 1360–80.

Green, J. "The Making of an Ice Princess." *New York Times*, December 18, 2005, sect. 6, p. 51.

Greene, Graham. *The Power and the Glory.* 1939. New York: Penguin Classics, 2003.

Gross, J. J. "The Emerging Field of Emotion Regulation: An Integrative Review." *Review of General Psychology* 2 (1998): 271–99.

Gross, J. J., and O. P. John. "Individual Differences in Two Emotion Regulation Processes: Implications for Affect, Relationships, and Well-Being." *Journal of Personality and Social Psychology* 85 (2003): 348–62.

——. "Mapping the Domain of Emotional Expressivity: Multi-Method Evidence for a Hierarchical Model." *Journal of Personality and Social Psychology* 74 (1998): 170–91.

Gross, J. J., and R. W. Levenson. "Hiding Feelings: The Acute Effects of Inhibiting Negative and Positive Emotion." *Journal of Abnormal Psychology* 106 (1997): 95–105.

Haggard, E. A., and K. S. Isaacs. "Micromomentary Facial Expressions as Indicators of Ego Mechanisms in Psychotherapy." In *Methods of Research in Psychotherapy*, edited by L. A. Gottschalk and A. H. Auerbach, 154–65. New York: Appleton-Century-Crofts, 1966.

Haidt, J. "The Emotional Dog and Its Rational Tail: A Social Intuitionist Approach to Moral Judgment." *Psychological Review* 108 (2001): 814–34.

Hall, J. A. "How Big Are Nonverbal Sex Differences? The Case of Smiling and Nonverbal Sensitivity." In *Sex Differences and Similarities in Communication*, edited by K. Dindia and D. J. Canary, 59–81. Mahwah, NJ: Lawrence Erlbaum Associates, 2006.

Hall, J. A., L. S. LeBeau, J. G. Reinoso, and F. Thayer. "Status, Gender, and Nonverbal Behavior in Candid and Posed Photographs: A Study of Conversations between University Employees." *Sex Roles* 44 (2001): 677–92.

Hammett, Dashiell. *The Maltese Falcon*. 1930. New York: Vintage Crime/Black Lizard, 1992.

Hankiss, E. *Social Traps*. Warsaw: Wiedza Powszechna, 1986.

Hardy, Thomas. *Far from the Madding Crowd*. London: Smith, Elder & Co., 1874.

Hare, R. D. "Psychopaths and Their Nature: Implications for Mental Health and Criminal Justice Systems." In *Psychopathy: Antisocial, Criminal and Violent Behavior*, edited by T. Millon, E. Simonsen, M. Birket-Smith, and R. D. Davis, 188–212. New York: Guilford Press, 1998.

Harlow, J. "The Smile That Says Where You're From." *Sunday Times* (London), February 20, 2005.

Harris, P. L., and D. Gross. "Children's Understanding of Real and Apparent Emotion." In *Developing Theories of Mind*, edited by J. W. Astington, P. L. Harris, and D. R. Olson. New York: Cambridge University Press, 1988.

Harvey, M. "Is Einstein Robot Too Human? Everything's Relative." *The Times* (London), February 27, 2009.

Hawthorne, Nathaniel. *The Scarlet Letter*. 1850. New York: Penguin Classics, 2003.

"Heard in the Halls; Toll-Taker Bonus: Paid for Smiling." *Patriot Ledger*, May 16, 1998.

Hecht, M. A., and M. LaFrance. "License or Obligation to Smile: The Effect of Power and Sex on Amount and Type of Smiling." *Personality and Social Psychology Bulletin* 24 (1998): 1332–42.

Heerey, E. A., and A. Kring. "Interpersonal Consequences of Social Anxiety." *Journal of Abnormal Psychology* 116 (2007): 125–34.

Heller, Joseph. *Catch-22: A Novel*. New York: Simon & Schuster, 1961.

Helquist, Brett [Lemony Snicket]. *The Bad Beginning*. A Series of Unfortunate Events, vol. 1. New York: HarperCollins, 2001.

Henderson, S. "Disregarding the Suffering of Others: Narrative, Comedy, and Torture." *Literature and Medicine* 24 (2005): 181–208.

Henig, T., M. Groth, M. Paul, and D. D. Gremier. "Are All Smiles Created Equal? How Emotional Contagion and Emotion Labor Affect Service Relationships." *Journal of Marketing* 70 (2006): 58–73.

Henley, N. M., and M. LaFrance. "Gender as Culture: Difference and Dominance in Nonverbal Behavior" In *Nonverbal Behavior: Perspectives, Applications, Intercultural Insights*, edited by A. Wolfgang, 351–72. Lewiston, NY: C. J. Hogrefe, 1984.

Henson, Kevin D. *Just a Temp*. Philadelphia: Temple University Press, 1996.

Hernandez-Reif, M., T. Field, M. Diego, Y. Vera, and J. Pickens. "Happy Faces Are Habituated More Slowly by Infants of Depressed Mothers." *Infant Behavior and Development* 29 (2006): 131–35.

Hertenstein, M. J., C. A. Hansel, A. M. Butts, and S. N. Hile. "Smile Intensity in Photographs Predicts Divorce Later in Life." *Motivation and Emotion* 33 (2009): 99–105.

Hess, U., and R. E. Kleck. "Differentiated Emotion Elicited and Deliberate Emotional Facial Expressions." *European Journal of Social Psychology* 20 (1990): 369–85.

Hildebrandt. K. H., D. A. Vogel, and M. A. Lake. "Parents' Gender-Stereotyped Perceptions of Newborns: The Eye of the Beholder Revisited." *Sex Roles* 33 (1995): 687–701.

Hill, A. "Actors Warned to Keep Off the Botox." *The Observer* (London), February 9, 2003. http://www.guardian.co.uk/uk/2003/feb/09/film.filmnews.

Hochschild, Arlie Russell. *The Managed Heart*. Berkeley: University of California Press, 1983.

Hofstede, Geert. *Culture's Consequences: International Differences in Work-Related Values*. Beverly Hills, CA: Sage Publications, 1980.

Holmes, R. "Voltaire's Grin." *New York Review of Books* 42 (1995): 49–55.

Holst-Warhaft, G. "Remembering the Dead: Laments and Photographs." *Comparative Studies of South Asia, Africa and the Middle East* 25 (2005): 152–60.

Holyfield, L. "Manufacturing Adventure: The Buying and Selling of Emotions." *Journal of Contemporary Ethnography* 28 (1999): 3–32.

House, R. J. "A Theory of Charismatic Leadership." In *Leadership: The Cutting Edge*, edited by J. G. Hunt and L. L. Larson, 189–207. Carbondale: Southern Illinois University Press, 1977.

Hrdy, Sarah Blaffer. *Mothers and Others: The Evolutionary Origins of Mutual Understanding*. Cambridge, MA: Harvard University Press, 2009.

Hudson, T. "Service with a Smile, or Else." *Hospitals and Health Networks* 72 (January 20, 1998): 62.

Hyde, J. "The Gender Similarities Hypothesis." *American Psychologist* 60 (2005): 581–92.

Hyers, Conrad. *The Laughing Buddha: Zen and the Comic Spirit.* Boston: Longwood Academic, 1991.

Intraub H., C. V. Gottesman, E. Willey, and I. J. Zuk. "Boundary Extension for Briefly Glimpsed Photographs: Do Common Perceptual Processes Result in Unexpected Memory Distortions?" *Journal of Memory and Language* 35 (1996): 118–34.

Ito, T. A., K. W. Chiao, P. G. Devine, T. S. Lorig, and J. T. Cacioppo. "The Influence of Facial Feedback on Race Bias." *Psychological Science* 17 (2006): 256–63.

Izard, C. E. "The Generality-Specificity Issue in Infants' Emotion Responses." *Infancy* 6 (2004): 417–23.

Jacob, T., and S. L. Johnson. "Sequential Interactions in the Parent-Child Communications of Depressed Fathers and Depressed Mothers." *Journal of Family Psychology* 15 (2001): 38–52.

James, Henry. *The Ambassadors.* 1903. Oxford, UK: Oxford University Press, 2008.

———. *The Portrait of a Lady.* 1881. Boston: Houghton Mifflin, 1909.

———. *The Wings of the Dove.* 1902. London: Penguin Classics, 2008.

James, William. *The Principles of Psychology.* 1890. New York: Dover, 1950.

Jamieson, Kathleen Hall. *Packaging the Presidency: A History and Criticism of Presidential Campaign Advertising.* New York: Oxford University Press, 1996.

Janes, L. M., and J. Olson. "Jeer Pressure: The Behavioral Effects of Observing Ridicule of Others." *Personality and Social Psychology Bulletin* 26 (2000): 474–84.

Jarymowicz, M., and D. Bar-Tal. "The Dominance of Fear over Hope in the Life of Individuals and Collectives." *European Journal of Social Psychology* 36 (2006): 367–92.

John, G. "Made in Japan." *Christian Science Monitor,* September 4, 1991.

Jones, B. C., L. M. DeBruine, A. C. Little, C. Conway, and D. R. Feinberg. "Integrating Gaze Direction and Expression in Preferences for Attractive Faces." *Psychological Science* 17 (2006): 588–91.

Jones, E. E., and T. S. Pittman. "Toward a General Theory of Strategic Self-Presentation." In *Psychological Perspectives on the Self,* vol. 1, edited by J. Suls, 231–62. Hillsdale, NJ: Lawrence Erlbaum Associates, 1982.

Jones, S. S., and H. W. Hong. "How Some Infant Smiles Get Made." *Infant Behavior and Development* 28 (2005): 194–205.

Jones, S. S., and T. Ragg. "Smile Production in Older Infants: The Importance of a Social Recipient for the Facial Signal." *Child Development* 60 (1989): 811–18.

Kagan, Jerome. *Galen's Prophecy: Temperament in Human Nature.* New York: Basic Books, 1994.

Kagan, Jerome, Norbert Herschkowitz, and Elinore Herschkowitz. *A Young Mind in a Growing Brain.* Mahwah, NJ: Lawrence Erlbaum Associates, 2005.

Kahana-Kalman, R., and A. S. Walker-Andrews. "The Role of Person Familiarity in Young Infants' Perception of Emotional Expressions." *Child Development* 72 (2001): 352–69.

Kaid, Lynda Lee, and Anne Johnston. *Videostyle in Presidential Campaigns: Style and Content of Televised Political Advertising.* Westport, CT: Frederick Praeger, 2001.

Kailey, Matt. *Just Add Hormones: An Insider's Guide to the Transsexual Experience.* Boston: Beacon Press, 2005.

Kanner, L. "Autistic Disturbances of Affective Contact." *Nervous Child* 2 (1943): 217–50.

Kappas, A., F. Bherer, and M. Theriault. "Inhibiting Facial Expressions: Limitations to the Voluntary Control of Facial Expressions of Emotion." *Motivation and Emotion* 24 (2000): 259–70.

Keating, C. F., A. Mazur, M. H. Segall, and P. G. Cysneiros. "Culture and the Perception of Dominance from Facial Expression." *Journal of Personality and Social Psychology* 40 (1981): 615–26.

Keillor, J. M., A. M. Barrett, G. P. Crucian, S. Kortenkamp, and K. M. Heilman. "Emotional Experience and Perception in the Absence of Facial Feedback." *Journal of the International Neuropsychological Society* 8 (2002): 130–35.

Kelley, R. "Show Them a 'Take Me Home' Face: Enlisting the Camera in the Adoption Quest." *New York Times*, March 21, 2005, p. A1.

Keltner, D., and B. N. Buswell. "Embarrassment: Its Distinct Form and Appeasement Functions." *Psychological Bulletin* 122 (1997): 250–70.

Keltner, D., and J. Haidt. "Social Functions of Emotions." In *Emotions: Current Issues and Future Directions*, edited by T. Mayne and G. Bonanno, 192–213. New York: Guilford Press, 2001.

Keltner, D., and L. A. Harker. "Expressions of Positive Emotion in Women's College Yearbook Pictures and Their Relationship to Personality and Life Outcomes." *Journal of Personality and Social Psychology* 80 (2001): 112–24.

Keltner, D., L. Capps, A. M. Kring, R. C. Young, and E. Heerey. "Just Teasing:

A Conceptual Analysis and Empirical Review." *Psychological Bulletin* 127 (2001): 229–48.

Keltner, D., D. H. Gruenfeld, and C. Anderson. "Power, Approach, and Inhibition." *Psychological Bulletin* 110 (2003): 265–84.

Keltner, D., R. C. Young, E. A. Heerey, and C. Oernig. "Teasing in Hierarchical and Intimate Relations." *Journal of Personality and Social Psychology* 75 (1998): 1231–47.

Kennedy, D. "Selling the Distant Other: Humanitarianism and Imagery." *Journal of Humanitarian Assistance*. http://jha.ac/2009/02/28/selling-the-distant-other-humanitarianism-and-imagery.

Kesey, Ken. *One Flew Over the Cuckoo's Nest*. 1962. New York: Penguin Classics, 2007.

Kincaid, J. "Girl." *The New Yorker*, June 26, 1978.

King, Florence. *Southern Ladies and Gentlemen*. New York: Stein & Day, 1975. Reprint, New York: St. Martin's Press, 1993.

Konner, M. J. "Biological Bases of Social Development." In *Social Competence in Children*, edited by M. W. Kent and J. E. Rolf. Hanover, NH: University of Vermont Press, 1979.

Kotchemidova, C. "From Good Cheer to 'Drive-By Smiling': A Social History of Cheerfulness." *Journal of Social History* 39 (2005): 5–37.

Kraus, M. W., and D. Keltner. "Signs of Socioeconomic Status." *Psychological Science* 20 (2009): 99–104.

Kraut, R. E., and R. E. Johnston. "Social and Emotional Messages of Smiling: An Ethological Approach." *Journal of Personality and Social Psychology* 13 (1979): 1539–53.

Kress, Gunther, ed. *Communication and Culture*. Sydney: University of New South Wales Press, 1998.

Krumhuber, E., A. S. R. Manstead, and A. Kappas. "Temporal Aspects of Facial Displays in Persona and Expression Perception: The Effects of Smile Dynamics, Head Tilt, and Gender." *Journal of Nonverbal Behavior* 31 (2007): 39–56.

Kruml, S. M., and D. Geddes. "Catching Fire Without Burning Out: Is There an Ideal Way to Perform Emotion Labor?" In *Emotions in the Workplace: Research, Theory, and Practice*, edited by N. M. Ashkanasy, C. E. J. Hartel, and W. J. Zerbe. Westport, CT: Quorum Books, 2000.

Kuleshov, Lev. *Kuleshov on Film: The Writings of Lev Kuleshov*. Edited and translated by Ronald Levaco. Berkeley: University of California Press, 1974.

Kundera, Milan. *The Book of Laughter and Forgetting*. New York: HarperPerennial, 1993.

Kwong, P., and D. Miscevic. "Globalization and Hong Kong's Future." *Journal of Contemporary Asia* 32 (2002): 323–37.

LaFrance, M. "Pressure to Be Pleasant: Effects of Sex and Power on Reactions to Not Smiling." *International Review of Social Psychology* 2 (1998): 95–108.

LaFrance, M., and B. Carmen. "The Nonverbal Display of Psychological Androgyny." *Journal of Personality and Social Psychology* 7 (1980): 36–49.

LaFrance, M., and M. A. Hecht. "Gender and Smiling: A Meta-analysis." In *Gender and Emotion: Social Psychological Perspectives*, edited by A. H. Fischer, 118–42. Cambridge, UK: Cambridge University Press, 2000.

———. "Why Smiles Generate Leniency." *Personality and Social Psychology Bulletin* 21 (1995): 207–14.

LaFrance, M., and J. Woodzicka. "No Laughing Matter: Women's Verbal and Nonverbal Responses to Sexist Humor." In *Prejudice: The Target's Perspective*, edited by J. Swim and C. Stangor, 61–80. New York: Academic Press, 1998.

LaFrance, M., M. A. Hecht, and E. L. Paluck. "The Contingent Smile: A Meta-analysis of Sex Differences in Smiling." *Psychological Bulletin* 129 (2003): 305–34.

Laird, J. D. "Self-Attribution of Emotion: The Effects of Expressive Behavior on the Quality of Emotional Experience." *Journal of Personality and Social Psychology* 29 (1974): 475–86.

Lander, K., and S. Metcalfe. "The Influence of Positive and Negative Facial Expression on Face Familiarity." *Memory* 15 (2007): 63–69.

Lardner, Ring. "The Big Town." 1920. In *Selected Stories*. New York: Penguin Classics, 1997.

Larned, W. L. "The Smile That Sells Goods." *Printers' Ink*, November 30, 1911, pp. 3–8.

Larsen, R. J., M. Kasimatis, and K. Frey. "Facilitating the Furrowed Brow: An Unobtrusive Test of the Facial Feedback Hypothesis Applied to Unpleasant Affect." *Cognition and Emotion* 6 (1992): 321–38.

Larson, E. B., and X. Yao. "Clinical Empathy as Emotional Labor in the Patient-Physician Relationship." *Journal of the American Medical Association* 293 (2005): 1100–1106.

Laski, Harold J. *American Democracy: A Commentary and an Interpretation*. New York: Viking Press, 1948.

Lee, D.-H. "Women's Creation of Camera Phone Culture." *Fibreculture*, issue 6 (2005). Available at http://journal.fibreculture.org/issue6/issue6_donghoo.html.

Leiderman P. H. "The Critical Period Hypothesis Revisited: Mother to Infant Social Bonding in the Neonatal Period." In *Early Developmental Hazards: Predictors and Precautions*, edited by F. D. Horowitz. Boulder, CO: Westview Press, 1978.

Lessing, Doris. *The Summer before the Dark*. New York: Alfred A. Knopf, 1973.

Levenson, R. W., and J. M. Gottman. "Marital Interaction: Physiological Linkage and Affective Exchange." *Journal of Personality and Social Psychology* 45 (1983): 587–97.

Lewis, M. "The Self-Conscious Emotions: Embarrassment, Shame, Pride and Guilt." In *The Handbook of Emotions*, 2nd ed., edited by M. Lewis and J. M. Haviland-Jones, 623–36. New York: Guilford Press, 2000.

Lill, M. M., and T. J. Wilkinson. "Judging a Book by Its Cover: Descriptive Survey of Patients' Preferences for Doctors' Appearance and Mode of Address." *British Medical Journal* 331 (2005): 1524–27.

Lincoln, Abraham. "Letter to Fanny McCullough, December 23, 1862." In *Lincoln Addresses and Letters*, edited by Charles W. Moores. New York: American Book Company, 1914.

Lindsay, D. S., L. Hagen, D. Read, K. A. Wade, and M. Garry. "True Photographs and False Memories." *Psychological Science* 15 (2004): 149–54.

Lipsitt, L. P. "Critical Conditions in Infancy." *American Psychologist* 34 (1979): 973–80.

Lorenz, Konrad. *King Solomon's Ring: New Light on Animal Ways*. 1961. New York: Routledge, 2002.

Lutz, C. "Depression and the Translation of Emotional Worlds." In *Culture and Depression: Studies in the Anthropology and Cross-Cultural Psychiatry of Affect and Disorder*, edited by A. Kleinman and B. Good, 63–100. Berkeley: University of California Press, 1985.

Lyons-Ruth, K., D. B. Connell, D. Zoll, and J. Stahl. "Infants at Social Risk: Relations among Infant Maltreatment, Maternal Behavior and Infant Attachment Behavior." *Developmental Psychology* 23 (1987): 223–32.

MacDonald, G., and M. R. Leary. "Why Does Social Exclusion Hurt? The Relationship between Social and Physical Pain." *Psychological Bulletin* 131 (2005): 202–23.

Machiavelli, Niccolò. *The Prince and the Discourses*. 1513. Translated by Luigi Ricci. New York: Random House, 1950.

Magnier, M. "As Olympics Loom, Beijing Outlaws Bad Manners." *Los Angeles Times*, January 14, 2007, p. 18.

Malatesta, C. Z., and C. E. Izard. "The Ontogenesis of Human Social Signals:

From Biological Imperative to Symbol Utilization." In *The Psychobiology of Affective Development*, edited by N. A. Fox and R. J. Davidson, 161–205. Mahwah, NJ: Lawrence Erlbaum Associates, 1984.

Malatesta, C. Z., M. J. Fiore, and J. Messina. "Affect, Personality, and Facial Expressive Characteristics of Older Individuals." *Psychology and Aging* 1 (1987): 64–69.

Mansfield, Harvey C. *Manliness*. New Haven, CT: Yale University Press, 2006.

Margolin, G., and E. B. Gordis. "Children's Exposure to Violence in the Family and Community." *Current Directions in Psychological Science* 13 (2004): 152–55.

Maris, R. "Roger Maris Quotes." *Baseball Almanac*. www.baseball-almanac .com.

Marsh, A. A., H. A. Elfenbein, and N. Ambady. "Separated by a Common Language: Nonverbal Accents and Cultural Stereotypes about Americans and Australians." *Journal of Cross-Cultural Psychology* 38 (2007): 284–301.

Marshall, J. "The Write Pose: Authors Can Think of a Lot of Things—But Not How to Get Out of Those Darn Book-Jacket Shots." *Seattle Post-Intelligencer*, February 1, 1996.

Master, S. L., N. I. Eisenberger, S. E. Taylor, B. D. Naliboff, D. Shirinyan, and M. D. Lieberman. "A Picture's Worth: Partner Photographs Reduce Experimentally Induced Pain." *Psychological Science* 20 (2009): 1316–18.

Masters, R. D. *The Nature of Politics*. New Haven, CT: Yale University Press, 1989.

Masters, R. D., and D. Sullivan. "Nonverbal Behavior and Leadership: Emotion and Cognition in Political Attitudes." In *Explorations in Political Psychology*, edited by S. Iyengar and W. McGuire, 150–82. Durham, NC: Duke University Press, 1993.

Masuda, T., and R. E. Nisbett. "Culture and Change Blindness." *Cognitive Science* 30 (2007): 381–99.

Masuda, T., P. C. Ellsworth, B. Mesquita, J. Leu, S. Tanida, and E. van de Veerdonk. "Placing the Face in Context: Cultural Differences in the Perception of Facial Emotion." *Journal of Personality and Social Psychology* 94 (2008): 365–81.

Matsumoto, D., T. Kudoh, K. Scherer, and W. Wallbott. "Antecedents of and Reactions to Emotions in the United States and Japan." *Journal of Cross-Cultural Psychology* 19 (1988): 267–86.

Matsumoto, D., S. H. Yoo, J. Fontaine, A. M. Anguas-Wong, M. Arriola, B. Ataca, M. H. Bond, et al. "Mapping Expressive Differences around the World:

The Relationship between Emotional Display Rules and Individualism versus Collectivism." *Journal of Cross-Cultural Psychology* 39 (2008): 55–74.

Mayes, S. "A Psychologist Says He Can Tell Which Marriages Will Last from the Wedding Couple's Smiles . . . Can You?" *Daily Mirror* (London), February 8, 2001, pp. 29–30.

McAlister, R. W., E. M. Harkness, and J. J. Nicoll. "An Ultrasound Investigation of Lip Levator Musculature." *European Journal of Orthodontics* 20 (1998): 713–20.

McCullers, Carson. *The Heart Is a Lonely Hunter.* Boston: Houghton Mifflin, 1940.

McDowell, D. J., and R. D. Park. "Differential Knowledge of Display Rules for Positive and Negative Emotions: Influences from Parents, Influences on Peers." *Social Development* 9 (2000): 415–32.

McElhinny, B. "Challenging Hegemonic Masculinities: Female and Male Police Officers Handling Domestic Violence." In *Gender Articulated: Language and the Socially Constructed Self*, edited by K. Hall and M. Bucholtz, 217–43. New York: Routledge, 1995.

McGinnis, Joe. *The Selling of the President, 1968.* New York: Pocket Books, 1970.

McGrew, William C. *The Cultured Chimpanzee: Reflections on Cultural Primatology.* Cambridge, UK: Cambridge University Press, 2004.

McIntosh, D. N. "Facial Feedback Hypothesis: Evidence, Implications and Directions." *Motivation and Emotion* 20 (1996): 121–47.

McLuhan, Marshall, and Quentin Fiore. *The Medium is the Massage.* New York: Random House, 1967.

Meade, Marion. *Buster Keaton: Cut to the Chase.* New York: HarperCollins, 1995.

Mehu, M., and R. I. M. Dunbar. "Smiles When Sharing." *Evolution and Human Behavior* 28 (2007): 415–22.

Meltzoff, A. N., and M. K. Moore. "Imitation, Memory and the Representation of Persons." *Infant Behavior and Development* 17 (1994): 83–94.

Mendoza-Denton, N. "Fighting Words: Latina Girls, Gangs, and Language Attitudes." In *Speaking Chicanas*, edited by D. L. Galindo and N. Gonzalez-Vasquez. Tucson: University of Arizona Press, 1999.

Mergen, B. "The Pullman Porter: From 'George' to Brotherhood." *South Atlantic Quarterly* 75 (1974): 224–35.

Merleau-Ponty, Maurice. *The Primacy of Perception.* 1945. Edited by James M. Edie. Evanston, IL: Northwestern University Press, 1964.

Messinger, D. S. "Positive and Negative: Infant Facial Expressions and Emotions." *Current Directions in Psychological Science* 11 (2002): 1–6.

Messinger, D. S., M. Dondi, G. C. Nelson-Goens, A. Beghi, A. Fogel, and F. Simion. "How Sleeping Neonates Smile." *Developmental Science* 5 (2002): 48–54.

Messinger, D. S., A. Fogel, and K. L. Dickson. "All Smiles Are Positive, But Some Smiles Are More Positive than Others." *Developmental Psychology* 37 (2001): 642–53.

Miles, L. "Who Is Approachable?" *Journal of Experimental Social Psychology* 45 (2009): 262–66.

Milgram, S. "The Image-Freezing Machine." In *The Individual in a Social World: Essays and Experiments*, edited by Stanley Milgram. Reading, MA: Addison-Wesley, 1977.

Miller, Arthur. *Death of a Salesman*. 1949. New York: Penquin Classics, 1998.

Minagawa-Kawai, Y., S. Matsuoka, I. Dan, N. Naoi, K. Nakamura, and S. Kojima. "Prefrontal Activation Associated with Social Attachment: Facial-Emotion Recognition in Mothers and Infants." *Cerebral Cortex* 19 (2009): 84–292.

Moeller, Susan D. *Shooting War: Photography and the American Experience of Combat*. New York: Basic Books, 1989.

Moore, G. A., J. F. Cohn, and S. B. Campbell. "Infant Affective Responses to Mother's Still Face at 6 Months Differentially Predict Externalizing and Internalizing Behaviors at 18 Months." *Developmental Psychology* 37 (2001): 706–14.

Morris, A. J., and D. C. Feldman. "Managing Emotions in the Workplace." *Journal of Managerial Issues* 9 (1997): 257–74.

Morris, Dick. *Behind the Oval Office: Winning the Presidency in the Nineties*. New York: Random House, 1997.

Mottet, T. P., S. A. Beebe, and P. C. Raffeld. "The Effects of Student Verbal and Nonverbal Responsiveness on Teachers' Liking of Students and Willingness to Comply with Student Requests." *Communication Quarterly* 52 (2004): 27–38.

Murphy, S. T., and R. B. Zajonc. "Affect, Cognition, and Awareness: Affective Priming with Optimal and Suboptimal Stimulus Exposures." *Journal of Personality and Social Psychology* 64 (1993): 723–39.

Nabokov, Vladimir. *Laughter in the Dark*. 1938. New York: New Directions, 1960.

Nagy, E., E. Nemeth, and P. Molnar. "From Unidentified to 'Misidentified' Newborn: Male Bias in Recognition of Sex." *Perception and Motor Skills* 90 (2000): 102–4.

Nelson, C., and M. De Haan. "A Neurobehavioral Approach to the Recognition of Facial Expressions in Infancy." In *The Psychology of Facial Expression*, edited by J. A. Russell and J. M. Fernández-Dols, 176–204. New York: Cambridge University Press, 1997.

Newman, A. "Kathy the Beluga, 34, Is Dead; Brought Smiles, and Gave Them." *New York Times*, April 10, 2004.

Newton, P., V. Reddy, and R. Bull. "Children's Everyday Deception and Performance on False-Belief Tasks." *British Journal of Developmental Psychology* 18 (2000): 297–317.

Nietzsche, Friedrich Wilhelm. *Beyond Good and Evil*. 1917. Chicago: H. Regnery Co., 1949.

Nijhof, G. "Parkinson's Disease as a Problem of Shame in Public Appearance." *Sociology of Health and Illness* 15 (2008): 193–205.

Nisbett, Richard. E., and Dov Cohen. *Culture of Honor: The Psychology of Violence in the South*. Boulder, CO: Westview Press, 1996.

Noller, P. "Channel Consistency and Inconsistency in the Communication of Married Couples." *Journal of Personality and Social Psychology* 43 (1982): 732–41.

Nucci, Larry P., Geoffrey B. Saxe, and Elliot Turiel, eds. *Culture, Thought, and Development*. Mahwah, NJ: Lawrence Erlbaum Associates, 2000.

Obama, B. "What I see in Lincoln's Eyes." *Time*, June 26, 2005. http://www .time.com/time/printout/0,8816,1077287,000.html.

O'Connor, Flannery. "Good Country People." 1955. In *The Complete Stories*, 271–91. New York: Farrar, Straus & Giroux, 1971.

O'Doherty, J. P., P. Dayan, K. Friston, H. Critchley, and R. J. Dolan. "Temporal Difference Models and Reward-Related Learning in the Human Brain." *Neuron* 28 (2003): 329–37.

Olson, S. L., J. E. Bates, and K. Bayles. "Early Antecedents of Childhood Impulsivity: The Role of Parent-Child Interaction, Cognitive Competence, and Temperament." *Journal of Abnormal Child Psychology* 18 (1990): 317–34.

Ordinary People (motion picture). Directed by Robert Redford. Screenplay by Alvin Sargent. 1980.

Orvaschel, H., G. Walsh-Allis, and W. Ye. "Psychopathology in Children of Parents with Recurrent Depression." *Journal of Abnormal Child Psychology* 16 (1988): 17–28.

Ottati, V., N. Terkildsen, and C. Hubbard. "Happy Faces Elicit Heuristic

Processing in a Televised Impression Formation Task: A Cognitive Tuning Account." *Personality and Social Psychology Bulletin* 23 (1997): 1144–57.

Owren, M. J., and J. A. Bachorowski. "Smiling, Laughter, and Cooperative Relationships: An Attempt to Account for Human Expressions of Positive Emotions Based on 'Selfish Gene' Evolution." In *Emotion: Current Issues and Future Development*, edited by T. Mayne and G. A. Bonanno, 152–91. New York: Guilford Press, 2001.

Paoli, Pascal. *Second European Survey on Working Conditions*. Dublin, Ireland: European Foundation for the Improvement of Living and Working Conditions, 1997.

Papa, A., and G. Bonanno. "Smiling in the Face of Adversity: The Interpersonal and Intrapersonal Functions of Smiling." *Emotion* 8 (2008): 1–12.

Parini, Jay. *Robert Frost: A Life*. New York: Macmillan, 2000.

Parker, S. W., and C. A. Nelson, with the Bucharest Early Intervention Project Core Group. "The Impact of Early Institutional Rearing on the Ability to Discriminate Facial Expressions of Emotion." *Child Development* 76 (2005): 54–72.

Parkinson, B. "Untangling the Appraisal-Emotion Connection." *Personality and Social Psychology Review* 1 (1997): 62–79.

Peace, V., L. Miles, and L. Johnston. "It Doesn't Matter What You Wear: The Impact of Posed and Genuine Expressions of Happiness on Product Evaluation." *Social Cognition* 24 (2006): 137–68.

Pellicer, Raynal. *Mug Shots: An Archive of the Famous, Infamous, and Most Wanted*. New York: Abrams/Putnam, 2009.

Pessa, J., V. Zadoo, E. J. Adrian, A. Dewitt, and J. Garza. "Double or Bifid Zygomaticus Major Muscle: Anatomy, Incidence, and Clinical Correlation." *Clinical Anatomy* 11 (1998): 310–13.

Phillips, R. D., and V. A. Sellitto. "Preliminary Evidence on Emotions Expressed by Children during Solitary Play." *Play and Culture* 3 (1990): 79–90.

Pickett, C. L., W. L. Gardner, and M. Knowles. "Getting a Clue: The Need to Belong and Enhanced Sensitivity to Social Cues." *Personality and Social Psychology Bulletin* 30 (2004): 1095–1107.

Pierce, J. L. "Emotional Labor among Paralegals." *Annals of the American Academy of Political and Social Science* 56 (1999): 127–42.

——. *Gender Trials: Emotional Lives in Contemporary Law Firms*. Berkeley: University of California Press, 1995.

Pierce, P. A. "Political Sophistication and the Use of Candidate Traits in Candidate Evaluation." *Political Psychology* 14 (1993): 21–35.

Polce-Lynch, M., B. J. Myers, C. T. Kilmartin, R. Forssmann-Falck, and W. Kliewer. "Gender and Age Patterns in Emotional Expression, Body Image, and Self-Esteem: A Qualitative Analysis." *Sex Roles* 38 (1998): 1025–48.

Pollack, A. "Happy in the East (^_^) or Smiling in the West :-)." *New York Times*, August, 12, 1996, p. D5.

Pollak, S. D., D. Cicchetti, K. Hornung, and A. Reed. "Recognizing Emotion in Faces: Developmental Effects of Child Abuse and Neglect." *Developmental Psychology* 36 (2000): 679–88.

Polsby, Nelson, Aaron Wildavsky, and David Hopkins. *Presidential Elections: Strategies and Structures of American Politics*. Lanham, MD: Rowman & Littlefield, 2007.

Preuschoft, S. "'Laughter' and 'Smile' in Barbary Macaques (*Macaca sylvanus*)." *Ethology* 91 (1992): 220–36.

Preuschoft, S., and J. van Hooff. "Homologizing Primate Facial Displays: A Critical View of Methods." *Folia Primatologica* 65 (1995): 121–37.

Price, S. "Cartoons from another Planet: Japanese Animation as Cross-Cultural Communication." *Journal of American and Comparative Cultures* 24 (2001): 153–69.

Prkachin, K. M., and B. E. Silverman. "Hostility and Facial Expression in Young Men and Women: Is Social Regulation More Important than Negative Affect?" *Health Psychology* 21 (2002): 33–39.

Provine, R. "Laughter Punctuates Speech: Linguistic, Social and Gender Contexts of Laughter." *Ethology* 95 (1993): 291–98.

Pugh, Marshall. *The Chancer*. New York: Hutchinson, 1959.

Pugh, S. D. "Service with a Smile: Emotional Contagion in the Service Encounter." *Academy of Management Journal* 44 (2001): 1018–27.

Rafaeli, A., and R. I. Sutton. "Expression of Emotion as Part of the Work Role." *Academy of Management Review* 12 (1987): 23–37.

———. "The Expression of Emotion in Organizational Life." *Research in Organizational Behavior* 11 (1989): 1–42.

Reddy, V. "Coyness in Early Infancy." *Developmental Science* 3 (2000): 186–92.

———. "Getting Back to the Rough Ground: Deception and 'Social Living.'" *Philosophical Transactions of the Royal Society: Biological Sciences* 362 (2007): 621–37.

Reed, John Shelton. *The Enduring South: Subcultural Persistence in Mass Society.* Lexington, MA: Lexington Books, 1972.

Register, Woody. *The Kid of Coney Island: Fred Thompson and the Rise of American Amusements.* New York: Oxford University Press, 2003.

Reis, H. T., I. M. Wilson, C. Monestere, S. Bernstein, K. Clark, E. Seidl, M. Franco, E. Cisioso, L. Freeman, and K. Radoane. "What Is Smiling Is Beautiful and Good." *European Journal of Social Psychology* 20 (1990): 259–67.

Repacholi, B. M. "Infants' Use of Attentional Cues to Identify the Referent of another Person's Emotional Expression." *Developmental Psychology* 34 (1998): 1017–25.

Richeson, J., and J. N. Shelton. "Thin Slices of Racial Bias." *Journal of Nonverbal Behavior* 29 (2006): 75–86.

Rind, B., and P. Bordia. "Effect on Restaurant Tipping of Male and Female Servers Drawing a Happy, Smiling Face on the Backs of Customer Checks." *Journal of Applied Social Psychology* 26 (1996): 218–25.

Rinn, W. "Neuropsychology of Facial Expression." In *Fundamentals of Nonverbal Behavior*, edited by R. S. Feldman and B. Rimé, 3–30. Cambridge, UK: Cambridge University Press, 1991.

Roach, Joseph. *It.* Ann Arbor: University of Michigan Press, 2007.

Robins, B., P. Dickerson, P. Stribling, and K. Dautenhahn. "Robot-Mediated Joint Attention in Children with Autism: A Case Study in Robot-Human Interaction." *Interaction Studies* 5 (2004): 161–98.

Robinson, J. L., and H. A. Demaree. "Physiological and Cognitive Effects of Expressive Dissonance." *Brain and Cognition* 63 (2007): 70–78.

Robson, K. S. "The Role of Eye-to-Eye Contact in Maternal-Infant Attachment." *Journal of Child Psychology and Child Psychiatry and Allied Disciplines* 8 (1967): 13–25.

Rose, Phyllis. "Milkmaid Madonnas: An Appreciation of Cameron's Portraits of Women." In *Julia Margaret Cameron's Women*, edited by Sylvia Wolf, 12–21. New Haven, CT: Yale University Press, 1999.

Roueche, B. "Pose." *The New Yorker*, June 24, 1950.

Rousseau, Jean-Jacques. In T. Edwards, *A Dictionary of Thoughts: Being a Cyclopedia of Laconic Quotations from the Best Authors of the World, Both Ancient and Modern.* London: Cassell Publishing Company, 1908.

Rubin, J. Z., F. J. Provenzano, and Z. Luria. "The Eye of the Beholder: Parents' Views on Sex of Newborns." *American Journal of Orthopsychiatry* 44 (1974): 512–19.

Rule, N. O., and N. Ambady. "Democrats and Republicans Can Be Differentiated from Their Faces." Poster presented at the annual meeting of the Association of Psychological Science, Boston, MA, May 29, 2010.

Ryan, A. M., and R. F. Ployhart. "Customer Service Behavior." In *Handbook of Psychology*, vol. 12, *Industrial and Organizational Psychology*, edited by W. C. Borman, C. Walter, and D. R. Ilgen, 377–97. New York: John Wiley and Sons, 2003.

Saarni, C. "Children's Understanding of Display Rules for Expressive Behavior." *Developmental Psychology* 15 (1979): 424–39.

Sacks, Oliver. *The Man Who Mistook His Wife for a Hat.* New York: Simon & Schuster, 1998.

Salinger, J. D. *The Catcher in the Rye.* 1951. New York: Bantam Books, 1984.

Santino, Jack. *Miles of Smiles, Years of Struggle: Stories of Black Pullman Porters.* Urbana: University of Illinois Press, 1991.

Sapir, Edward. *Selected Writings of Edward Sapir: Language, Culture and Personality.* Edited by David G. Mandelbaum. Berkeley: University of California Press, 1984.

Schacter, Daniel L. *Searching for Memory: The Brain, the Mind, and the Past.* New York: Basic Books, 1996.

Schmidt, K. L., Z. Ambadar, J. F. Cohn, and L. I. Reed. "Movement Differences between Deliberate and Spontaneous Facial Expressions: Zygomaticus Major Action in Smiling." *Journal of Nonverbal Behavior* 30 (2006): 37–52.

Schmidt, R. "A New Wrinkle in Welfare Reform." *Chronicle of Higher Education*, April 23, 1999, p. A42.

Schwartz, G. E., G. L. Ahern, and S. Brown. "Lateralized Facial Muscle Response to Positive and Negative Emotional Stimuli." *Psychophysiology* 16 (1979): 561–71.

Scott, C., and K. K. Myers. "The Socialization of Emotion: Learning Emotion Management at the Fire Station." *Journal of Applied Communication* 33 (2007): 67–92.

Seaford, H. "Facial Expression Dialect: An Example." In *Organization of Behavior in Face-to-Face Interaction*, edited by A. Kendon, R. M. Harris, and M. R. Key. The Hague, Netherlands: Mouton Publishers, 1975.

Sedaris, David. *Holidays on Ice.* Milan: Mondadori, 2003.

Seiter, J. S., and E. Dutson. "The Effect of Compliments on Tipping Behavior in Hairstyling Salons." *Journal of Applied Social Psychology* 37 (2007): 1999–2007.

Sendak, Maurice. *Where the Wild Things Are.* New York: Harper & Row, 1963.

Shakepeare, William. *The Oxford Shakespeare: The Complete Works*. 2nd edition. Edited by John Jowett, William Montgomery, Gary Taylor, and Stanley Wells. Oxford, UK: Oxford University Press, 2005.

Shamay-Tsoory, S. G., Y. Tibi-Elhanany, and J. Aharon-Peretz. "The Green-Eyed Monster and Malicious Joy: The Neuroanatomical Bases of Envy and Gloating (Schadenfreude)." *Brain* 130 (2007): 1663–78.

Shaver, P. R., H. J. Morgan, and S. Wu. "Is Love a Basic Emotion?" *Personal Relationships* 3 (2005): 81–96.

Shepard, Sam. *Motel Chronicles*. San Francisco, CA: City Lights, 1982.

Shipler, D. K. "A Poor Cousin of the Middle Class." *New York Times Magazine*, January 18, 2004.

Shookman, Ellis, ed. *The Faces of Physiognomy: Interdisciplinary Approaches to Johann Caspar Lavater*. New York: Camden, 1993.

Simonton, D. K. "Presidential Personality: Biographical Use of the Gough Adjective Check List." *Journal of Personality and Social Psychology* 51 (1986): 149–60.

Simpson, J., S. Gangestad, and M. Biek. "Personality and Nonverbal Social Behavior: An Ethological Perspective of Relationship Initiation." *Journal of Experimental Social Psychology* 29 (1993): 434–61.

Sloan, D. M., M. M. Bradley, E. Dimoulas, and P. J. Lang. "Looking at Facial Expressions: Dysphoria and Facial EMG." *Biological Psychology* 60 (2002): 79–90.

"Smile! William Photo Touched Up." BBC, June 21, 1999. Available at http://news.bbc.co.uk/2/hi/uk_news/374584.stm.

Smith, C. A., and H. S. Scott. "A Componential Approach to the Meaning of Facial Expression." In *The Psychology of Facial Expression*, edited by J. A. Russell and J. M. Fernández-Dols, 229–54. Cambridge, UK: Cambridge University Press, 1997.

Smith, F., and P. G. Schyns. "Smile through Your Fear and Sadness: Transmitting and Identifying Facial Expression Signals over a Range of Viewing Distances." *Psychological Science* 20 (2009): 1202–8.

Smith, R. H., T. J. Turner, R. Garonzik, C. W. Leach, V. Urch-Druskat, and C. M. Weston. "Envy and Schadenfreude." *Personality and Social Psychology Bulletin* 22 (1996): 158–68.

Solomon, S., J. Greenberg, and T. Pyszczynski. "The Cultural Animal: Twenty Years of Terror Management Theory and Research." In *Handbook of Experimental Existential Psychology*, edited by J. Greenberg, S. L. Koole, and T. Pyszczynski. New York: Guilford Press, 2004.

Sontag, Susan. *On Photography.* New York: Farrar, Straus & Giroux, 1973.

Sorce, J. F., R. N. Emde, J. Campos, and M. D. Klinnert. "Maternal Emotional Signaling: Its Effect on the Visual Cliff Behavior of 1-Year-Olds." *Developmental Psychology* 21 (1985): 195–200.

Spinrad, T. L., C. A. Stifter, and N. Donelan-McCall. "Mothers' Regulation Strategies in Response to Toddlers' Affect: Links to Later Emotion Self-Regulation." *Social Development* 13 (2004): 40–55.

Spitz, R. A. *The First Year of Life.* New York: International Universities Press, 1965.

Spitz, R. A., and K. M. Wolf. "The Smiling Response: A Contribution to the Ontogenesis of Social Relations." *General Psychology Monograph* 34 (1946): 57–125.

Sroufe, L. Alan. *Emotional Development.* New York: Cambridge University Press, 1995.

Stanislavski, Constantin. *An Actor Prepares.* Translated by E. R. Hapgood. New York: Theatre Arts, 1936.

Steiner, J. E. "Facial Expressions of the Neonate Infant Indicating the Hedonics of Food-Related Chemical Stimuli." In *Taste and Development*, edited by J. M. Weiffenbach. Bethesda, MD: U.S. Department of Health, Education, and Welfare, 1977.

Stel, M., and A. van Knippenberg. "The Role of Facial Mimicry in the Recognition of Affect." *Psychological Science* 19 (2008): 984–85.

Stengel, R. "Mandela: His 8 Lessons of Leadership." *Time*, July 21, 2008. http://www.time.com/time/printout/0,8816,1821467,00.html.

Stern, D. N. "Affect Attunement." In *Frontiers of Infant Psychiatry*, vol. 2, edited by J. D. Call, E. Galenson, and R. T. Tyson, 3–14. New York: Basic Books, 1984.

Stevenson, Robert Louis. *Treasure Island.* 1883. New York: Macmillan, 1922.

Strack, R., L. L. Martin, and S. Stepper. "Inhibiting and Facilitating Conditions of the Human Smile: A Non-Obtrusive Test of the Facial Feedback Hypothesis." *Journal of Personality and Social Psychology* 54 (1988): 768–77.

Striano, T., and A. Vaish. "Seven- to 9-Month-Old Infants Use Facial Expressions to Interpret Others' Actions." *British Journal of Developmental Psychology* 24 (2006): 753–60.

Striano, T., P. A. Brennan, and E. J. Vanman. "Maternal Depressive Symptoms and 6-Month-Old Infants' Sensitivity to Facial Expressions." *Infancy* 3 (2002): 115–26.

Suthrell, Charlotte A. *Unzipping Gender: Sex, Cross-Dressing and Culture*. Oxford, UK: Berg Publishers, 2004.

Sweeny, T., M. Grabowecky, K. A. Paller, and S. Suzuki. "Within-Hemifield Perceptual Averaging of Facial Expressions Predicted by Neural Averaging." *Journal of Vision* 9 (2009): 1–11.

Tarkington, Booth. *Alice Adams*. Garden City, NY: Doubleday, Page & Co., 1921.

Tartter, V. V. "Happy Talk: Perceptual and Acoustic Effects of Smiling on Speech." *Perceptual Psychophysiology* 27 (1980): 24–27.

Tavuchis, Nicholas. *Mea Culpa: A Sociology of Apology and Reconciliation*. Stanford, CA: Stanford University Press, 1991.

Taylor, P., C. Funk, and P. Craighill. "Are We Happy Yet?" Pew Research Center, 2006. http://pewresearch.org/assets/social/pdf/AreWeHappyYet.pdf (accessed August 19, 2007).

Terry, D. A., and P. L. Pirtle. "Learning to Smile: The Neuroanatomical Basis for Smile Training." *Journal of Esthetic and Restorative Dentistry* 13 (2001): 20–27.

Theroux, Paul. *The Happy Isles of Oceania*. New York: G. P. Putnam's Sons, 1992.

Thompson, J. B. "The New Visibility." *Theory, Culture and Society* 22 (2005): 31–51.

Thurow, R., and L. Lescaze. "Frosty Mugs: Winter Olympics Hosts Are Known for Skiing, Not Sunny Disposition." *Wall Street Journal* (Eastern edition), January 17, 1994, p. A1.

Tickle-Degnen, L., and K. Doyle-Lyons. "Practitioners' Impressions of Patients with Parkinson's Disease: The Social Ecology of the Expressive Mask." *Social Science and Medicine* 58 (2004): 603–14.

Tidd, K. L., and J. D. Lochard. "Monetary Significance of the Affiliative Smile: A Case for Reciprocal Altruism." *Bulletin of the Psychonomic Society* 11 (1978): 344–46.

Todorov, A., A. N. Mandisodza, A. Goren, and C. C. Hall. "Inferences of Competence from Faces Predict Election Outcomes." *Science* 308 (2005): 1623–26.

Torr, D., and J. Czyzselska. "Drag Kings and Subjects." *Journal of Lesbian Studies* 2 (1998): 235–38.

Tourangeau, R., and P. C. Ellsworth. "The Role of the Facial Response in the Experience of Emotion." *Journal of Personality and Social Psychology* 37 (1979): 1519–31.

Tracy, J. L., and R. W. Robins. "Show Your Pride: Evidence for a Discrete Emotion Expression." *Psychological Science* 15 (2004): 194–97.

Trousdale, A. M. "Teacher as Gatekeeper—Schoolteachers in Picture Books for Young Children." In *Images of Schoolteachers in Twentieth-Century America—Paragons, Polarities, Complexities*, edited by P. B. Joseph and G. E. Burnaford, 195–214. New York: St. Martin's Press, 1994.

Tsai, J. L., B. Knutson, and H. H. Fung. "Cultural Variation in Affect Valuation." *Journal of Personality and Social Psychology* 90 (2006): 288–307.

Tsai, J. L., J. Y. Louie, E. E. Chen, and Y. Uchida. "Learning What Feelings to Desire: Socialization of Ideal Affect through Children's Storybooks." *Personality and Social Psychology Bulletin* 33 (2007): 17–30.

Tsai, W. C. "Determinants and Consequences of Employee Displayed Positive Emotions." *Journal of Management* 27 (2001): 497–512.

Underwood, G. "Subliminal Perception on TV." *Nature* 370 (1994): 103–10.

Updike, John. "Gesturing." 1974. In *The Early Stories: 1953–1975*. New York: Alfred A. Knopf, 2003.

van Dijk, A. "Discourse and Manipulation." *Discourse and Society* 17 (2006): 359–83.

van Dijk, W. W., J. W. Ouwerkerk, S. Gosling, M. Nieweg, and M. Gallucci. "When People Fall from Grace: Reconsidering the Role of Envy in Schadenfreude." *Emotion* 6 (2006): 156–60.

Van Hooff, J. "A Comparative Approach to the Phylogeny of Laughter and Smiling." In *Non-Verbal Communication*, edited by R. A. Hinde, 209–37. Cambridge, UK: Cambridge University Press, 1972.

Van Kleef, G. A., C. K. W. Dreu, and A. S. R. Manstead. "The Interpersonal Effects of Anger and Happiness in Negotiations." *Journal of Personality and Social Psychology* 86 (2004): 57–76.

Van Maanen, J. "The Smile Factory: Work at Disneyland." In *Reframing Organizational Culture*, edited by P. J. Frost, L. F. Moore, M. R. Louis, C. C. Lundberg, and J. Martin. Newbury Park, CA: Sage Publications, 1991.

Vanman, E. J., B. Y. Paul, T. A. Ito, and N. Miller. "The Modern Face of Prejudice and Structural Features That Moderate the Effect of Cooperation on Affect." *Journal of Personality and Social Psychology* 73 (1997): 941–59.

Venezia, M., D. Messinger, D. Thorp, and P. Mundy. "The Development of Anticipatory Smiling." *Infancy* 6 (2004): 397–406.

Vidal, Gore. *The Best Man*. New York: Dramatists Play Service, 1960.

Vorauer, J. D., and C. Turpie. "Disruptive Effects of Vigilance on Dominant Group Members' Treatment of Outgroup Members: Choking versus Shining under Pressure." *Journal of Personality and Social Psychology* 87 (2004): 384–99.

Vrij, Aldert. *Detecting Lies and Deceit: The Psychology of Lying and the Implications for Professional Practice*. Chichester, UK: John Wiley and Sons, 2000.

Wade, K. A., M. Garry, J. D. Read, and D. S. Lindsay. "A Picture Is Worth a Thousand Lies: Using False Photographs to Create False Childhood Memories." *Psychonomic Bulletin and Review* 9 (2002): 597–603.

Walker, W. R., J. J. Skowronski, and C. P. Thompson. "Life Is Pleasant—And Memory Helps to Keep It That Way!" *Review of General Psychology* 7 (2003): 203–10.

Walker-Andrews, A. S. "Perceiving Social Affordances: The Development of Emotional Understanding." In *The Development of Social Cognition and Communication*, edited by B. D. Homer and C. S. Tamis-LeMonda, 93–116. Mahwah, NJ: Lawrence Erlbaum Associates, 2005.

Wallace, P. S., and S. P. Taylor. "Reduction of Appeasement-Related Affect as a Concomitant of Diazepam-Induced Aggression: Evidence for a Link between Aggression and the Expression of Self-Conscious Emotions." *Aggressive Behavior* 35 (2009): 203–12.

Waters, E., J. Wippman, and L. A. Sroufe. "Attachment, Positive Affect and Competence in the Peer Group: Two Studies in Construct Validation." *Child Development* 50 (1979): 821–29.

Watson, J. S. "Smiling, Cooing, and the Game." *Merrill-Palmer Quarterly* 18 (1972): 323–39.

Weeks, S. J., and R. P. Hobson. "The Salience of Facial Expression for Autistic Children." *Journal of Child Psychology and Psychiatry* 28 (1987): 137–52.

Weikum, W. M., A. Vouloumanos, J. Navarra, S. Soto-Faraco, N. Sebastián-Gallés, and J. F. Werker. "Visual Language Discrimination in Infancy." *Science* 25 (2007): 1159.

Weinzweig, Ari. *Zingerman's Guide to Good Eating*. Boston: Houghton Mifflin, 2003.

Weisfeld, C. C., and M. A. Stack. "When I Look into Your Eyes: An Ethological Analysis of Gender Differences in Married Couples' Nonverbal Behaviors." *Psychology, Evolution and Gender* 4 (2002): 125–47.

Weissman, M. "Advances in Psychiatric Epidemiology: Rates and Risks for Major Depression." *American Journal of Public Health* 77 (1987): 445–51.

Whitehead, G. I., and S. H. Smith. "The Use of Hand Gestures and Smiles in the Inaugural Addresses of Presidents of the United States." *Journal of Social Psychology* 142 (2002): 670–72.

Wilde, Oscar. *The Picture of Dorian Gray*. 1891. Charleston, SC: Bibliolife, 2008.

Wilson, D. S., D. Near, and R. Miller. "Machiavellianism: A Synthesis of the

Evolutionary and Psychological Literatures." *Psychological Bulletin* 119 (1998): 285–99.

Wilson, E. L. "To My Patrons." 1871. In *Photography: Essays and Images*, edited by B. Newhall, 129–33. New York: MoMA, 1980.

Wolfe, Tom. *I Am Charlotte Simmons*. New York: Picador, 2005.

Wolff, P. H. "Observation on Newborn Infants." *Psychosomatic Medicine* 21 (1959): 110–18.

Woodzicka, J. A., and M. LaFrance. "The Effects of Subtle Sexual Harassment on Women's Performance in a Job Interview." *Sex Roles* 53 (2005): 67–77.

Woolf, Virginia. *A Room of One's Own*. 1930. New York: Houghton Mifflin, 2005.

Wylie, Laurence, and Rick Stafford. *Beaux Gestes: A Guide to French Body Talk*. Cambridge, MA: Undergraduate Press, 1977.

Wyly, M. Virginia. *Infant Assessment*. Boulder, CO: Westview Press, 1997.

Ye, Z. "The Chinese Folk Model of Facial Expressions." *Culture & Psychology* 10 (2004): 197–222.

Yuki, M., W. W. Maddux, and T. Masuda. "Are the Windows to the Soul the Same in the East and West? Cultural Differences in Using the Eyes and Mouth as Cues to Recognize Emotions in Japan and the United States." *Journal of Experimental Social Psychology* 43 (2006): 303–11.

Zapf, D. "Emotion Work and Psychological Well-Being. A Review of the Literature and Some Conceptual Considerations." *Human Resource Management Review* 12 (2002): 237–68.

Zeigler, M. "Pair Au Contraire: Zimmerman and Ina Broke the Ice during Restaurant Chatfests." *San Diego Union-Tribune*, February 9, 2002.

Zelazo, P. R., and M. J. Komer. "Infant Smiling to Nonsocial Stimuli and the Recognition Hypothesis." *Child Development* 42 (1971): 1327–39.

index

Page numbers in *italics* refer to illustrations.